FOODS, NUTRITION AND SPORTS PERFORMANCE

An International Scientific Consensus
organized by Mars, Incorporated
with International Olympic Committee patronage

Edited by

CLYDE WILLIAMS
and
JOHN T. DEVLIN

E & FN SPON

An Imprint of Chapman & Hall

Foods, Nutrition and Sports Performance

Foods, Nutrition and Sports Performance

An International Scientific Consensus
held 4–6 February 1991 and
organized by Mars, Incorporated,
with International Olympic Committee patronage

Edited by

Clyde Williams
*Department of Physical Education, Sports Science
and Recreation Management
Loughborough University
UK*

and

John T. Devlin
*University of Vermont College of Medicine
Maine
USA*

E & FN SPON
An Imprint of Chapman & Hall
London · Glasgow · New York · Tokyo · Melbourne · Madras

Published by
E & FN Spon, an imprint of Chapman & Hall, 2–6 Boundary Row, London
SE1 8HN

Chapman & Hall, 2–6 Boundary Row, London SE1 8HN, UK

Blackie Academic & Professional, Wester Cleddens Road, Bishopbriggs, Glasgow G64 2NZ, UK

Chapman & Hall, 29 West 35th Street, New York NY10001, USA

Chapman & Hall Japan, Thomson Publishing Japan, Hirakawacho Nemoto Building, 6F, 1–7–11 Hirakawa-cho, Chiyoda-ku, Tokyo 102, Japan

Chapman & Hall Australia, Thomas Nelson Australia, 102 Dodds Street, South Melbourne, Victoria 3205, Australia

Chapman & Hall India, R. Seshadri, 32 Second Main Road, CIT East, Madras 600 035, India

First published as a special supplement to the *Journal of Sports Sciences*, Summer 1991

First edition 1992

© 1992 E & F N Spon

Typeset in 10/12 Times by Intype, London
Printed in Great Britain by Page Bros, Norwich

ISBN 0 419 17890 2

A catalogue record for this book is available from the British Library

Library of Congress Cataloging-in-Publication data

Foods, nutrition, and sports performance: an international scientific
  consensus conference, held 4–6 February, 1991 / organized by Mars,
  Incorporated with International Olympic Committee patronage; edited
  by Clyde Williams and John T. Devlin.
      p. cm.
    Includes bibliographical references (p.   ) and index.
    ISBN 0–419–17890–2
    1. Athletes—Nutrition—Congresses. 2. Sports—Physiological
  aspects—Congresses. I. Williams, Clyde. II. Devlin, John T.
  III. Mars, Incorporated. IV. International Olympic Committee.
  TX361.A8F67 1992
  613.2′024796—dc20   92–13358
                                                          CIP

Contents

Contributors

SCIENTIFIC CO-CHAIRMEN

Clyde Williams
Department of Physical Education, Sports Science and
Recreation Management
Loughborough University
Loughborough
Leicestershire
LE11 3TU

John T. Devlin
University of Vermont College of Medicine
Diabetes Center
Maine Medical Center
Portland
Maine 04102
USA

AUTHORS

Eric J. van der Beek
Department of Human Nutrition
TNO Toxicology and Nutrition Institute
P.O. Box 360
3700 AJ Zeist
The Netherlands

Per Bjorntorp
Department of Medicine I
Sahlgren's Hospital
University of Göteborg
43045 Göteborg
Sweden

F. Brouns
Nutrition Research Center
Department of Human Biology
University of Limburg
Postbus 616
6200 MD
Maastricht
The Netherlands

Priscilla M. Clarkson
Department of Exercise Science
University of Massachusetts
Amherst
MA 01003
USA

Edward F. Coyle
Human Performance Laboratory
The University of Texas at Austin
Austin
Texas 78712
USA

Mark Hargreaves
Department of Physiology
Parkville 3052
Australia

Peter W.R. Lemon
Applied Physiology Research Laboratory
Schools of Biomedical Sciences and Physical Education
Kent State University
Ohio 44242
USA

R.J. Maughan
Department of Environment and Occupational Medicine
University Medical School
University of Aberdeen
Foresterhill
Aberdeen
AB9 2ZD
Scotland

Wim H.M. Saris
Nutrition Research Center
Department of Human Biology
University of Limburg
Postbus 616
6200 MD Maastricht
The Netherlands

Klaas R. Westerterp
Nutrition Research Center
Department of Human Biology
University of Limburg
Postbus 616
6200 MD Maastricht
The Netherlands

Preface

The material in this book is the peer reviewed proceedings of the International Scientific Consensus Conference on Foods, Nutrition and Sports Performance. It first appeared as a special supplement to the *Journal of Sports Sciences* in the Summer 1991. The supplement is in huge demand and reflects the growing interest in the links between nutrition and sports performance.

Our aim in reproducing the proceedings in book form is to make it more widely available, especially to students, teachers, coaches and dietitians. One of its unique features is that the nutritional recommendations are based on the results of research studies thoroughly scrutinized by all the contributing authors and experts in sports nutrition who attended the Conference. Therefore, the implementation of the recommended nutritional strategies during the preparation for, the participation in, and the recovery from sport and exercise can be undertaken with confidence. In addition, the information and insights contained in this book provide researchers with a solid base from which they can launch new, well controlled research studies in sports nutrition.

It is our hope that the interest in this subject will continue to grow, so much so that it will be necessary to convene a second International Scientific Consensus Conference on Foods, Nutrition and Sports Performance before the end of this decade.

Clyde Williams
Loughborough University

Introduction

This Consensus Conference on *Foods, Nutrition and Sports Performance* held in Lausanne on 4–6 February 1991, and under the patronage of the Medical Commission of the International Olympic Committee, brought together leading international scientists to review the current state of knowledge regarding the role of nutrition in improving sports performance. Under the direction of the Scientific Co-chairmen, scientists, widely recognized as experts in their respective fields, presented reviews of current scientific knowledge in their areas of expertise. Seven additional research scientists and four delegates of the International Olympic Committee were also invited to participate as discussants. The list of participants represented fifteen individual countries in four continents.

All participants received, in advance, copies of the scientific manuscripts for review prior to the Consensus Conference. They were requested to prepare written comments to be discussed at the meeting. The topics covered included recommendations for optimum carbohydrate, protein, fat, total energy, fluid and electrolyte, and vitamin and mineral intakes to maximize sports performance. The topics of carbohydrate and fluid intake included a review of the general state of current knowledge in the area (descriptive), and a separate discussion of the practical application of this knowledge in the training regimen (prescriptive).

Although the primary focus of this Consensus Conference was centred on optimum food intakes for the competitive athlete, the recommendations made in the following papers may be applicable to the recreational athlete as well. This is especially true for the individuals engaged in high-intensity forms of endurance exercise, in whom the higher intakes of carbohydrates, protein and fluids may enhance physical performance and possibly decrease the risk of injury. General recommendations can be made regarding those dietary modifications shown to improve various classes of sports performance (e.g. team sports, endurance sports, body building), but advice for the individual athlete cannot be made without specific information on the type, duration and intensity of the athletic event.

Concern was raised during the Conference about the limited data available on female athletes. Additional research is clearly needed better to define optimum training and food intake regimens to achieve desired body weight goals, and to limit the risks of reducing the body stores of calcium and iron, in particular.

For two productive days the manuscripts were individually presented, and open discussions were enjoined by all the participants. Only after the modifications recommended by the group had been incorporated into a revised manuscript was a final version approved for publication.

The Consensus Statement (p. xv) was reached after full participant discussion. A final draft of this statement was circulated prior to its presentation by the Scientific Co-chairmen at the International Olympic Committee headquarters in Lausanne on 6 February 1991. In the presence of Juan Antonio Samaranch, President of the International Olympic Committee and IOC delegates, Prince Alexandre de Merode, Chairman of the IOC Medical Commission, introduced the Consensus Statement by expressing his gratitude and support for this Conference on *Foods, Nutrition and Sports Performance*. This marks an important milestone in officially recognizing the important role of food intake in optimizing athletic performance, and reflects the positive message so urgently needed after the recent pre-occupation of the Medical Commission with illicit drug use. As stated by Prince de Merode, this Conference and its proceedings set the precedent for a new era of co-operation and mutual support between the International and National Olympic Committees and the scientific community leading to a better definition of proper nutrition for optimum sports performance.

ACKNOWLEDGEMENTS

The participants gratefully acknowledge the support of Mars, Incorporated in convening this important conference.

Foods, nutrition and sports performance: final consensus statement

Diet significantly influences athletic performance. An adequate diet, in terms of quantity and quality, before, during and after training and competition will maximize performance. In the optimum diet for most sports, carbohydrate is likely to contribute about 60–70% of total energy intake and protein about 12%, with the remainder coming from fat.

Total energy intake must be raised to meet the increased energy expended during training and maintenance of energy balance can be assessed by monitoring body weight, body composition and food intake. Where there is a need to reduce body weight this should be done gradually, and not immediately before competition.

In athletic events of high intensity and long duration (such as multiple sprint sports and endurance sports) performance is generally limited by carbohydrate availability. High carbohydrate diets (even in excess of two-thirds of total energy) maximize carbohydrate (glycogen) stores and improve performance in such activity. A high carbohydrate diet is also necessary to sustain high-intensity training on a daily basis. After each bout of exercise, the diet should contain sufficient carbohydrate to replenish the glycogen stores and to maximize subsequent performance. The requirement for sugars and starches, in both solid and liquid forms, will vary, depending on the timing and nature of the physical activity.

Increased fluid intake is necessary to avoid dehydration, and may improve performance during prolonged exercise, especially when sweat loss is high. These fluids may contain some carbohydrate, the concentration of which will be dictated by both duration of exercise and climatic conditions. If exercise is of short duration and sweat losses are small, the replacement of salts can be achieved from a normal food intake after exercise.

Protein requirements are higher in individuals involved in physical training programmes than in inactive people. However, most athletes already consume sufficient protein as a consequence of their increased energy intakes.

Fat consumption should be no greater than 30% of total energy intake. Supplementary fat beyond this intake is not recommended for training or competition because the body is able to mobilize its large reserve of this energy store. Except where there is a need to reduce body fat content, it is important to maintain these stores by ingesting sufficient energy between periods of exercise.

Vitamin supplements are not necessary for athletes eating a diet adequate in respect of quality and quantity. Of the minerals and trace elements essential for health, particular attention should be paid to iron and calcium status in those individuals who may be at risk.

There is no good evidence to support the use of other nutritional supplements, including those commonly assumed by athletes to have ergogenic effects.

1

Limits of energy turnover in relation to physical performance, achievement of energy balance on a daily basis

Klaas R. Westerterp and Wim H.M. Saris

1.1 INTRODUCTION

The main component of the daily energy turnover (ADMR = average daily metabolic rate) in the average subject is the energy expenditure for maintenance processes, usually called basal metabolic rate (BMR). This is the energy expenditure for the ongoing processes in the body in the resting state, when no food is digested and no energy is needed for temperature regulation, i.e. in the post-absorptive state in a thermoneutral environment. BMR is usually expressed as a function of body size to allow comparisons between subjects and even between species. The remaining components of ADMR are the diet induced thermogenesis (DIT) and the energy expenditure for (physical) activity (EEA). DIT is a fraction of energy intake of about 10% depending on the macronutrient composition of the food consumed. EEA is the most variable component of the daily energy turnover, ranging between an average value of 25–30% up to 75% in extreme situations during heavy sustained exercise. Table 1.1 shows some examples of energy intake in endurance, strength and team sport athletes.

Food, Nutrition and Sports Performance
Edited by Clyde Williams and John T. Devlin
Published in 1992 by E & F N Spon, London. ISBN 0 419 17890 2

Table 1.1 Energy intake data of different endurance, strength, and team sport athletes[a]

Type of sport[b]	Sex	Energy intake (kJ kg^{-1} day^{-1}) Mean	Range
Endurance (E)			
1 Tour de France	M	347	286–388
2 Tour de l'Avenir	M	316	247–378
3 Triathlon	M	272	246–295
4 Cycling, amateur	M	253	207–314
5 Marathon skating	M	222	175–294
6 Swimming	M	221	119–300
7 Rowing	M	189	167–225
8 Running	M	193	127–311
9 Rowing	F	186	140–200
10 Cycling, amateur	F	164	115–215
11 Running	F	168	123–218
12 Sub-top swimming	F	200	92–338
Strength (S)			
1 Body building	M	157	106–183
2 Judo	M	157	76–210
3 Weight lifting	M	167	99–203
4 Judo	M	177	60–325
5 Top gymnastics	F	158	91–216
6 Sub-top gymnastics	F	206	113–334
7 Body building	F	110	91–133
Team Sport (T)			
1 Water polo	M	194	92–299
2 Soccer	M	192	118–287
3 Hockey	M	181	167–217
4 Volley	F	140	101–229
5 Hockey	F	145	91–199
6 Handball	F	142	78–271

[a]From Erp-Baart *et al.* (1989).
[b]Subjects were élite athletes including European, World and Olympic medal winners. Data were obtained by a 4 or 7 day food diary. Recently we were able to compare recorded intake with measured expenditure using the doubly labelled water method. The results from the comparison often show recorded intake to be a lower estimate of energy requirements (see below).

In this paper we will focus on energy turnover in relation to physical performance during sports activities where body composition and energy supply are often limiting factors. Body composition is a limiting factor in sports like gymnastics, body building and judo, where a low body mass or fat mass is preferable for the performance or when competing in specific weight classes is mandatory. In these types of sport, subjects often try to maintain a negative energy balance to lose weight. The other extreme includes endurance sports like cycling and the triathlon, where the only way to success is the maintenance of energy balance at the upper limit of human performance in terms of energy turnover. Both topics, the consequences of a limiting energy intake on energy turnover and the upper limit of energy turnover during endurance exercise, will be discussed. Finally we will focus on two topics encountered by the average athlete, namely, changes in energy metabolism during the preparation period when physical activity is gradually increased and how energy intake is regulated at a changing energy expenditure from day to day.

1.2 THE LOWER LIMIT OF ENERGY EXPENDITURE

Energy intake, especially for females, gymnasts and ballet dancers is often extremely low (Erp-Baart *et al.*, 1989; Dahlstrom *et al.*, 1990). Energy expenditure in the average sedentary subject ranges between 1.4 and 1.6 BMR (WHO, 1985), while reported energy intake in top gymnasts is usually below this level despite the fact that they trained for 3–4 h a day. This can probably be explained by two factors: under-reporting and the urge to limit energy intake, the first being a result of the latter. Whether the intake data are realistic or not, in some sports the athletes often limit energy intake to reduce body mass and fat mass with consequences for energy turnover and, probably, performance. The lower limit of ADMR is set by the sum of BMR, DIT and a minimum EEA. Reducing intake to lose mass reduces directly DIT and indirectly BMR while it is probably difficult to mobilize energy for physical activity, resulting in a lowered EEA as well.

Subjects on a weight reducing diet show a reduction in their resting metabolic rate, not only through a loss of metabolic active tissue but also per unit active tissue. The efficiency of energy turnover goes up. There are indications that this phenomenon is more pronounced when energy restriction periods are repeated as practised in some sports where weight control takes place before matches and regained afterwards. The result is weight cycling and it may get increasingly difficult to lose weight while regaining it is facilitated (Steen *et al.*, 1988).

Intensely training female élite athletes often encounter other problems when energy intake is restricted, namely, menstrual dysfunction, related decrease in bone density and iron deficiency anaemia. There is a close relation between total energy intake and iron intake. Most male athletes meet their requirements, whereas some women, mainly due to menstruation losses, may have a negative balance between intake and losses. This may lead to iron deficiency anaemia. A high percentage of élite female athletes experience secondary amenorrhea. Though energy restriction is probably not the only reason, nutritional intake in amenorrheic athletes tends to be lower than in eumenorrheic athletes (Deuster *et al.*, 1986). One of the important consequences of the amenorrhea is a decrease in bone density which predisposes a subject to stress fractures. Resumption of the menstrual function does not result in a complete regain of lost bone mass (Drinkwater *et al.*, 1990).

Some studies have been done on the effects of acute energy restriction on different performance parameters in wrestlers and runners. In general the outcome of these studies is that performance capacity decreases either as a consequence of reduced carbohydrate intake and availability or as a result of the effects on fluid balance. There is also evidence for a reduction in spontaneous activity and so the body defends itself against a negative energy balance through a reduction of resting energy expenditure. People in a negative energy balance get slower and this cannot be the goal of an athlete. The long term effect of a negative energy balance is not only the loss of body fat but also the loss of fat-free mass, i.e. of muscle mass. Wrestlers wanting to reduce their weight by a decrease in energy intake show a diminished protein nutritional status (Craig *et al.*, 1990). The practice of starvation in order to achieve a rapid weight loss in the days before competition in weight class sports is well known. Several methods are used including an increase in exercise instead of tapering off the training intensity, and food restriction sometimes combined with deprivation or total absence of fluid intake. Besides the excessive loss of lean body mass, depletion of glycogen stores, the most important energy substrate for high-intensity performance, will occur. Therefore, the net result is a diminished body reserve for athletic events which more than offsets any advantages of competing in a lower weight classification (Houston *et al.*, 1981).

1.3 THE UPPER LIMIT OF ENERGY EXPENDITURE

The limiting factors for human performance depend on the type of exercise. Nutrition is an important determinant during the preparation phase and, for endurance exercise, also during the exercise itself. Athletes can only sustain a high level of exercise when they manage to maintain energy balance. Here we will focus only on the latter. What is the limit of energy expenditure which can be maintained over several days up to several weeks? In this case, the energy intake should meet the energy requirements.

The limit of human performance was originally encountered during hard work such as that performed by lumberjacks (Dill, 1936). They were supposed to work for eight or more hours per day at a level of energy expenditure of eight times BMR. Assuming a daily sleep period of 8 h at 1 BMR and the remaining hours at 2 BMR, their ADMR reached a level of four times BMR. This is nearly three times higher than the minimum level of 1.4 BMR in a subject who is minimally active. Nowadays, the upper limit of energy turnover is reached in endurance sports like cycle racing and triathlon. Here, athletes work at a high level of energy expenditure for up to 8 h per day, sometimes for several weeks.

The level of energy expenditure during endurance sports has been measured in the world's most demanding cycle race, the Tour de France, a race of more than 20 stages lasting about 3 weeks. Energy expenditure was measured with a doubly labelled water technique (Westerterp *et al.*, 1986) and calculated from recorded activities and dietary intake (Saris *et al.*, 1989). The doubly labelled water method allows measurement of energy expenditure under field conditions without any effect on performance (see Appendix).

Energy expenditure in the Tour de France reached values of 35 MJ per day, measured over weekly intervals. The highest recorded mean energy intake for the four observed cyclists was 32 MJ per day. Athletes remain weight stable over the race and if not, e.g. during a period of gastro-intestinal distress, then they do not manage to finish the tournament. Body composition does not show detectable changes either, suggesting subjects are in energy balance though measured expenditure is systematically higher than recorded activities and food intake. Whatever is the right value for energy turnover, subjects operate over 3 weeks at a level of 3.5–5.5 times BMR. This is in accordance with a suggested interspecies limit for working capacity on a sustained basis (Kirkwood, 1983).

It is not known what sets the upper limit of energy turnover, energy intake or energy expenditure, i.e. the capacity to eat and process food or the capacity to supply energy through oxidation. It is evident that the power output of the human muscle is higher on carbohydrate than on fat and protein and that the body store of carbohydrate energy in the form of glycogen can cover energy expenditure over 1–2 h only. Thus the upper limit of power output during endurance exercise with an intensity higher than 60% of the aerobic power is increased when one can eat energy-dense, carbohydrate-rich foods while one works, a common practice in cycle races.

It is clear that the energy turnover is directly related to the power output of the body. Brouns *et al.* (1989) did a simulation study, measuring the influence of diet manipulation on performance in subjects cycling for 2 days reaching a level of energy expenditure of 26 MJ per day. Subjects received *ad libitum* a conventional solid diet with a high carbohydrate content (62.5% En) supplemented with water or the same diet supplemented with a 20% enriched carbohydrate liquid (total CHO 80% En). Subjects were able to maintain energy balance during the exercise days on the carbohydrate-supplemented diet while on the water-supplemented solid diet the energy intake was 5–10 MJ per day too low.

Under such circumstances the athlete must drink and eat to maintain body CHO stores during the exercise as well as to replete the stores within 18 h for the exercise performance on the next day. From respiratory exchange measurements, an oxidation rate of nearly 13 g CHO kg^{-1} day^{-1} was calculated

The actual intake in the CHO-supplemented experiment was 16 g CHO kg^{-1} day^{-1} suggesting that also with respect to CHO intake there is a ceiling in the energy intake above which other factors play a role in relation to fatigue. The alternative, a higher intake of fat, which has a higher energy density is not appropriate in top sport performance because for maximal power output the muscle needs carbohydrate instead of fat. From these experiments it became clear that energy intake cannot meet energy expenditure at high working levels even when high-carbohydrate conventional foods are consumed unless energy-dense, carbohydrate-rich liquid formulae are supplemented, which can be ingested in large enough quantities.

Subjects working for long hours at high intensity do not have enough time to consume and process food outside the exercise period to balance the energy expenditure. Therefore, the practice of consuming large quantities of liquid CHO-rich formulations is one of the appropriate nutritional strategies to optimize performance during extreme sustained exercise.

1.4 CHANGES IN ENERGY EXPENDITURE DURING A TRAINING PROGRAMME

Novice athletes starting a training programme change their physical activity with consequences for the energy turnover, depending on the intensity and the duration of training bouts. Again, the most profound effects are to be expected in those taking up endurance training. Two recent studies provide data on this, both in novice athletes preparing for running a marathon (Janssen *et al.*, 1989) and half-marathon (Westerterp *et al.*, 1991, submitted).

Energy expenditure, as measured before, 8, 20 and 40 weeks after the start of the training period with doubly labelled water, showed an initial increase of on average 30% and remained stable afterwards (Fig. 1.1). The training 'volume' of the subjects doubled after the energy turnover had stabilized at 1.3 times the pre-training level. We postulate that the subjects already in the beginning of the training period, after 8 weeks,

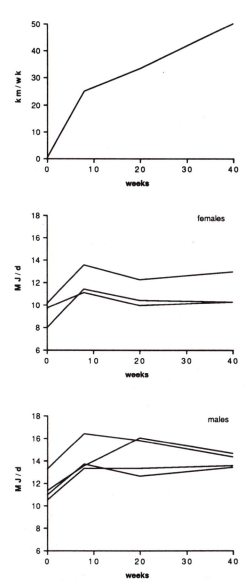

Fig. 1.1 Training distance and energy expenditure in novice athletes from before until the end of a training period in preparation for the half-marathon. Training distance as scheduled weekly during one supervised session and energy expenditure as measured in three female and four male individuals before and 8, 20 and 40 weeks after the start of the training period (Westerterp *et al.*, 1991, submitted).

reached a natural limit of their daily energy turnover. Afterwards, they could increase their training volume without an increase of the energy expenditure by an increasing efficiency as a mere result of the training.

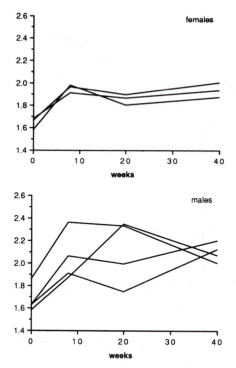

Fig. 1.2 Physical activity index (PAI) in novice athletes from before until the end of a training period in preparation for the half-marathon. PAI (average daily metabolic rate/basal metabolic rate) as measured in three female and four male individuals before and 8, 20 and 40 weeks after the start of the training period (Westerterp *et al.*, 1991, submitted).

Thus the result of the training means an increase in the efficiency of the exercise, in this case running.

Initially the increase in ADMR was two to three times higher than one would expect from training distance and running costs measured on a treadmill (Meijer, 1990). There were no indications that the training had an influence on the level of spontaneous physical activity (Meijer *et al.*, 1991).

Subjects in the two studies were real novice athletes. At the start of the training period they were sedentary as can be seen from their physical activity index (PAI = ADMR/BMR, Fig. 1.2). The initial PAI value was 1.66 ± 0.07 (mean $\pm$ s.D.), close to the value of 1.54 for sedentary subjects (WHO, 1985). The PAI value after 8 weeks of training was 2.03 ± 0.18, close to the value of 2.14 for the subjects engaged in hard work.

One indication for the increase in the efficiency of energy turnover after the start of the training, apart from changes during the training itself, is a change in resting metabolic rate. Though there are indications for an increase in resting metabolic rate directly after an exercise bout, in the long term subjects showed a decrease in their resting energy expenditure. In males resting metabolic rate, as measured in a respiration chamber, was 4% lower ($P<0.05$) after 40 weeks of training. In females we observed the same tendency, though here the variation between individuals was higher and the change probably had an even longer delay. The decrease in resting metabolic rate is surprising for another reason. Resting metabolic rate is closely related to the lean body mass. All subjects showed an increase in their lean body mass during the training period, as measured with underwater weighing and isotope dilution. Females gained 2.1 ± 0.4 kg ($P<0.01$) and males gained 3.2 ± 0.5 kg ($P<0.01$). The decrease in resting metabolic rate combined with the increase in lean body mass, especially in the males who even gained significantly more lean body mass than the females ($P<0.05$), is more evidence for an increase in energy efficiency during the training period.

Energy intake does not seem to be a reliable measure for energy turnover during the training period. Before the training started, there was a non-significant under-reporting of intake as measured with a 7-day dietary record compared with simultaneous measurement of energy expenditure with doubly labelled water ($-12+17\%$). After 40 weeks of training the discrepancy was ($-19+17\%$). Thus subjects did not show a significant change in reported intake between the measurement before and during the training when energy expenditure had increased by as much as 30%.

Despite the lack of change in the quantity of energy consumed as measured by self-report there are systematic changes in the quality of food consumption in dietary records in the course of a training programme. Janssen *et al.* (1989) reported an increase in the %En carbohydrate from 47% to 55% and 48% to 52% in females and males, respectively, over 18 months while preparing for the marathon. The increase in carbohydrate consumption was at the expense of dietary fat. Thus the increase in physical activity caused a favourable change in food habits with regard to the nutritional guidelines for good health. There were no indications of a gender difference in substrate utilization as suggested by Tarnapolsky *et al.* (1990). They got indications of a higher capacity for fat utilization during endurance exercise in females compared with males, suggesting a lower need for dietary carbohydrate in the former group.

1.5 REGULATION OF ENERGY BALANCE AT A CHANGING ENERGY TURNOVER

Man does not balance energy intake and energy expenditure on a daily basis (Edholm, 1977), whereas smaller animals do. Apparently man can afford to rely on body reserves while smaller species sooner show signs of energy shortage like a lowered body temperature and a reduced physical activity. Smaller species have a higher energy expenditure on a kg body mass basis plus a relatively smaller body energy reserve. Thus a mouse does not survive a period of 3 days without food while a normal adult survives more than 30 days.

Of course many people maintain a perfect energy balance in the long term as shown by a constant body weight in adult life. Edholm (1977) showed how energy intake highly correlates with energy expenditure on a weekly basis. Discrepancies on a daily basis between intake and expenditure are especially large when days with a high energy expenditure are alternated with quieter intervals. Military cadets did not show an increase in energy intake on days with a higher energy expenditure when they joined a drill competition. The 'matching' increase in energy intake came about 2 days afterwards (Edholm *et al.*, 1955). Based on 69 subjects from six energy balance studies, Durnin (1961) concluded that there is no precise short-term control mechanism.

Even during hard sustained exercise, like the earlier mentioned cycle race the Tour de France where is it essential for success to match energy intake with energy expenditure, there are day to day discrepancies between energy intake and energy expenditure. Despite the fact that cycle racers eat while they work they do not always manage to cover energy needs on days with the highest energy expenditure, i.e. on those days with the longest stages. However, overall matching between energy intake and energy expenditure is striking compared to the early studies on a lower exercise level (Saris *et al.*, 1989), indicating that at higher levels of exercise the risk of deregulation of the energy balance is smaller.

We suggest that possibly two mechanisms are involved: firstly the physiological regulation system and secondly the fact that highly trained athletes have learned how to eat the maximum amount of food during hard physical work. The digestive system is limiting and a negative energy balance on one day is difficult to compensate later on. In a study of food intake and energy expenditure in four amateur cyclists in the Tour de l'Avenir race in France it was shown that with increasing energy expenditure two cyclists had great difficulties in keeping energy balance (Erp-Baart *et al.*, 1989, personal communication). Therefore one of the factors endurance athletes have to adapt to is the consumption of energy-dense CHO-rich foods and/or CHO-rich liquid formulas in order to compete at top level.

REFERENCES

Brouns, F., Saris, W.H.M., Stroecken, J., Beckers, E., Thijssen, R., Rehrer, N.J. and ten Hoor, F. (1989). Eating, drinking, and cycling. A controlled Tour de France simulation study. Part II. Effect of diet manipulation. *International Journal of Sports Medicine*, **10**, S41–S48.

Craig, A.H., Park, S.H. and Roemmich, J.N. (1990). Changes in protein nutritional status of adolescent wrestlers. *Medicine and Science in Sports and Exercise*, **22**, 599–604.

Dahlstrom, M.E., Jansson, E., Nordevang, E. and Kaijser, L. (1990). Discrepancy between estimated energy intake and requirement in female dancers. *Clinical Physiology*, **10**, 11–25.

Deuster, P.A., Kyle, S.B., Moser, P.B., Vigersky, R.A., Singh, A. and Schoomaker, E.B. (1986). Nutritional intakes and status of highly trained amenorrheic and eumenorrheic women runners. *Fertility and Sterility*, **46**, 636–43.

Dill, D.B. (1936). The economy of muscular exercise. *Physiological Reviews*, **16**, 263–91.

Drinkwater, B.L., Bruemmer, B. and Chesnut, C.H. (1990). Menstrual history as a determinant of current bone density in young athletes. *Journal of the American Medical Association*, **263**, 545–8.

Durnin, J.V.G.A. (1961). Appetite and the relationship between expenditure and intake of calories. *Journal of Physiology*, **156**, 294–306.

Edholm, O.G. (1977). Energy balance in man. *Human Nutrition*, **31**, 413–31.

Edholm, O.G., Fletcher, J.G., Widdowson, E.M. and McCance, R.A. (1955). The energy expenditure and food intake of individual men. *British Journal of Nutrition*, **9**, 286–300.

Erp-Baart, A.M.J. van, Saris, W.H.M., Binkhorst, R.A., Vos, J.A. and Elvers, J.W.H. (1989). Nationwide survey on nutritional habits in élite athletes, part I: Energy, carbohydrate, protein, and fat intake. *International Journal of Sports Medicine*, **10**, S3–S10.

Houston, M.E., Marrin, D.A., Green, H.J. and Thomson, J.A. (1981). The effect of rapid weight loss on physiological functions in wrestlers. *Physician and Sportmedicine*, **91**, 73–8.

Janssen, G.M.E., de Graef, C.J.J. and Saris, W.H.M. (1989). Food intake and body composition in novice athletes during a training period to run a marathon. *International Journal of Sports Medicine*, **10**, S17–S21.

Kirkwood, J.K. (1983). A limit to metabolisable energy intake in mammals and birds. *Comparative Biochemistry and Physiology*, **75A**, 1–3.

Meijer, G.A.L. (1990). *Physical activity, implications for human energy metabolism*. Thesis University of Limburg, Maastricht, The Netherlands.

Meijer, G.A.L., Janssen, G.M.E., Westerterp, K.R., Verhoeven, F., Saris, W.H.M., ten Hoor, F. (1991). The effect of a 5-month endurance training programme on physical activity: evidence for a sex-difference in the metabolic response to exercise. *European Journal of Applied Physiology*, **62**, 11–17.

Saris, W.H.M., van Erp-Baart, M.A., Brouns, F., Westerterp, K.R. and ten Hoor, F. (1989). Study on food intake and energy expenditure during extreme sustained exercise: the Tour de France. *International Journal of Sports Medicine*, **10**, S26–S31.

Steen, S.E., Oppliger, R.A. and Brownell, K.D. (1988). Metabolic effects of repeated weight loss and regain in adolescent wrestlers. *JAMA*, **260**, 47–50.

Tarnapolsky, L.J., MacDougall, J.D., Atkinson, S.A., Tarnapolsky, M.A. and Sutton, J.R. (1990). Gender differences in substrate for endurance exercise. *Journal of Applied Physiology*, **68**, 302–8.

Westerterp, K.R., Saris, W.H.M., van Es, M. and ten Hoor, F. (1986). Use of the doubly labelled water technique in humans during heavy sustained exercise. *Journal of Applied Physiology*, **61**, 2162–7.

Westerterp, K.R., Meijer, G.A.L., Janssen, G.M.E., Saris, W.H.M. and ten Hor, F. (1991). Long term effect of physical activity on energy balance and body composition. *British Journal of Nutrition* (submitted).

World Health Organization (1985). Energy and protein requirements, report of a joint FAO/WHO/UNU expert consultation. Technical Report Series 724, Geneva.

APPENDIX: DOUBLY LABELLED WATER AS A TOOL IN ENERGY BALANCE STUDIES IN MAN

Introduction

Energy expenditure can be measured under field conditions using the doubly labelled water (DLW) method. Basically, the oxygen of expired CO_2 is in isotopic equilibrium with the oxygen of body water. When a subject is loaded with $^2H_2{}^{18}O$, the decrease in ^{18}O in the body water is a measure for H_2O plus CO_2 outputs and the decrease in ^2H is a measure for H_2O output alone. Hence the CO_2 output can be obtained by difference (Lifson and McLintock, 1966). Both markers, ^{18}O and ^2H, are stable isotopes which occur naturally in the body water at a level around 2000 and 150 p.p.m., respectively. The required excess enrichment of 200–400 p.p.m. does not have any measurable health consequences. Initially the method was used only in small animals due to the high cost of ^{18}O enriched water. Nowadays, with the current prices and the use of high-precision Isotope Ratio Mass Spectrometry, the cost of an isotope dose for one observation in an adult is US$300–600. The method has been applied in humans from the early 1980s onwards and has been validated in several laboratories. It has been recently standardized in a workshop where all users in the field of human energy metabolism were represented (Prentice, 1990).

Method

Body water is enriched with the stable isotopes ^{18}O and ^{2}H and their disappearance rate from a body fluid (e.g. blood, urine or saliva) is measured. The difference between the two disappearance rates $(k_O - k_D)$ is a measure of CO_2 production as k_O reflects H_2O plus CO_2 output and k_D reflects H_2O output alone. The optimal observation period is 1–3 biological half-lifes of the isotopes.

An observation starts by collecting a baseline sample. Then a weighed isotope dose is administered, usually a mixture of 10 APE ^{18}O and 5 APE ^{2}H. Subsequently the isotopes equilibrate with the body water and the initial sample is collected. The equilibration time is, depending on body size and metabolic rate, for adults 4–8 h. During equilibration the subject usually does not consume any food or drink. After collecting the initial sample the subject resumes his routine according to the instructions of the experimenter and collects body water samples at regular intervals until the end of the observation period.

Calculating CO_2 production from k_O and k_D one has to correct for isotope fractionation and isotope incorporation in compartments other than H_2O. Physical fractionation occurs when the relative abundance of the isotope is a function of its mass. Thus, ^{2}H and ^{18}O are relatively more abundant in liquid water than in water vapour and ^{18}O is relatively more abundant in CO_2 than in H_2O. The fractionation factors f_1, f_2 and f_3 at body temperature are 0.941, 0.992 and 1.039, respectively. Incorporation of the isotopes, calculated from the difference between total body water and the dilution space, is 1% for ^{18}O and 4% for ^{2}H. Thus, CO_2 production can be calculated from isotope elimination with the equation (Schoeller *et al.*, 1986):

$$rCO_2 = \left(\frac{k_O \cdot D_O - k_H \cdot D_H}{2f_3} \right) \left(\frac{f_2 - f_1}{2f_3} \right) rGf$$

where k_O, D_O, k_H and D_H are elimination rates and dilution spaces for ^{18}O and ^{2}H, respectively. Factors f_1, f_2 and f_3 are for fractionation of ^{2}H in water vapour, ^{18}O in water vapour and ^{18}O in CO_2, respectively. rGf is the rate of isotopically fractionated gaseous water loss. When

$$rGf = 1.3 \times 1.77 \times rCO_2$$

assuming that breath is saturated with water and contains 3.5% CO_2 (fractionated breath water $= 1.77 \times rCO_2$), transcutaneous fractionated (non-sweat) water loss amounts to about 50% of breath water. Then

$$rCO_2 = 0.455 N(1.01 k_O - 1.04 k_H)$$

where N is the total body water calculated from the isotope dilution spaces: $N = (D_O/1.01 + D_H/1.04)/2$.

Results

Validation studies in four laboratories resulted in an accuracy of 1–3% and a precision of 2–8%, comparing the method with respirometry. The method has now been applied in subjects at a wide age range and at different activity levels, from premature infants to elderly and from hospitalized patients to participants in a cycle race.

The method needs high-precision Isotope Ratio Mass Spectrometry, working at low levels of isotope enrichment for many reasons mentioned above. Another reason is the fact that the difference between k_O and k_D is relatively small. Table 1.2 presents the k_D/k_O ratio in the full age range and activity range. In prematures the k_D/k_O ratio is highest indicating a greater risk for error. Judging the k_O/k_D ratios, the potential error is smaller in applications with children and active adults. The optimal observation period is 1–3 biological half-lifes, i.e. 2.5–7.5 days in Tour de France conditions and 10–30 days in the elderly (Table 1.3).

There is still discussion on the ideal sampling protocol, i.e. multi-point *vs* two-point method. We prefer a combination of both, taking two independent samples at the start, in the midpoint, and at the end of the observation period. Thus an independent comparison can be made within one run, calculating rCO_2 from the first samples and the second samples over the first half and the second half of the observation interval.

Table 1.2 The ratio between the elimination rate of ^2H (k_H) and ^{18}O (k_O) in different subject categories

Subjects	n	Age (yr)	k_H/k_O	s.e.m.
Prematures[a]	8	0	0.86	0.005
Children[b]	10	11	0.75	0.007
Adults				
sedentary[c]	5	20–40	0.78	0.010
active[c]	9	20–40	0.75	0.003
(tour)[d]	4	20–40	0.75	0.003
Elderly[e]	10	65–80	0.77	0.004

[a]Westerterp *et al.* (submitted).
[b]Blaak *et al.* (submitted).
[c]Westerterp *et al.* (1988).
[d]Westerterp *et al.* (1986).
[e]Pannemans *et al.* (in preparation).

Table 1.3 Biological half-life of ^{18}O ($T_{1/2}O$) in different subject categories (see Table 1.2 for further details about references)

Subjects	n	Age (yr)	$T_{1/2}O$ (d)	s.e.m.
Prematures	8	0	3.4	0.1
Children	10	11	5.2	0.1
Adults				
sedentary	5	20–40	7.4	0.6
active	9	20–40	4.4	0.1
(tour)	4	20–40	2.6	0.1
Elderly	5	65–80	9.8	0.3

Discussion and conclusion

The DLW method gives precise and accurate information on carbon dioxide production. Converting rCO_2 to energy expenditure needs information on the energy equivalent of CO_2, which can be calculated with additional information on the substrate mixture being oxidized. One option is the calculation of the Food Quotient from the macronutrient composition of the diet. In energy balance the value of the FQ equals the RQ. Alternatively the RQ can be measured over a representative interval in a respiration chamber.

In conclusion, DLW is an excellent method to measure energy expenditure in unrestrained humans in their normal surroundings over a time period of 1–3 weeks.

References

Blaak, E.E., Westerterp, K.R., Bar-Or, O. and Saris, W.H.M. (1991). Effect of training on total energy expenditure and spontaneous activity in obese boys. *American Journal of Clinical Nutrition* (submitted).

Lifson, N. and McClintock, R. (1966). Theory of use of the turnover rates of body water for measuring energy and material balance. *Journal of Theoretical Biology*, **12**, 46–74.

Prentice, A.M. (ed.) (1990). The doubly-labelled water method for measuring energy expenditure, technical recommendations for use in humans. A consensus report by the IDECG working group. International Atomic Energy Agency, Vienna.

Schoeller, D.A., Ravussin, E. Schutz, Y., Acheson, K.J., Baertschi, P. and Jéquier, E. (1986). Energy expenditure by doubly labeled water: validation in humans and proposed calculation. *American Journal of Physiology*, **250**, R823–R830.

Westerterp, K.R., Saris, W.H.M., van Es, M. and ten Hoor, F. (1986). Use of the doubly labeled water technique in humans during heavy sustained exercise. *Journal of Applied Physiology*, **61**, 2162–7.

Westerterp, K.R., Brouns, F., Saris, W.H.M. and ten Hoor, F. (1988). Comparison of doubly labeled water with respirometry at low- and high-activity levels. *Journal of Applied Physiology*, **65**, 53–6.

Westerterp, K.R., Lafeber, H.N., Sulkers, E.J. and Sauer, P.J.J. (1991). Comparison of short term indirect calorimetry and doubly labelled water method for the assessment of energy expenditure in preterm infants. *Biology of the Neonate* (in press).

COMMENTARY BY KIENS, RODRIGUEZ, AND HAMM

Weight reduction in athletes

In several sports a low body weight has to be maintained or a weight reduction is required for participating in specific weight categories.

In a weight reducing period it is important for athletes to be capable of maintaining their daily high physical performance. Thus a long-term planned weight reduction programme must be followed, because the length of energy restriction increases the contribution of fat stores to total body weight lost substantially. If body weight is lost rapidly over short periods of time, this would minimize the loss of fat and lead to substantial losses of lean tissue and water. Thus weight loss should therefore be limited to 500–1000 g per week.

To obtain this weight loss energy restriction must be in the range of 2–4 MJ day^{-1} below normal energy intake. The composition of the diet is not different from recommendations to other athletes. An adequate carbohydrate and protein intake should be guaranteed, in order to prevent performance impairment due to glycogen stores depletion or an imbalance between protein synthesis and degradation. The daily dietary carbohydrate intake of 65–70% E should mainly be covered by food items of high glycaemic index.

Water intake restriction, dehydration, high-intensity or high-volume training sessions immediately before competition, or the use of laxatives or diuretics are strongly discouraged.

Dietary intake should be closely assessed, using food composition tables or appropriate computer programs available, and food intake recalled at least on a weekly basis. Anthropometric and other body composition assessment methods can be used in order to monitor changes. In already lean subjects, there may be a risk of reducing the muscle mass when the energy intake is limited. Also these changes have to be monitored and prevented when possible, by means of reducing the training volume or introducing strength training loads.

Eating disorders in athletes

Eating disorders – in particular anorexia nervosa and bulimia – are complex, closely related alterations of the eating behaviour. Anorexia nervosa is an extremely unhealthy mental and physical state, characterized by weight loss, poor body image, and an intense fear of obesity and weight gain (Health and Public Policy Committee, 1987; Herzog and Copeland, 1985). A high number of anorectic persons (6–20%) die prematurely – from suicide, heart diseases, or infections. It affects mainly, but not exclusively, adolescent girls, and some clinicians believe that no person with anorexia ever completely recovers. Bulimia, an eating disorder characterized by eating large quantities of food at one time (binging) which are soon purged from the body by means of vomiting, use of laxatives, diuretics, or other means, is a recurrent state frequently related to weight reduction diets. Most health problems in bulimia arise from

Table 1.4 Criteria for eating disorder[a]

Anorexia nervosa

A   Refusal to maintain body weight over a minimum normal weight for age and height, for example, weight loss leading to maintenance of body weight 15% below that expected; or failure to make expected weight gain during period of growth, leading to body weight 15% below that expected.

B   Intense fear of gaining weight or becoming fat, even though underweight.

C   Disturbance in the way in which one's body weight, size or shape is experienced. The person claims to 'feel fat' even when emaciated, believes that one area of the body is 'too fat' even when obviously underweight.

D   In females, absence of at least three consecutive menstrual cycles when otherwise expected to occur (primary or secondary amenorrhea). (A woman is considered to have amenorrhea if her periods occur only following hormone administration, such as estrogen.)

Bulimia nervosa

A   Recurrent episodes of binge eating (rapid consumption of a large amount of food in a discrete period of time).

B   A feeling of lack of control over eating behaviour during the eating binges.

C   The person regularly engages in either self-induced vomiting, use of laxatives or diuretics, strict dieting or fasting, or vigorous exercise to prevent weight gain.

D   A minimum average of two binge eating episodes a week for at least 3 months.

E   Persistent overconcern with body shape and weight.

[a]*Source*: Diagnostic and Statistical Manual for Mental Disorders, DSM IIIR.

vomiting – tooth decay, low blood potassium level causing heart rhythm problems, salivary gland swelling, oesophageal and stomach ulcers, etc.

Both disorders are complex and rooted in multiple causes – biological, psychological and social (Health and Public Policy Committee, 1987; Herzog and Copeland, 1985). In Table 1.4 are diagnostic criteria for eating disorders, as in the *Diagnostic and Statistical Manual for Mental Disorders* (DSM IIIR) (American Psychiatric Association, 1989)

In a recent study, élite athletes competing in weight category sports, and other athletes for whom weight or body composition are relevant for performance, were shown to have a higher prevalence of 'risk' of eating disorders than athletes involved in sports which are not body weight dependent (Rodriguez *et al.*, 1991, unpublished).

An effort has to be made to prevent such disorders by means of adequate nutritional education of the coaches and athletes, information about the clinical signs for the coaches and athletes, and by avoiding uncontrolled weight reduction diets.

References

American Psychiatric Association (1989). Diagnostic and Statistical Manual for Mental Disorders. Press Syndicate of the University of Cambridge, Cambridge, UK.

Health and Public Policy Committee, American College of Physicians (1987). Eating disorders: anorexia nervosa and bulimia. *Nutrition Today*, March/April, **29**.

Herzog, D. and Copeland, P. (1985). Eating disorders. *The New England Journal of Medicine*, **318**, 295.

2

Carbohydrates and exercise

Mark Hargreaves

2.1 INTRODUCTION

For many years the importance of carbohydrates as substrates for contracting skeletal muscle has been recognized (Christensen and Hansen, 1939a
and 1939b; Krogh and Lindhard, 1920), the classical studies of Christensen
and Hansen in the 1930s clearly demonstrating the importance of carbohydrate availability during prolonged exercise and the potential influence
of dietary carbohydrate on endurance exercise performance. Their work
was expanded in the late 1960s with the use of the percutaneous muscle
biopsy technique to examine skeletal muscle glycogen metabolism during
exercise in human volunteers (Bergstrom and Hultman, 1967; Bergstrom
et al., 1967; Hermansen *et al.*, 1967). These studies demonstrated the
critical role of muscle glycogen as a determinant of endurance exercise
performance and the benefit of increasing dietary carbohydrate intake
prior to prolonged exercise. Since that time, numerous studies have been
undertaken and there is little doubt that adequate carbohydrate availability is essential for heavy training and successful athletic performance
(Costill, 1988).

2.2 SOURCES AND BODY STORES OF CARBOHYDRATE

As the name implies, carbohydrates are molecules containing carbon in a
ratio to hydrogen and oxygen as found in water (i.e. CH_2O). Carbohydrate

Food, Nutrition and Sports Performance
Edited by Clyde Williams and John T. Devlin
Published in 1992 by E & F N Spon, London. ISBN 0 419 17890 2

foods have been traditionally classified on the basis of the chemical structure of the constituent carbohydrates, being either monosaccharides ($C_6H_{12}O_6$), such as glucose and fructose, and disaccharides, such as sucrose (simple carbohydrates) or polysaccharides, such as starch (complex carbohydrates). Glycogen is the major storage form of glucose in animal tissues and differs slightly from plant starch. Glucose polymers, consisting of chains of 7–13 glucose units, do not occur in great amounts in nature. Technically oligosaccharides, they are produced from the hydrolysis of starch and have been introduced in the athlete's diet through products such as carbohydrate-electrolyte replacement beverages. Of course, foods do not always occur exclusively as simple or complex carbohydrates. Both in nature (e.g. bananas) and as the result of food processing (e.g. cakes) many foods contain a mixture of carbohydrate types.

Table 2.1 Foods containing 50 g of either simple or complex carbohydrate

Simple carbohydrates	Complex carbohydrates
50 g sugar	130 g wholemeal bread
75 g jam	100 g cornchips/crisps
90 g pastry	250 g baked potato
500 ml soft drink	500 g baked beans
700 ml sports drink (7%)	150 g boiled wholemeal rice
75 g chocolate bar	200 g boiled pasta
50 g jelly beans	200 ml maltodextrins (25%)
3 medium pieces of fruit (apple)	
600 ml fruit juice	
1000 ml skim milk	

It has been suggested that in order to promote good health, the intake of complex carbohydrate should be increased and indeed this can provide for optimal training nutrition (Burke and Read, 1989). Such a diet should provide sufficient amounts of other nutrients (e.g. fibre, protein, vitamins, minerals), while being relatively low in fat. During times of increased carbohydrate need (e.g. heavy training, intense competition, multi-day endurance events), however, it will become necessary for athletes to rely more heavily on carbohydrate-dense liquids and food which may contain predominantly simple carbohydrates. In a recent study of Tour de France cyclists it was observed that 30–35% of the total carbohydrate intake came from carbohydrate-rich liquids such as sports drinks and 'carboloaders' (Saris *et al.*, 1989). Although during such supplementation micronutrient intake may become marginal (Snyder *et al.*, 1989), in the short term this is probably of little functional significance.

In the past it has been assumed that the chemical composition could predict the blood glucose and insulin responses following ingestion of carbohydrate foods; simple carbohydrates producing a rapid rise and fall in glucose and insulin, while complex carbohydrates produce a flatter response. Recent work has questioned this assumption and it has been observed that carbohydrate foods elicit very individual metabolic responses, based upon various factors that influence their rate of digestion and absorption. The glycemic index has been devised to account for these differences in individual blood glucose responses and is derived by comparing the area under the blood glucose curve following ingestion of a carbohydrate food with that obtained after ingesting the same amount of carbohydrate as glucose or bread (Jenkins *et al.*, 1984). Under this scheme, it is possible to have both simple and complex carbohydrates that are easily absorbed and therfore have a high glycaemic index. Furthermore, there are simple carbohydrates with a low glycaemic index (e.g. fructose). Thus, during times of increased carbohydrate requirement, athletes should ingest carbohydrates that are easily absorbed and have a high glycaemic index (see Chapter 3).

The vast majority of ingested carbohydrate enters the bloodstream as glucose and in the resting state is directed towards the sites of carbohydrate storage within the body. In animal tissues the storage form of carbohydrate is glycogen, a branched polymer of glucose containing a mixture of alpha-1,4 and 1,6 linkages between glucose units. The liver has the highest concentration of glycogen (approx. 250 mmol kg^{-1}); however, because of the large mass of skeletal muscle (40–50% of body weight), this tissue contains the largest reserve of glycogen (Table 2.2). The muscle glycogen concentration is influenced by exercise, dietary carbohydrate intake and training status and can be anywhere between 20–200 mmol kg^{-1} wet muscle depending upon the interaction between these factors.

Table 2.2. Sites and magnitude of carbohydrate stores in a rested, 70 kg reference man on a mixed diet. Numbers in parentheses refer to possible ranges following extremes in dietary carbohydrate intake

Tissue	Wt. or Vol.	CHO store
Liver	1.8 kg	70 g (0–135)
ECF	12 l	10 g (8–11)
Muscle	32 kg	450 g (300–900)

The principal role of the liver glycogen reserve is to maintain a constant blood glucose level between meals, thereby ensuring adequate substrate supply for those organs dependent upon glucose for their energy needs (brain and CNS, blood cells, kidney). At rest these tissues account for approximately 75% of the peripheral glucose utilization; resting skeletal muscle accounts for about 15–20%. The majority of hepatic glucose output is derived from glycogenolysis (75%), but there is also an important contribution from gluconeogenesis (25%), this fraction increasing during prolonged exercise and fasting. Obviously during exercise the liver plays a key role in maintaining blood glucose homeostasis. Muscle glycogen utilization in the resting state is negligible and its major function is to provide substrate during periods of increased skeletal muscle activity. Although muscle glycogen cannot contribute directly to the maintenance of blood glucose, the release of lactate during moderate and intense exercise provides an important gluconeogenic precursor for the liver.

2.3 CARBOHYDRATE UTILIZATION DURING EXERCISE

Muscle glycogen is initially degraded to glucose 1-phosphate by the action of phosphorylase and then converted to glucose 6-phosphate. Glucose is taken from the blood by a carrier-mediated process and phosphorylated to glucose 6-phosphate in a reaction catalysed by hexokinase. Thus, glucose 6-phosphate represents a common entry point for glucose and glycogen into the series of cytosolic reactions, known as glycolysis or the Embden–Meyerhof pathway, which produce pyruvate. The major fate of pyruvate is oxidation in the Krebs cycle and electron transport chain; however, if the rate of pyruvate formation exceeds the rate of pyruvate oxidation lactate will be produced. The degradation of 1 mole of glucose and glycogen to lactate results in the generation of 2 and 3 moles of ATP, respectively. In contrast, the complete oxidation of glucose and glycogen to carbon dioxide and water produces 38 and 39 moles of ATP, respectively. The oxidation of carbohydrate yields 21.1 kJ (5.05 kcal) per litre of oxygen consumed.

During high intensity, dynamic exercise (e.g. sprinting, track cycling, interval training, 'multiple-sprint' sports such as football, hockey), the breakdown of the high-energy phosphagens (ATP, CP) and the degradation of glycogen are the predominant energy yielding pathways. Although metabolic acidosis and ionic disturbances are thought to be the primary causes of fatigue during such exercise, carbohydrate availability may also play a role. It is possible that subpopulations of the fast twitch muscle fibres are depleted of glycogen during intense exercise. Furthermore, it has been demonstrated that increased dietary carbohydrate intake can improve high-intensity exercise performance while inadequate carbohydrate intake impairs performance (Maughan, 1990). There is also greater reliance on phosphagens and muscle glycogen during static contractions above 20–30% MVC, where increased intramuscular pressure results in occlusion of the arterial blood supply, thereby limiting oxygen and blood-borne substrate delivery. During prolonged exercise requiring 60–85% of maximal oxygen uptake, muscle glycogen is an important substrate for oxidative metabolism. Its rate of utilization is most rapid during the early stages of exercise (Vøllestad *et al.*, 1984) and is exponentially related to exercise intensity (Saltin and Karlsson, 1971; Vøllestad and Blom, 1985). Fatigue during such exercise is often associated with depletion of glycogen in the contracting muscle, specifically in those fibres recruited during exercise (Hermansen *et al.*, 1967; Vøllestad *et al.*, 1984). In addition, the pattern of muscle glycogen depletion is influenced by the mode of exercise. Cycling exercise results in glycogen loss predominantly in vastus lateralis; during running it is greater in gastrocnemius and soleus. The close relationship between muscle glycogen depletion and fatigue appears to be due to the inability of glycogen-depleted muscle cells to maintain a sufficient rate of ATP resynthesis. Recent studies have observed increases in the ATP breakdown products IMP and ammonia in muscles depleted of glycogen (Broberg and Sahlin, 1989; Norman *et al.*, 1987). Furthermore, another possible effect of lowered muscle glycogen availability is the loss of substrate, in particular pyruvate, for anaplerotic reactions that provide Krebs cycle intermediates necessary for the continued oxidation of acetyl units derived from other substrates (Sahlin *et al.*, 1990).

The increase in skeletal muscle glycogenolysis that occurs during exercise is the result of a number of local and systemic regulatory factors. These include calcium and cyclic-AMP mediated activation of phosphorylase, allosteric activation of phosphorylase and phosphofructokinase by a number of muscle metabolites and alterations in substrate availability (for a review see Hargreaves and Richter, 1988; Hargreaves, 1990). Although muscle glycogen is the predominant carbohydrate energy source during the early stages of exercise, blood glucose becomes more important as exercise continues (Wahren *et al.*, 1971). Muscle glucose uptake can increase up to 30–40 times the resting level, depending upon the exercise intensity and duration (Katz *et al.*, 1986; Wahren *et al.*, 1971). This increase in glucose uptake is achieved by activation of the membrane mechanisms involved in glucose transport and the enzymes responsible for glucose disposal. The important regulatory factors include membrane glucose transporter numbers and activity, sarcoplasmic calcium, circulating insulin levels, intramuscular and blood-borne substrate levels and glucose availability (for a review see Hargreaves, 1990; Holloszy *et al.*, 1986). Accompanying the increased peripheral utilization of glucose during exercise is an increase in hepatic glucose output. Initially this is due to accelerated glycogenolysis, but as exercise continues gluconeogenesis becomes more important with lactate, pyruvate, glycerol and alanine being the major gluconeogenic precursors (Felig and Wahren, 1975). During prolonged exercise lasting several hours, hepatic glucose output may fall

Carbohydrates and exercise

INTESTINE

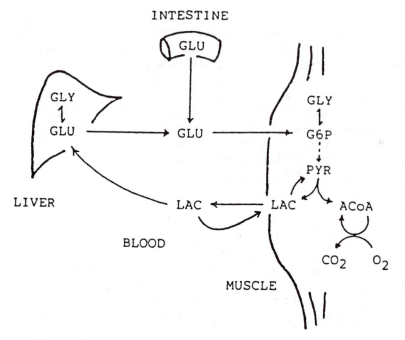

Fig. 2.1 Overview of carbohydrate interactions during exercise.

behind peripheral glucose utilization resulting in hypoglycaemia (Felig *et al.*, 1982). Although the breakdown of muscle glycogen and blood glucose provides pyruvate for oxidation, another important function during exercise is the generation of lactate which can be used as a gluconeogenic precursor and a substrate for contracting muscle (Brooks, 1986).

The importance of muscle glycogen and blood glucose during exercise is demonstrated by the observations that muscle glycogen loading (Bergstrom *et al.*, 1967; Karlsson and Saltin, 1971) and glucose ingestion (Coyle *et al.*, 1983; 1986) result in improved endurance exercise performance. In view of the importance of carbohydrates during exercise, the resynthesis of carbohydrate reserves, in particular muscle glycogen, following exercise is a critical metabolic process in the recovery period. Although exercise will activate glycogen synthase in muscle (Bak and Pedersen, 1990), full restoration of muscle glycogen during recovery is dependent upon an adequate carbohydrate intake. There are a number of factors influencing the rate of muscle glycogen resynthesis, most notably the type and amount of carbohydrate ingested and the timing of carbohydrate ingestion (Costill, 1988; see also Chapter 3). It has been reported that exercise-induced muscle damage can impair muscle glycogen resynthesis, an effect that is partially overcome by increasing carbohydrate intake (Costill *et al.*, 1990). There appears to be a preferential resynthesis of muscle glycogen reserves following exhaustive exercise; however, once this process is complete, liver glycogen levels will return to normal as long as carbohydrate intake is adequate.

2.4 FACTORS INFLUENCING CARBOHYDRATE UTILIZATION DURING EXERCISE

The general pattern of muscle glycogen and glucose utilization outlined above is influenced by a number of factors. These include exercise intensity and duration, training status, diet, environment, age and gender.

2.4.1 Exercise intensity and duration

It has been known for many years, from measurements of the respiratory exchange ratio during exercise, that as exercise intensity increases there is increased reliance on carbohydrate. The biochemical mechanism(s) responsible for this transition are not well understood; however, it makes sense, since the energy yield per litre of oxygen is greater from the oxidation of carbohydrates than from fats. Furthermore, as exercise intensity reaches and exceeds maximal oxygen uptake, muscle glycogen utilization increases markedly and blood glucose utilization declines. Again, this provides an energetic advantage since slightly more ATP is generated from the breakdown of glycogen compared with glucose. The critical role of carbohydrate, in particular muscle glycogen, during exercise above 65–70% of maximal oxygen uptake is demonstrated by the observation that patients suffering from a glycogen phosphorylase deficiency (McArdle's disease) have a maximal exercise capacity that is 40–50% of the expected normal value (Lewis and Haller, 1986). Furthermore, there is evidence that the dominant use of fat as a substrate cannot normally support exercise above 60–65% of maximal oxygen uptake (Davies and Thompson, 1979). Thus, the intense training loads undertaken by competitive athletes place a large demand on their carbohydrate reserves and necessitate increased dietary carbohydrate intake if they are to avoid carbohydrate deficiency that will impair their ability to train effectively.

There is an inverse relationship between exercise intensity and duration. As exercise duration increases there is a declining contribution from carbohydrates, related, in part, to the decreased levels of muscle glycogen and glucose, but also to the increased availability of plasma-free fatty acids. Nevertheless, even during prolonged exercise lasting several hours there is a reliance on carbohydrate to provide pyruvate for ongoing free fatty acid oxidation (see above). The majority of studies on carbohydrate metabolism during exercise have been conducted using continuous exercise. In game situations, however, intermittent high-intensity efforts are performed over 30–90 min and under such conditions there is also likely to be a heavy dependence upon carbohydrate reserves.

2.4.2 Training status

The metabolic consequences of endurance training have been extensively studied for many years (Holloszy and Coyle, 1984). There is a marked decrease in muscle glycogen utilization and lactate production during exercise at the same absolute and relative intensity following endurance training (Hurley *et al.*, 1986; Jansson and Kaijser, 1987). Furthermore, isotopically determined glucose turnover, disposal and oxidation during exercise are lower following endurance training (Coggan *et al.*, 1990), a finding in agreement with the observation of lower leg glucose uptake during exercise in trained, compared with untrained, men (Jansson and Kaijser, 1987). The reduction in glucose turnover is likely to result in a smaller liver glycogen utilization during exercise, although no data are available in humans. The reduction in carbohydrate utilization is generally believed to be due to the increase in muscle oxidative capacity that occurs in response to training. Such adaptation promotes an increase in the aerobic breakdown of carbohydrates, an increased reliance on fat oxidation and less stimulation of glycolysis during exercise (Holloszy and Coyle, 1984). Although the reliance on carbohydrate is lower following training, athletes still need to be aware of the need for adequate dietary carbohydrate since, as a consequence of training, they will be able to train and complete at higher exercise intensities.

2.4.3 Diet

The early work of Christensen and Hansen (1939a) demonstrated the important influence of diet on exercise metabolism and performance. Following consumption of a high carbohydrate diet, respiratory exchange ratios during exercise were higher and exercise time to exhaustion longer than those observed following consumption of a high fat diet. Subsequent work by Bergstrom *et al.* (1967) showed that such dietary manipulation produced marked differences in the pre-exercise muscle glycogen levels and that exercise time to exhaustion was directly related to these initial glycogen levels. Largely on the basis of these results, glycogen loading regimes for endurance events were popularized. Carbohydrate oxidation and muscle glycogen utilization during exercise are greater following consumption of a high carbohydrate diet, presumably due to the relative hyperinsulinemia and increased carbohydrate availability. The increase in muscle glycogen utilization (Sherman *et al.*, 1981) appears to be counteracted by the greater glycogen availability, since endurance performance

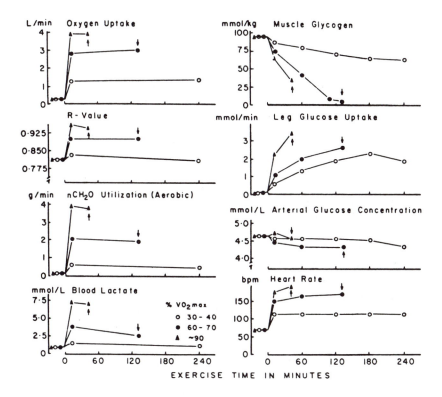

Fig. 2.2 Metabolic responses to exercise of varying intensity and duration (from Saltin and Gollnick (1988) with permission).

is enhanced by glycogen loading (Bergstrom *et al.*, 1967; Karlsson and Saltin, 1971). In contrast, following consumption of a high fat diet or after a 3–4 day fast, carbohydrate oxidation, muscle glycogen utilization and glucose turnover during exercise are lower than after a mixed diet or in the post-absorptive state, respectively (Bergstrom *et al.*, 1967; Jansson and Kaijser, 1982; Knapik *et al.*, 1988). These effects appears to be due to a reduction in carbohydrate availability and the inhibitory effects of lipid metabolites on carbohydrate utilization, the so-called 'glucose–fatty acid cycle'. Recent work has demonstrated reduced muscle glucose uptake during exercise in the presence of elevated plasma levels of lipid metabolites (Hargreaves *et al.*, 1991), although their effect on muscle glycogen utilization during exercise is less clear (Costill *et al.*, 1977; Hargreaves *et al.*, 1991).

2.4.4 Environment

Extremes in the external environment can also influence carbohydrate metabolism during exercise. During exercise in the heat there is an increase in muscle glycogen utilization (Fink *et al.*, 1975), although this has not been observed in all studies (Nielsen *et al.*, 1990; Young *et al.*, 1985). A reduction in muscle blood flow, although controversial (Nielsen *et al.*, 1990), increased muscle temperature and elevated catecholamines may all contribute to a stimulation of muscle glycogenolysis during exercise in the heat. It has recently been demonstrated that muscle glycogen is an important substrate for shivering thermogenesis in humans during cold exposure (Martineau and Jacobs, 1988) and that muscle glycogen utilization is greater during light exercise at 9°C compared with 21°C, although this difference is not seen at higher exercise intensities (Jacobs *et al.*, 1985). The increased circulating catecholamines observed in cold environments may account, in part, for these observations. Exposure to hypoxic environments is associated with an increase in blood lactate, which may reflect an accelerated glycogenolysis or a reduction in lactate clearance. Glucose disposal, as measured using tracer techniques, is greater during exercise under hypoxic conditions (Cooper *et al.*, 1986); however, this may not necessarily result in increased blood glucose utilization, since there is intracellular accumulation of glucose in contracting muscle under such conditions (Katz and Sahlin, 1989). Following adaptation to altitude there appears to be a 'sparing' of muscle glycogen (Young *et al.*, 1982), which may reflect either increased mobilization and utilization of free fatty acids (Young *et al.*, 1982) or an inability to fully activate skeletal muscle during exercise (Green *et al.*, 1989). These observed effects of environment on carbohydrate metabolism during exercise may well have implications for the dietary carbohydrate requirements of athletes who have to train and perform under such conditions.

2.4.5 Age and gender

The majority of studies on carbohydrate metabolism during exercise have been conducted on young, healthy, male subjects. Accordingly, there are relatively few studies examining the influence of age and gender on metabolic responses during exercise. Ageing is associated with a deterioration in glucose tolerance and insulin sensitivity which is attenuated by regular exercise (Seals *et al.*, 1984). Muscle glycogen levels have been reported to be lower in older subjects, but do increase in response to exercise training (Meredith *et al.*, 1989). Glycogen utilization, expressed per unit of energy expenditure during submaximal exercise, is higher in the elderly (Meredith *et al.*, 1989). It remains to be determined whether there are differences in dietary carbohydrate requirements between physically active young and older individuals.

It has often been suggested that there is a greater reliance on fat oxidation during exercise in female, compared with male, subjects, although studies have produced conflicting results (Costill *et al.*, 1979; Froberg and Pedersen, 1984). In a recent study, the metabolic responses of male and female subjects, matched for training status and diet, were studied during exercise at 60–65% of maximal oxygen uptake (Tarnopolsky *et al.*, 1990). Muscle glycogen utilization was 25% lower and estimated total carbohydrate oxidation was 43% lower in the female subjects. In contrast, Brewer *et al.* (1988) have observed no differences in the metabolic responses to treadmill running and increased dietary carbohydrate intake between male and female runners. The divergent results in the literature may reflect difficulties in matching male and female subjects for maximal aerobic power, body composition and exercise intensity. Further work is required to examine the extent of gender differences in the metabolic response to exercise and whether such differences, if they exist, result in differences in dietary carbohydrate requirements.

In summary, muscle glycogen and blood glucose are important substrates for contracting skeletal muscle during exercise and fatigue often coincides with depletion of these carbohydrate reserves. Carbohydrate utilization during exercise is influenced by several factors including exercise intensity and duration, training status, diet, environment and gender. In view of the importance of carbohydrates for exercise performance, active individuals should ensure their diet contains sufficient carbohydrate. For athletes engaged in heavy training the daily carbohydrate requirement may be as high as 9–10 g carbohydrate per kg body mass in order to guarantee adequate carbohydrate availability prior to and during exercise and to allow full recovery of carbohydrate reserves following exercise.

ACKNOWLEDGEMENT

The helpful contribution of Dr Louise Burke, Australian Institute of Sport, during the preparation of this manuscript is gratefully acknowledged.

REFERENCES

Bak, J.F. and Pedersen, O. (1990). Exercise-enhanced activation of glycogen synthase in human skeletal muscle. *American Journal of Physiology*, **258**, E957–E963.

Bergstrom, J. and Hultman, E. (1967). A study of the glycogen metabolism during exercise in man. *Scandinavian Journal of Clinical Laboratory Investigation*, **19**, 218–28.

Bergstrom, J., Hermansen, L., Hultman, E. and Saltin, B. (1967). Diet, muscle glycogen and physical performance. *Acta Physiologica Scandanavica*, **71**, 140–50.

Brewer, J.C., Williams, C. and Patton, A. (1988). The influence of high carbohydrate diets on endurance running performance. *European Journal of Applied Physiology*, **57**, 698–706.

Broberg, S. and Sahlin, K. (1989). Adenine nucleotide degradation in human skeletal muscle during prolonged exercise. *Journal of Applied Physiology*, **67**, 116–22.

Brooks, G.A. (1986). The lactate shuttle during exercise and recovery. *Medicine and Science in Sports and Exercise*, **18**, 360–8.

Burke, L. and Read, R.S.D. (1989). Sports nutrition: approaching the nineties. *Sports Medicine*, **8**, 80–100.

Christensen, E.H. and Hansen, O. (1939a). Arbeitsfahigkeit und Ernahrung. *Scandinavian Archives for Physiology*, **81**, 160–71.

Christensen, E.H. and Hansen, O. (1939b). Hypoglykamie, Arbeitsfahigkeit und Ermudung. *Scandinavian Archives for Physiology*, **81**, 172–9.

Coggan, A.R., Kohrt, W.M., Spina, R.J., Bier, D.M. and Holloszy, J.O. (1990). Endurance training decreases plasma glucose turnover and oxidation during moderate-intensity exercise in man. *Journal of Applied Physiology*, **68**, 990–6.

Cooper, D.M., Wasserman, D.H., Vranic, M. and Wasserman, K. (1986). Glucose turnover in response to exercise during high- and low-F102 breathing in man. *American Journal of Physiology*, **251**, E209–E214.

Costill, D.L. (1988). Carbohydrates for exercise: dietary demands for optimal performance. *International Journal of Sports Medicine*, **9**, 1–18.

Costill, D.L., Coyle, E., Dalsky, G., Evans, W., Fink, W. and Hoopes, D. (1977). Effects of elevated plasma FFA and insulin on muscle glycogen usage during exercise. *Journal of Applied Physiology*, **43**, 695–9.

Costill, D.L., Fink, W.J., Getchell, L., Ivy, J. and Witzmann, F. (1979). Lipid metabolism in skeletal muscle of endurance-trained males and females. *Journal of Applied Physiology*, **47**, 787–91.

Costill, D.L., Pascoe, D.D., Fink, W.J., Robergs, R.A., Barr, S.I. and Pearson, D. (1990). Impaired muscle glycogen resynthesis after eccentric exercise. *Journal of Applied Physiology*, **69**, 46–50.

Coyle, E.F., Hagberg, J.M., Hurley, B.F., Martin, W.H., Ehsani, A.A. and Holloszy, J.O. (1983). Carbohydrate feeding during prolonged strenuous exercise can delay fatigue. *Journal of Applied Physiology*, **55**, 230–5.

Coyle, E.F., Coggan, A.R., Hemmert, M.K. and Ivy, J.L. (1986). Muscle glycogen utilization during prolonged strenuous exercise when fed carbohydrate. *Journal of Applied Physiology*, **61**, 165–72.

Davies, C.T.M. and Thompson, M.W. (1979). Aerobic performance of female and male ultramarathon athletes. *European Journal of Applied Physiology*, **41**, 233–45.

Felig, P. and Wahren, J. (1975). Fuel homeostasis in exercise. *New England Journal of Medicine*, **293**, 1078–84.

Felig, P., Cherif, A., Minagawa, A. and Wahren, J. (1982). Hypoglycemia during prolonged exercise in normal men. *New England Journal of Medicine*, **306**, 895–900.

Fink, W.J., Costill, D.L. and van Handel, P.J. (1975). Leg muscle metabolism during exercise in the heat and cold. *European Journal of Applied Physiology*, **34**, 183–90.

Froberg, K. and Pedersen, P. (1984). Sex difference in endurance capacity and metabolic response to prolonged, heavy exercise. *European Journal of Applied Physiology*, **52**, 446–50.

Green, H.J., Sutton, J., Young, P., Cymerman, A. and Houston, C.S. (1989). Operation Everest II: muscle energetics during maximal exhaustive exercise. *Journal of Applied Physiology*, **66**, 142–50.

Hargreaves, M. (1990). Skeletal muscle carbohydrate metabolism during exercise. *Australian Journal of Science and Medicine in Sport*, **22**, 35–8.

Hargreaves, M. and Richter, E.A. (1988). Regulation of skeletal muscle glycogenolysis during exercise. *Canadian Journal of Sports Science*, **13**, 197–203.

Hargreaves, M., Kiens, B. and Richter, E.A. (1991). Effect of increased plasma free fatty acid concentrations on muscle metabolism in exercising man. *Journal of Applied Physiology*, **70**, 194–201.

Hermansen, L., Hultman, E. and Saltin, B. (1967). Muscle glycogen during prolonged severe exercise. *Acta Physiologica Scandanavica*, **71**, 129–39.

Holloszy, J.O. and Coyle, E.F. (1984). Adaptations of skeletal muscle to endurance exercise and their metabolic consequences. *Journal of Applied Physiology*, **56**, 831–8.

Holloszy, J.O., Constable, S.H. and Young, D.A. (1986). Activation of glucose transport in muscle by exercise. *Diabetes/Metabolism Reviews*, **1**, 409–23.

Hurley, B.F., Nemeth, P.M., Martin, W.H., Hagberg, J., Dalsky, G. and Holloszy, J.O. (1986). Muscle triglyceride utilization during exercise: effect of training. *Journal of Applied Physiology*, **60**, 562–7.

Jacobs, I., Romet, T.T. and Kerrigan-Brown, D. (1985). Muscle glycogen depletion during exercise at 9°C and 21°C. *European Journal of Applied Physiology*, **54**, 35–9.

Jansson, E. and Kaijser, L. (1982). Effect of diet on the utilization of bloodborne and intramuscular substrate during exercise in man. *Acta Physiologica Scandanavica*, **115**, 19–30.

Jansson, E. and Kaijser, L. (1987). Substrate utilization and enzymes in skeletal muscle of extremely endurance-trained men. *Journal of Applied Physiology*, **62**, 999–1005.

Jenkins, D.J.A., Wolever, T.M.S., Jenkins, A.L., Josse, R.G. and Wong, G.S. (1984). The glycaemic response to carbohyrate foods. *Lancet*, **2**, 388–91.

Katz, A. and Sahlin, K. (1989). Effect of hypoxia on glucose metabolism in human skeletal muscle during exercise. *Acta Physiologica Scandanavica*, **136**, 377–82.

Katz, A., Broberg, S., Sahlin, K. and Wahren, J. (1986). Leg glucose uptake during maximal dynamic exercise in humans. *American Journal of Physiology*, **251**, E65–E70.

Karlsson, J. and Saltin, B. (1971). Diet, muscle glycogen and endurance performance. *Journal of Applied Physiology*, **31**, 203–6.

Knapik, J.J., Meredith, C.N., Jones, B.H., Suek, L., Young, V.R. and Evans, W.J. (1988). Influence of fasting on carbohydrate and fat metabolism during rest and exercise in men. *Journal of Applied Physiology*, **64**, 1923–9.

Krogh, A. and Lindhard, J. (1920). The relative value of fat and carbohydrates as sources of muscular energy. *Biochemical Journal*, **14**, 290–363.

Lewis, S.F. and Haller, R.G. (1986). The pathophysiology of McArdle's disease: clues to regulation in exercise and fatigue. *Journal of Applied Physiology*, **61**, 391–401.

Martineau, L. and Jacobs, I. (1988). Muscle glycogen utilization during shivering thermogenesis in humans. *Journal of Applied Physiology*, **65**, 2046–50.

Maughan, R.J. (1990). Effects of diet composition on the performance of high intensity exercise. In *Nutrition and Sport* (ed. H. Monod), pp. 200–11. Masson, Paris.

Meredith, C.N., Frontera, W.R., Fisher, E.C., Hughes, V.A., Herland, J.C., Edwards, J. and Evans, W.J. (1989). Peripheral effects of endurance training in young and old subjects. *Journal of Applied Physiology*, **66**, 2844–9.

Nielsen, B., Savard, G., Richter, E.A., Hargreaves, M. and Saltin, B. (1990). Muscle blood flow and muscle metabolism during exercise and heat stress. *Journal of Applied Physiology*, **69**, 1040–6.

Norman, B., Sollevi, A., Kaijser, L. and Jansson, E. (1987). ATP breakdown products in human skeletal muscle during prolonged exercise to exhaustion. *Clinical Physiology*, **7**, 503–9.

Sahlin, K., Katz, A. and Broberg, S. (1990). Tricarboxylic acid cycle intermediates in human muscle during prolonged exercise. *American Journal of Physiology*, **259**, C834–C841.

Saltin, B. and Gollnick, P.D. (1988). Fuel for muscular exercise: role of carbohydrate. In *Exercise, Nutrition and Energy Metabolism* (eds. E.S. Horton and R.L. Terjung), pp. 45–71. Macmillan, New York.

Saltin, B. and Karlsson, J. (1971). Muscle glycogen utilization during work of different intensities. In *Muscle Metabolism During Exercise* (eds. B. Pernon and B. Saltin), pp. 289–99. Plenum Press, New York.

Saris, W.M., van Erp-Baart, M.A., Brouns, F., Westerterp, K.R. and ten Hoor, F. (1989). Study on food intake and energy expenditure during extreme sustained exercise. *International Journal of Sports Medicine*, **10**, S26–S31.

Seals, D.R., Hagberg, J.M., Allen, W.K., Hurley, B.F., Dalsky, G.P., Ehsani, A.A. and Holloszy, J.O. (1984). Glucose tolerance in young and older athletes and sedentary men. *Journal of Applied Physiology*, **56**, 1521–5.

Sherman, W.M., Costill, D.L., Fink, W.J. and Miller, J.M. (1981). The effect of exercise and diet manipulation on muscle glycogen and its subsequent utilization during performance. *International Journal of Sports Medicine*, **2**, 114–18.

Snyder, A.C., Schultz, L.O. and Foster, C. (1989). Voluntary consumption of a carbohydrate supplement by elite speed skaters. *Journal of American Dietrics Association*, **89**, 1125–7.

Tarnolpolsky, L.J., MacDougall, J.D., Atkinson, S.A., Tarnopolsky, M.A. and Sutton, J.R. (1990). Gender differences in substrate for endurance exercise. *Journal of Applied Physiology*, **68**, 302–8.

Vøllestad, N.K. and Blom, P.C.S. (1985). Effect of varying exercise intensity on glycogen depletion in human muscle fibres. *Acta Physiologica Scandanavica*, **125**, 395–405.

Vøllestad, N.K., Vaage, O. and Hermansen, L. (1984). Muscle glycogen depletion patterns in type I and subgroups of type II fibres during prolonged severe exercise in man. *Acta Physiologica Scandanavica*, **122**, 433–41.

Wahren, J., Felig, P. Ahlborg, G. and Jorfeldt, L. (1971). Glucose metabolism during leg exercise in man. *Journal of Clinical Investigations*, **50**, 2715–25.

Young, A.J., Evans, W.J., Cymerman, A., Pandolf, K.B., Knapik, J.J. and Maher, J.T. (1982). Sparing effect of chronic high-altitude exposure on muscle glycogen utilization. *Journal of Applied Physiology*, **52**, 857–62.

Young, A.J., Sawka, M.N., Levine, L., Cadarette, B.S. and Pandolf, K.B. (1985). Skeletal muscle metabolism during exercise is influenced by heat acclimation. *Journal of Applied Physiology*, **59**, 1929–35.

3

Timing and method of increased carbohydrate intake to cope with heavy training, competition and recovery

Edward F. Coyle

3.1 INTRODUCTION

Proper nutrition is critical for optimal physical performance. A person's diet must contain adequate amounts of various nutrients which are used to regenerate bodily tissue and provide fuel for many processes, particularly muscular exercise. Carbohydrate is the most important nutrient in an athlete's diet because it is the only fuel that can power intense exercise for prolonged periods, yet its stores within the body are relatively small. Athletes are frequently undernourished with respect to carbohydrate and therefore their training and performance suffer (Costill *et al.*, 1988). The purpose of this chapter is to discuss methods for increasing carbohydrate intake to speed recovery from heavy training and to improve performance during competition. The conditions which require carbohydrate supplementation, the critical timing of supplementation, as well as the amount and type of carbohydrate that is best will be discussed. The various regimes of carbohydrate intake should be judged by how well they allow the athlete to exercise intensely during the latter stages of exercise when success hangs in the balance and carbohydrate stores are often limiting. As such, these guidelines apply mostly to athletes who frequently train intensely and often experience muscle glycogen depletion, sometimes on a daily basis. However, these recommendations can also apply to the average

Food, Nutrition and Sports Performance
Edited by Clyde Williams and John T. Devlin
Published in 1992 by E & F N Spon, London. ISBN 0 419 17890 2

person, who for a brief period may participate in strenuous activities. They too may benefit by dietary carbohydrate supplementation for the same reason that athletes benefit.

In this chapter, carbohydrate intake is quantified in grams to better illustrate food portions; however, ideally it should be made relative to body weight (i.e. in g per kg). All recommendations are made for a reference person weighing 70 kg (154 lbs). Therefore, when applying these recommendations to others, the extent to which their body weight differs from 70 kg should be factored in. For example, a person weighing 100 kg should multiple the recommended intake by 1.4 (i.e. 100/70 kg), whereas a person weighing 50 kg should multiply the recommended intake by 0.7 (i.e. 50/70 kg).

3.2 CARBOHYDRATE TYPES AND METABOLIC RATES

Glucose is the only type of carbohydrate (i.e. sugar or starch) which skeletal muscle can readily metabolize for energy and which it can store as glycogen. The liver can metabolize both glucose and fructose. Carbohydrates are eaten before, during and after exercise for the primary purpose of providing glucose to skeletal muscle. A secondary purpose is to present glucose and fructose to the liver for glycogen synthesis in that organ. Carbohydrates can be functionally classified according to the extent to which they increase blood glucose concentration (i.e. glycaemic index) and by the extent to which they trigger insulin secretion which responds to and reflects the rate of glucose entry into the blood.

The glycaemic index is generally determined by the rate at which the ingested carbohydrate is made available to intestinal enzymes for hydrolysis and intestinal absorption (O'Dea *et al.*, 1980; Gatti *et al.*, 1987). This is a function of the gastric emptying time (Mourot *et al.*, 1988) and the physical availability of the sugar or starch to hydrolytic enzymes. The latter is influenced by cooking which alters the integrity of the starch granule (Wursch *et al.*, 1986) and the degree of gelatinization (O'Dea *et al.*, 1980). Another factor is the amylose against amylopectin content of food (Behall *et al.*, 1988; Goddard *et al.*, 1984). It is a misconception to think that the glycaemic index is simply a function of whether the carbohydrate is complex (i.e. starch) or a simple sugar.

Some starchy foods produce glycaemic responses which are identical to that of glucose (i.e. baked potato, maltodextrins) (Crapo *et al.*, 1977; Guezennec *et al.*, 1989). On the other hand, the rise in blood glucose after eating fructose or sucrose is less than that observed for a wide range of starchy complex carbohydrates (e.g. potato, bread, cornflakes) (Jenkins *et al.*, 1984). These points are summarized in Tables 3.1, 3.2 and 3.3

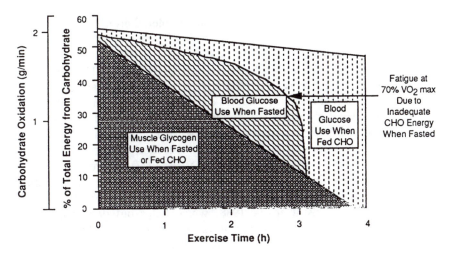

Fig. 3.1 The percentage of energy and the absolute rate of carbohydrate oxidation which is derived from muscle glycogen and blood glucose during prolonged cycling. When exercising at 70–75% of maximal oxygen uptake, approximately 50% of the energy is derived from carbohydrate and 50% is derived from fat. The contribution of muscle glycogen to energy is similar with and without carbohydrate ingestion during exercise. The energy derived from blood glucose is shown when fasted and when fed carbohydrate. Fatigue occurs after 3 h of exercise in the fasted state because blood glucose concentration declines and its contribution to energy declines below 30%. Carbohydrate ingestion which maintains blood glucose concentration allows blood glucose oxidation to increase to where it supplies almost all of the carbohydrate energy during the 3–4 h period of exercise. Adapted from Coyle *et al.* (1986).

which display various foods classified as having a high, moderate or low glycaemic index (Jenkins *et al.*, 1984) whereas Table 3.4 contains common food which the author does not have sufficient information to classify. The amount of food which contains 50 g of carbohyrate is also reported so that practical recommendations can be quantified.

3.3 MUSCLE GLYCOGEN RESYNTHESIS FOLLOWING EXERCISE

The restoration of muscle glycogen after heavy training or competition quite often dictates the time needed to recover between intense bouts of exercise. It is commonly stated that muscle glycogen becomes depleted after about 2–3 h of continuous exercise performed at intensities of approximately 60–80% VO_2 max. Although true, it is not usually appreciated that muscle glycogen can also become depleted after only 15–30 min of exercise, which is performed at very high intensities (90–130% VO_2 max) in 'intervals' of 1–5 min exercise bouts followed by a rest period and then another 'interval' and rest, etc. (Keizer *et al.*, 1986). These patterns of intense exercise are typical of many individual and team sports. As such, it is not uncommon for athletes participating in soccer or hockey to become somewhat glycogen depleted by the half-time of the game or after a hard practice. There is some good evidence that low muscle glycogen levels are associated with increased injury risk in alpine downhill skiing, especially in recreational skiers (Eriksson *et al.*, 1977). Therefore, athletes who attempt to train daily at intensities which deplete muscle glycogen, must increase their carbohydrate consumption from 50–60% to 70–80% of their calories (Costill *et al.*, 1988) which helps but does not always guarantee optimal muscle glycogen storage (Kirwan *et al.*, 1988).

Exhaustive exercise in athletes usually causes muscle glycogen concentration to decline about 100 mmol kg^{-1} (e.g. from 130 to 30 mmol kg^{-1}). Therefore, for sake of simplicity, the rate of glycogen resynthesis in units of mmol kg^{-1} h^{-1} generally agrees with the percentage restoration per hour. In people, muscle glycogen is resynthesized to normally high levels at a rate of only about 5 mmol kg muscle^{-1} h^{-1} which corresponds to a rate of about 5% per h (i.e. 5 mmol kg muscle^{-1} h^{-1} when attempting to increase muscle glycogen to 100 mmol kg^{-1}). Therefore, approximately 20 h are required to recover muscle glycogen stores. A longer time will be necessary if the diet is not optimal. The important dietary factors to consider are: (a) the rate of carbohydrate ingestion, (b) carbohydrate type, and (c) timing of carbohydrate ingestion after exercise.

3.3.1 Rate of carbohydrate ingestion

Blom *et al.* (1987) and Ivy *et al.* (1988b) fed subjects different amounts of high-glycaemic carbohydrates (i.e. glucose or maltodextrins) every 2 h after exercise and measured the rates of muscle glycogen synthesis during the first 6 h. They reported that glycogen synthesis increased from 2% per h (i.e. 2 mmol kg^{-1} h^{-1}) when 25 g was ingested every 2 h to 5–6% per h (i.e. 5–6 mmol^{-1} h^{-1}) when 50 g was ingested every 2 h. However, they did not observe muscle glycogen synthesis to increase to more than 5–6% per h (i.e. 5–6 mmol kg^{-1} h^{-1}) when 100, 112 or 225 g were ingested every 2 h.

This plateau in glycogen synthesis does not appear to be due simply to an accumulation of carbohydrate in the gastrointestinal tract because Reed *et al.* (1989) reported that intravenous glucose infusion at about 100 g every 2 h also failed to increase muscle glycogen synthesis above 7–8 mmol kg^{-1} h^{-1}. Additionally, this failure of muscle glycogen synthesis to increase with increased carbohydrate ingestion or intravenous glucose infusion (100 g per 2 h) occurred despite the fact that increased carbohydrate administration promoted progressively greater increases in blood glucose and plasma insulin concentration, which remained within the physiological range (Blom *et al.*, 1987; Ivy *et al.*, 1988a; Reed *et al.*, 1989).

Therefore, other factors besides glucose entry into blood (within the normal range) seem to limit muscle glycogen resynthesis after exercise. One possibility is that glucose presentation to muscle is limited by muscle blood flow and that increased glucose administration does little to markedly increase glucose presentation to muscle yet it increases the insulin response which causes increased glucose oxidation and glucose disposal by tissue other than the previously exercised muscle (Bourey *et al.*, 1990; Constable *et al.*, 1984; Reed *et al.*, 1989). This suggests that the muscle glycogen synthesis is near optimal (5–7 mmol kg^{-1} h^{-1}) when at least 50 g of glucose is ingested every 2 h, most of which enters the blood. This forms the basis for the recommendation that the amount and type of food to be eaten after exercise for near optimal muscle glycogen resynthesis should be that which promotes glucose entry into the blood and systemic circulation at a rate of at least 50 g every 2 h. This goal can be achieved by considering both the glycaemic index, which reflects the rate of absorption, and the amount of carbohydrate ingested. Tables 3.1–3.4 present the portions of various foods which contain 50 g of carbohydrate.

3.3.2 Carbohydrate type and glycogen resynthesis

As discussed, the rate of glycogen synthesis after exercise and ingestion of glucose, or food with a high glycaemic index (Table 3.1), is 5–6% per h (i.e. 5–6 mmol kg^{-1} h^{-1}) (Blom *et al.*, 1987; Ivy *et al.*, 1988a; Ivy *et al.*, 1988b; Reed *et al.*, 1989). When sucrose is ingested, it is hydrolysed to equal amounts of glucose and fructose. Its ingestion elicits a similar rate of glycogen synthesis as glucose ingestion, despite the fact that the glycaemic index of sucrose is 60–70% of that of glucose (Blom *et al.*, 1987; Jenkins *et al.*, 1984), which classifies it as having a moderate to high glycaemic index (Tables 3.1 and 3.2). A possible explanation for the similar rates of post-exercise glycogen synthesis with glucose and sucrose is that the fructose moiety formed during the hydrolysis of sucrose reduces glucose uptake by the liver, thereby allowing a sufficient presentation of glucose moieties to the muscle for glycogen synthesis.

However, fructose ingestion alone promotes muscle glycogen to be resynthesized at only 3% per h (i.e. 3 mmol kg^{-1} h^{-1}) because of its low glycaemic index (20–30% of that of glucose; Table 3.3) (Blom *et al.*, 1987; Jenkins *et al.*, 1984). It appears that fructose ingestion, even in large amounts which causes diarrhoea, cannot produce sufficient entry of glucose into the blood (i.e. 50 g every 2 h) probably because of the relatively slow rate with which the liver converts fructose to blood glucose. Concerning simple sugars, it appears that glucose and sucrose, which possess high and moderate glycaemic indexes, are equally effective in the partial restoration of muscle glycogen during the 4–6 h period after exercise yet fructose is only one-half as effective due to a low glycaemic index.

A limited amount of information is available about the rates of glycogen synthesis elicited by eating common foods containing various starches and sugars. When the type of carbohydrate ingested elicits a high and moderate glycaemic index (Tables 3.1 and 3.2), it makes little difference if the carbohydrate is in liquid or solid form (Keizer *et al.*, 1986; Reed *et al.*, 1989). The rate of muscle glycogen resynthesis after eating rice (100 g every 2 h), which possesses a moderate glycaemic index (Table 3.2), is not different from that observed when an equal amount of maltodextrins (high glycaemic index) is ingested (i.e. 4.6 ± 0.5 against 5.1 ± 1.0 mmol $kg^{-1} h^{-1}$; Coyle and Ivy, unpublished observations). Based upon our present knowledge, it appears that foods with a moderate glycaemic index (Table 3.2) produce a sufficient rate of glucose entry into blood to promote a rate of glycogen resynthesis which is similar to that after eating food with a high glycaemic index (Table 3.1). This is supported by studies which have found muscle glycogen resynthesis to be similar during the 24 h period after exercise when ingesting approximately 600 g of sucrose/glucose/fructose compared to moderate glycaemic starches (Costill *et al.*, 1981). Additionally, Brewer *et al.* (1988) have found that a diet high in carbohydrate, obtained either from simple sugars or complex carbohydrate, was equally effective in improving endurance performance.

Little data exist as to the extent to which carbohydrate foods with a low glycaemic index (Table 3.3) promote muscle glycogen resynthesis (Kiens *et al.*, 1990). As discussed, fructose is converted to glucose relatively slowly, which explains the relatively low glycaemic index of numerous fruits and the fact that it stimulates muscle glycogen resynthesis to only one-half the rate elicited by high glycaemic foods. Legumes possess a low glycaemic index largely because the carbohydrate granule is not as accessible to digestive enzymes (Wursch *et al.*, 1986), a factor which can be influenced by food processing and cooking. It appears that low glycaemic legumes can promote a sufficient rate of glucose entry into blood for optimal muscle glycogen synthesis by the 20–44 h period after exercise, but the rate of glycogen synthesis may be suboptimal during the first 6 h (Kiens *et al.*, 1990). However, until more direct data becomes available, it is assumed that foods with a low glycaemic index (Table 3.3) should not comprise the bulk of carbohydrate ingested after exercise, when appetite is suppressed, because it is likely that muscle glycogen synthesis would be compromised. It is estimated, somewhat arbitrarily, that no more than one-third of the carbohydrate consumed should be derived from low-glycaemic foods (Table 3.3) when attempting to maximize muscle glycogen resynthesis.

Table 3.1 Carbohydrate-containing foods with a High Glycaemic Index (foods listed as eaten)

Food group	Food item	Serving size (g or ml) giving 50 g carbohydrate	Fat per serving (g)
Cereals	White bread	201 g	2
	Wholemeal bread	120 g	3
	Rye bread (light)	104 g	4
	Bagel	89 g	2
	Pastry (shortcrust)	90 g	29
	Rice (wholegrain)	196 g	1
	Rice (white)	169 g	0.5
Breakfast	Cornflakes	59 g	1
Cereals	Muesli	76 g	6
	Shredded Wheat	74 g	2
	Weetabix	71 g	2
Biscuits and	Wholewheat semi-sweet		
Confectionery	biscuits	76 g	16
	Crispread – rye	71 g	1.5
	Plain cracker	66 g	8
	Chocolate nougat bar (contains sucrose and glucose)	75 g	14
Vegetables	Sweetcorn	219 g	5
	Broad beans	704 g	4
	Parsnips	370 g	Trace
	Potato (instant)	310 g	0.5
	Potato (boiled)	254 g	Trace
	Potato (baked)	200 g	Trace
Fruit	Raisins	78 g	Trace
	Banana	260 g	1
Sugars	Glucose	50 g	0
	Maltose	50 g	0
	Honey	67 g	wax only, 3
	Sucrose	50 g	0
	Molasses	113 ml	0
	Corn syrup	63 g	0
Beverages	6% sucrose solution	833 ml	0
	7.5% maltodextrin and sugar	666 ml	0
	10% Corn syrup – Carbonated drink	500 ml	0
	20% maltodextrin	250 ml	0

According to Jenkins et al. (1988 and 1984) where foods are classified against white bread with an equivalent of 100. Foods with values at >85 are considered to have 'high glycaemic indices'. Nutritional values from McCance and Widdowson's, *The Composition of Foods*, 4th revised edition by A.A. Paul and D.A.T. Southgate (1978), London: HMSO and *Food Values of Portions Commonly Used*, by Jean A.T. Pennington, New York: Harper and Row, 15th Edition.

Table 3.2 Carbohydrate-containing foods with a Moderate Glycaemic Index (foods listed as eaten)

Food group	Food item	Serving size (g) giving 50 g carbohydrate	Fat per serving (g)
Cereals	Spaghetti/Macaroni	198	1
	Noodles (oriental)	370	14
Breakfast cereals	Wheatbran nuggets	232	13
	Porridge (oatmeal)	69	1
Biscuits and confectionery	Oatmeal biscuits	79	15
	Sweet, plain	67	11
	Sponge cake	93	6
Vegetables	Potato (Sweet)	249	1
	Yam	168	Trace
	Potato chips	100	40
Fruit	Grapes (Black)	323	Trace
	Grapes (Green)	310	Trace
	Orange	420–600	Trace

According to Jenkins *et al.* (1984 and 1988) where foods are classified against white bread with an equivalent of 100. Foods with values between 60–85 are considered to have 'moderate glycaemic indices'. Nutritional values from McCance and Widdowson's, *The Composition of Foods*, 4th revised edition by A.A. Paul and D.A.T. Southgate (1978), London: HMSO and *Food Values of Portions Commonly Used*, by Jean A.T. Pennington, New York: Harper and Row, 15th Edition.

3.3.3   Timing of carbohydrate ingestion after exercise

During the first 2 h following exercise, the rate of muscle glycogen resynthesis is 7–8% per h (i.e. 7–8 mmol kg^{-1} h^{-1}), which is somewhat faster than the normal rate of 5–6% per h, but certainly not rapid (Ivy *et al.*, 1988b). A recovering athlete should ingest sufficient carbohydrate as soon after exercise as is practical. The most important reason for this is that it will provide more total time for resynthesis.

Since eating more than 50 g of carbohydrate (with a high or moderate glycaemic index) every 2 h does not seem beneficial for increasing muscle glycogen resynthesis, one might think it best that small frequent meals be eaten until a sufficient total amount of carbohydrate has been consumed (i.e. >600 g for a 70 kg person). However, this does not appear to be the case. Costill *et al.* (1981) fed subjects 525 g of carbohydrate over the course of 24 h (which comprised 70% of the caloric intake) and reported that muscle glycogen synthesis was similar when two large meals were eaten as compared to when seven smaller meals were eaten.

3.3.4 Practical considerations and specific recommendations

People are not usually hungry immediately following exhaustive exercise and often prefer to drink fluids rather than to eat solid foods (Keizer *et al.*, 1986). Therefore, beverages which contain glucose, sucrose, maltodextrins or corn syrups in concentrations of 6 g/100 ml or higher should be made available. Table 3.1 lists the volumes of various high-glycaemic solutions which should be ingested every 2 h to obtain at least 50 g of carbohydrate. If preferred, there is no reason why an athlete should not eat solid food. However, since appetite is usually suppressed, foods which

Table 3.3 Carbohydrate-containing foods with a Low Glycaemic Index (foods listed as eaten)

Food group	Food item	Serving size (g, ml or l) giving 50 g carbohydrate	Fat per serving (g)
Fruits	Apples	400 g	Trace
	Apple sauce (sweet)	290 g	Trace
	Cherries	420 g	Trace
	Dates (dried)	78 g	Trace
	Figs (raw)	526 g	Trace
	Grapefruit (canned)	300 g	Trace
	Peaches	450–550 g	Trace
	Plums	400–550 g	Trace
Legumes	Butter beans	292 g	1
	Baked beans	485 g	2
	Haricot beans	301 g	2
	Chick peas	305 g	5
	Red lentils	294 g	2
	Navy beans	238 g	1
Sugars	Fructose	50 g	0
Dairy Products	Ice cream	202 g	13
	Milk (whole)	1.1 l	40
	Milk (skim)	1.0 l	1
	Yoghurt (plain, low fat)	800 g	8
	Yoghurt (fruit, low fat)	280 g	3
Soup	Tomato soup	734 ml	6

According to Jenkins *et al.* (1984 and 1988) where foods are classified against white bread with an equivalent of 100. Foods with values at <60 are considered to have 'low glycaemic indices'. Nutritional values from McCance and Widdowson's, *The Composition of Foods*, 4th revised edition by A.A. Paul and D.A.T. Southgate (1978), London: HMSO and *Food Values of Portions Commonly Used*, by Jean A.T. Pennington, New York: Harper and Row, 15th Edition.

are more concentrated in carbohydrate and which have a high glycaemic index should be available. These foods generally have a relatively small amount of fat, protein and fibre (i.e. bananas, raisins, high carbohydrate confectionery candy bars). When the desire for solid food returns, the athletes should eat enough to ensure that a total of approximately 600 g of carbohydrate is eaten within 24 h. Most of the food chosen should have a moderate or high glycaemic index (Tables 3.1 and 3.2), although a certain amount of low-glycaemic carbohydrate is acceptable (e.g. one-

Table 3.4 Carbohydrate-containing foods with an Undetermined Glycaemic Index (foods listed as eaten)

Food group	Food item	Serving size (g or ml) giving 50 g carbohydrate	Fat per serving (g)
Beverages	Apple juice	366 ml	0
	Grape juice	311 ml	Trace
	Papaya nectar	326 ml	0
	Pineapple juice	371 ml	0.5
	Prune juice	269 ml	Trace
	Grapefruit juice (sweetened)	515 ml	Trace
Cereal/Grain Products	Rice cakes	60 g	2.2
	Pancakes	138 g	2.2
	Cream of rice	340 g	9
Biscuit Confectionery	Shortbread	76 g	20
	Cream crackers	73 g	12
	Rich fruit cake	86 g	9
	Madeira cake	86 g	15
	Jam tart	80 g	12
	Christmas pudding	105 g	12
	Scones	89 g	13
	Fruit pie	88 g	14
	Boiled sweets (Sugar confectionery)	57 g	Trace
Miscellaneous	Pizza (cheese and tomato)	202 g	23
Fruit	Apricots (stewed with sugar)	320 g	Trace
	Apricots (dried)	115 g	Trace

Nutritional values from McCance and Widdowson's, *The Composition of Foods*, 4th revised edition by A.A. Paul and D.A.T. Southgate (1978), London: HMSO and *Food Values of Portions Commonly Used*, by Jean A.T. Pennington, New York: Harper and Row, 15th Edition.

third of total carbohydrate). The athlete should avoid eating meals which contain less than 70% carbohydrate, and thus have high fat and protein content, especially during the first 6 h after exercise because this often suppresses hunger and limits carbohydrate intake.

Realistically, due to other daily activities including sleep, it is usually not possible to eat meals frequently (every 2 h) which contain at least 70% and 50 g of carbohydrate. Therefore, when a person must go for an extended period between meals, their last meal should contain enough carbohydrate to suffice for that period (i.e. 50 g per 2 h and therefore 150 g for a 6 h period or 250 g for a 10 h period). To ensure a more uniform rate of gastric emptying, carbohydrate digestion and blood glucose availability throughout this extended period, it is probably helpful for this meal to contain a limited amount of fat and protein because they slow the gastric emptying of a large carbohydrate meal.

This may explain why Costill *et al.* (1981) found glycogen synthesis to be similar with two large meals compared to seven smaller meals. However, if a person chooses to eat only twice a day, it should be realized that each of these two huge meals has the potential to be quite bulky if obtained solely from starchy food (i.e. bread, potato, rice, spaghetti, cereal, etc.). This is why it is often necessary to drink solutions with concentrated carbohydrate.

Given the limited rate of muscle glycogen recovery post-exercise, it is not possible to train with optimal muscle glycogen when two or more workouts are performed per day. Even when carbohydrate intake is very high, muscle glycogen will probably be suboptimal in direct relation to the volume of high-intensity exercise performed during the extra session. As a result, athletes will not be able to tolerate training at peak competitive intensities. Therefore, it is well known that sufficient time must be allowed between training sessions performed at race pace during the 'peak' of the competitive season, and it would be counterproductive not to reduce training volume.

3.4 MAXIMIZING MUSCLE GLYCOGEN PRIOR TO COMPETITION

A few days prior to a prolonged and intense competitive event, athletes should regulate their diets and training in an attempt to maximize ('super compensate' or 'load') muscle glycogen stores. High pre-exercise glycogen levels will allow athletes to exercise for longer periods by delaying fatigue. The most practical method (Sherman *et al.*, 1981) of 'glycogen loading' involves altering training and diet for 7 days. On days 7, 6, 5 and 4 before competition one should train moderately hard (e.g. 1–2 h) and consume a moderately low carbohydrate diet (i.e. 350 g day^{-1}). This will make the muscle sufficiently carbohydrate deprived and ready to supercompensate, without making the person sick as sometimes occurs when all carbohydrate is eliminated. However, the extent to which carbohydrates must be restricted has not been determined. During the 3 days prior to competition, training should be tapered (30–60 min day^{-1} of low to moderate intensity) and a high-carbohydrate diet consumed (i.e. 500–600 g day^{-1}). Such a regimen will increase muscle glycogen stores 20–40% or more above normal. This 'modified' glycogen loading regimen is as effective as the 'classic' regimen (Bergstrom and Hultman, 1966), and more practical since it does not require athletes to attempt to maintain training while consuming a high-fat diet. It has also been suggested that muscle glycogen supercompensation improves performance during maximal exercise of only several minutes in duration (Maughan, 1990).

3.5   PRE-EVENT NUTRITION

Although it is agreed that athletes should eat sufficient carbohydrate the day before exercise, there is less agreement as to when, how much and what type of carbohydrate should be eaten during the hours before exercise.

3.5.1   When fuel stores are adequate

The only rationale for eating fat or protein during the several hours before exercise is to control hunger which is not trivial because it promotes a sense of well-being. When participating in sports and activities which are not prolonged and not intense and which therefore do not require more carbohydrate than is normally available in the fasted state, the choice of food consumption before exercise should be made by the athlete based upon past experience as to what minimizes hunger yet prevents the sensation of stomach fullness.

3.5.2   Exercise which is limited by carbohydrate availability

The goal of a pre-exercise carbohydrate meal is to optimize the supply of muscle glycogen and blood glucose late in the subsequent exercise bout. Pre-exercise carbohydrate meals have the following effects: (1) promote additional muscle glycogen synthesis when stores are not already supercompensated; (2) replenish liver glycogen and store glucose in the body (i.e. intestines and glucose space) for potential oxidation during exercise; and (3) cause increases in carbohydrate oxidation during exercise and decreases in fat oxidation.

Although these first two responses to pre-exercise carbohydrate feeding are beneficial because more carbohydrate is stored within the body, controversy remains as to whether the increase in carbohydrate oxidation is advantageous or disadvantageous. It would seem disadvantageous if the increases in carbohydrate oxidation were greater than the increases in carbohydrate storage because bodily carbohydrate stores would become depleted more rapidly compared to when carbohydrate is not consumed before exercise.

3.5.3 Sugar feedings during the hour before exercise

Fasting overnight followed by eating sugar during the hour before moderately intense exercise (i.e. 60–75% VO_2 max) may cause a decline in blood glucose concentration at the onset of exercise (Costill *et al.*, 1977). This is due to the effects of the concomitant hyperinsulinaemia which increases glucose uptake by the contracting muscles at a time when liver glucose output may be reduced thus creating an imbalance and hypoglycaemia (Ahlborg and Felig, 1976; Ahlborg and Bjorkman, 1987; Costill *et al.* 1977). This is usually not perceived by the individual and it does not cause muscle weakness. Hyperinsulinaemia also has the long-lasting effect of reducing the release of free fatty acids (FFA) from adipocytes and the rate of fat oxidation (Coyle *et al.*, 1985).

Thus there is a shift in blood-borne fuels from FFA to glucose. There has been much debate as to whether these processes alter muscle glycogen use. Theoretically, muscle glycogen use would be increased if the decline in fat oxidation was not offset by a proportional increase in blood glucose uptake and oxidation by muscle. The two studies which have found pre-exercise feedings to slightly increase muscle glycogen use also reported a relatively large decline in blood glucose concentration, which may have limited increases in muscle glucose uptake (Costill *et al.*, 1977; Hargreaves *et al.*, 1985). Several other studies have not found sugar feedings during the hour before exercise to increase muscle glycogen use, possibly because the hypoglycaemia was not as pronounced (Levine *et al.*, 1983; Koivisto *et al.*, 1985; Gleeson *et al.*, 1986; Fielding *et al.*, 1987; Hargreaves *et al.*, 1987).

More importantly, in examining the studies which have measured endurance performance following sugar ingestion during the hour before exercise (Table 3.5), only one study has reported a negative effect (Foster *et al.*, 1979); four studies have observed no significant effect (McMurray *et al.*, 1983; Keller and Schwarzkopf, 1984; Devlin *et al.*, 1986; Hargreaves *et al.*, 1987); and three studies reported improvements in performance (Gleeson *et al.*, 1986; Okano *et al.*, 1988; Peden *et al.*, 1989). Therefore, there is little support for the idea that sugar ingestion before exercise impairs performance.

3.5.4   Carbohydrate ingestion during the 6 h period before exercise

In an attempt to avoid a decline in blood glucose at the onset of exercise, it is sometimes recommended that carbohyrate meals be eaten 3–4 h before exercise so as to allow enough time for plasma insulin concentration to return to basal levels. However, the insulin effects of a pre-exercise carbohydrate meal lasts for several hours after plasma insulin has returned to basal levels and thus blood glucose still declines when exercise (i.e. 70% VO_2 max) is begun 4 h after a meal (Coyle *et al.*, 1985). It appears that at least 6 h of fasting are necessary after consuming a 150 g high-glycaemic meal before carbohydrate oxidation and plasma glucose homeostasis during exercise at 70% VO_2 max are similar to values after an 8–12 h fast (Montain *et al.*, 1991). There is no reason, however, to recommend that people fast this long before exercise. The decline in blood glucose is not problematic (Brouns *et al.*, 1989b). Actually, it can be prevented simply by having the subjects exercise slightly more intensely, which probably causes liver glucose output to increase and match blood glucose uptake by muscle (Montain *et al.*, 1991). Additionally, the elevation in carbohydrate oxidation should not cause problems if enough carbohydrate was stored in the body as a result of the meal. When muscle glycogen is suboptimal, a substantial amount of the pre-exercise carbohydrate meal can be converted to muscle glycogen in a four-hour period (Coyle *et al.*, 1985; Neufer *et al.*, 1987). Liver glycogen undoubtedly increases as well.

Accumulating evidence suggests performance is improved when a relatively large carbohydrate meal is eaten 3–4 h before prolonged exercise compared to when nothing is consumed (Table 3.6). Neufer *et al.* (1987) reported that a 200 g carbohydrate meal of bread, cereal and fruit eaten 4 h before exercise, as well as a confectionery candy bar (containing 43 g of sucrose) eaten 5 min before exercise, resulted in a 22% increase in cycling power compared to placebo. This 22% increase was also greater than the 11% increase above placebo which occurred when only the candy bar was ingested. Additionally, Sherman *et al.* (1989) fed cyclists various amounts of carbohydrate 4 h before exercise and found that a 312 g feeding of maltodextrin improved power (15%) during the last 45 min of exercise (Table 3.6).

Mixed meals containing either 45 g or 156 g of carbohydrate did not significantly improve performance. Apparently, eating approximately 150 g of carbohydrate (i.e., bread and juice) 4 h before exercise does not produce a marked elevation of muscle glycogen, blood glucose or carbohydrate oxidation after 105 min of exercise (Coyle *et al.*, 1985), which may explain why Sherman *et al.* (1989) did not observe an improvement in performance with this amount. Finally, Wright and Sherman (1989) have reported that a 350 g feeding of maltodextrins 3 h before exercise dramatically improves performance (Table 3.6).

Table 3.5 Effect of sugar feedings during the hour before exercise

Reference	Time of feeding before exercise	Amount and type of carbohydrate	Exercise protocol	Effect on performance
Negative Effect				
Foster et al., 1979	30 min	70 g glucose	Cycling at 80% VO$_2$ max	19% decrease in time to fatigue
No Effect				
McMurray et al., 1983	45 min	100 g glucose or fructose	Running to exhaustion	no effect
Keller and Schwarzkopf, 1984	60 min	100 g glucose	Intermittent cycling	no effect
Devlin et al., 1986	30 min	Candy bar: 43 g sucrose, 9 g fat, 3 g protein	Cycling at 70% VO$_2$ max	no effect
Hargreaves et al., 1987	45 min	75 g of glucose or 75 g of fructose	Cycling at 75% VO$_2$ max	no effect either glucose or fructose
Positive Effect				
Gleeson et al., 1986	45 min	70 g of glucose	Cycling at 70% VO$_2$ max	13% increase in exercise time to fatigue
Okano et al., 1988	60 min	60–85 g fructose in non-fasted subjects	Cycling at 62–81% VO$_2$ max	7% increase in exercise time
Peden et al., 1989	60 min	80 or 160 g of glucose polymers	Cycling at 70–80% VO$_2$ max	12–13% increase in power during last 45 min

Table 3.6 Effect of carbohydrate feedings 3–4 h before exercise on performance

Reference	Time of feeding before exercise	Amount and type of carbohydrate	Exercise protocol	Effect on performance
Neufer et al., 1987	4 h and/or	200 g of cereal, bread, fruits and	45 min of cycling at 77% VO_2 max and 15 min performance	22% greater power than placebo and 11% greater power than placebo with just the candy bar
	5 min before	candy bar (43 g sucrose, 9 g fat, 3 g protein)		
Sherman et al., 1989	4 h	45 g of carbohydrate from fruit. Total 733 kcal.	95 min of cycling at 52–70% VO_2 max followed by an approx. 45 min power test	45 g No effect
		156 g of carbohydrate from maltodextrin and fruit. Total 733 kcal.		156 kg No effect
		312 g of mostly maltodextrins. Total 1248 kcal.		312 g 15% increase
Wright and Sherman, 1989	3 h	350 g maltodextrin	Cycling at 70% VO_2 max with high intensity intervals every 45 min	Total work increased by 24%

A relatively large pre-exercise carbohydrate meal (i.e., > 200 g) appears to increase performance by maintaining the ability to oxidize carbohydrates at high rates, late in exercise. It is not clear if this is simply due to a greater availability of muscle glycogen. It could also be due to increased blood glucose uptake and oxidation despite the observation that blood glucose concentration is not increased (Neufer *et al.*, 1987; Sherman *et al.*, 1989). Preliminary studies suggest that large pre-exercise carbohydrate feedings in combination with continued feeding during exercise, which does increase blood glucose concentration, produce even more dramatic improvements in performance than when carbohydrate is only eaten before exercise or when carbohydrate feedings are provided only after exercise has begun (Wright and Sherman, 1989).

3.5.5 Types of carbohydrate to ingest during the 6 h before exercise

Foods ingested during this period should be low in fat, fibre and bulk and well tolerated. If muscle glycogen stores are not supercompensated, these foods should have a high or moderate glycaemic index to best stimulate synthesis. It is sometimes recommended that low glycaemic foods, particularly fructose, be consumed during this period so as to minimize an insulin response (Okano *et al.*, 1988). This would seem advisable only in situations when muscle glycogen cannot be further increased and carbohydrate feedings will not be ingested during exercise. The rationale is to make more glucose available during exercise by storing carbohydrate in the body which can be slowly absorbed as glucose during exercise. However, if more glucose is needed during exercise it makes more sense to simply ingest glucose during exercise as discussed below.

3.5.6 Specific recommendations

High and moderate glycaemic food should be ingested prior to competitive events which will result in fatigue due to carbohydrate depletion. It is generally recommended that approximately 200–300 g of carbohydrate be ingested during the 4 h before exercise. Most importantly, the meals should be low in fat, protein and fibre and they should not cause gastrointestinal discomfort.

3.6 CARBOHYDRATE FEEDING DURING EXERCISE

3.6.1 Prolonged continuous intense exercise

After 1–3 h of continuous exercise at 60–80% VO_2 max, it is clear that athletes fatigue due to carbohydrate depletion. Carbohydrate feedings during exercise will delay fatigue by 30–50 min (Coyle *et al.*, 1983; Coyle *et al.*, 1986; Coggan and Coyle, 1987). However, this improvement in performance is not due to a sparing of muscle glycogen use during exercise (Coyle *et al.*, 1986; Fielding *et al.*, 1985; Flynn *et al.*, 1987; Hargreaves and Briggs, 1988; Mitchell *et al.*, 1989a; Noakes *et al.*, 1988; Slentz *et al.*, 1990). Instead, it appears that the exercising muscles rely mostly upon blood glucose for energy late in exercise (Coyle *et al.*, 1986).

These concepts are summarized in Fig. 3.1 based upon recent findings (Coyle *et al.*, 1986). In well-trained cyclists, approximately 50% of energy for exercise at 70% VO_2 max is derived from fat, whereas the remaining 50% is derived from carbohydrate. During the early portions of exercise, the majority of carbohydrate energy is derived from muscle glycogen. As exercise progresses, muscle glycogen is reduced and contributes less to the carbohydrate requirements of exercise and there is increased reliance upon blood glucose. After 3 h of exercise while drinking only water (i.e. fasting), the majority of carbohydrate energy appears to be derived from the metabolism of glucose, which is transported from the circulating blood into the exercising muscles. When drinking only water, fatigue occurs after approximately 3 h due to a lowering of blood glucose which causes an inadequate supply of this carbohydrate energy. However, when carbohydrate is ingested throughout exercise and glucose remains high in the blood stream, the subjects maintain the necessary reliance upon carbohydrate for energy and fatigue is delayed by 1 h (Fig. 3.1). Remarkably, muscle glycogen use was minimal during the additional hour of exercise despite the fact that carbohydrate oxidation was maintained. This suggests that blood glucose was the predominant carbohydrate fuel during the latter stages of exercise.

It should be realized that during the latter stages of exercise, when muscle glycogen is low, athletes rely heavily upon blood glucose for energy, their muscles feel tired and they must concentrate to maintain exercise at intensities that are ordinarily not stressful when muscle glycogen stores are filled. Additionally, cyclists do not appear to be able to exercise more intensely than 75% VO_2 max for several minutes late in exercise (Coggan and Coyle, 1988). Carbohydrate feedings delay but do not prevent fatigue, which can arise from many factors besides carbohydrate depletion (Coyle *et al.*, 1986).

This model emphasizes that carbohydrate feeding during prolonged exercise improves performance in events which results in hypoglycaemia. Thus, carbohydrate feeding is clearly beneficial when cycling is performed for longer than 2 h. The extent to which carbohydrate feedings improve performance when running and in events which are less than 2 h in duration and which are not obviously limited by carbohydrate availability, is less clear. Blood glucose concentration does not appear to decline as readily during prolonged running as it does during prolonged cycling

(Coggan, 1991); consequently, there may be less of a need for supplemental carbohydrate, especially if the duration of running is not longer than 2 h (Maughan *et al.*, 1989). This may explain why some world-class marathon (42 km) runners, who finish in approximately 2.1 to 2.5 h, do not emphasize carbohydrate ingestion during exercise. Some of these runners find that the difficulty in drinking carbohydrate solutions while racing, outweighs the benefits. However, Williams *et al.* (1990) observed that blood glucose concentration declined by the end of a 30 km treadmill run when subjects were provided with only water to drink, whereas glucose ingestion throughout exercise maintained blood glucose concentration and enabled the runners to complete the last 5 km significantly faster than when only water was consumed. Future research should focus on running events of 2–4 h duration.

Several recent studies, employing mostly cycling exercise, have also observed carbohydrate ingestion to improve performance even when blood glucose availability and carbohydrate energy were not obviously limiting when only water was consumed (Davis *et al.*, 1988; Mitchell *et al.*, 1989a; Murray *et al.*, 1987; Murray *et al.*, 1989a; Murray *et al.*, 1989b). When fed carbohydrate in these studies, the subjects had a higher blood glucose concentration, higher rates of carbohydrate oxidation and were able to maintain a higher exercise intensity late in exercise. This suggests that the amount of carbohydrate which is available late in exercise will directly influence performance and that it might be beneficial to ingest carbohydrates in events which are longer than 60 min in duration (particularly cycling). If body carbohydrate stores are reduced prior to the onset of exercise, due to inadequate diet and previous exercise, carbohydrate supplementation can improve performance during exercise of 60 min duration (Neufer *et al.*, 1987).

3.6.2 Timing of carbohydrate feedings during continuous intense exercise

Consuming carbohydrate during prolonged continuous exercise will ensure that sufficient carbohydrate will be available during the later stages of exercise. If carbohydrate supplementation is withheld until the point of exhaustion, fatigue can only be reversed, and exercise continued for another 45 min, if glucose is intravenously infused at a high rate (i.e. over 1 g min^{-1}). This delivers glucose to the muscles at the rate needed to maintain its energy requirements. This of course is not practical. When cyclists wait until they are exhausted and then drink 400 ml of a 50% maltodextrin solution, which is a huge load (200 g), they are unable to absorb this meal rapidly enough to maintain the energy needs of the exercising muscles. This is reflected by a decline in plasma glucose concentration and fatigue after an additional 26 min of exercise. Therefore, people should ingest carbohydrate well in advance of the estimated point of fatigue. The latest that a cyclist can delay carbohydrate ingestion is 30 min before the time of fatigue when ingesting only water (Coggan and Coyle, 1989). In this case, a large and highly concentrated carbohydrate feeding is required (100–200 g of glucose, sucrose or maltodextrins in a 50% solution) to delay fatigue in this situation. Although this is an alternative in situations where it is not possible to ingest carbohydrate earlier in exercise, it is not ideal. A better approach is to ingest carbohydrate at regular intervals throughout exercise according to the guidelines given below.

3.6.3 Carbohydrate feeding during intermittent exercise

Although it does not appear that carbohydrate feedings alter the net rate of decline in muscle glycogen concentration during prolonged exercise maintained at a constant high intensity (Coyle *et al.*, 1986; Hargreaves and Briggs, 1988; Slentz *et al.*, 1990), they may affect intermittent exercise. It has been demonstrated in rats and in man that carbohydrate feedings given during low-intensity exercise, which followed prolonged high-intensity exercise, can promote glycogen resynthesis within non-active muscle fibres with low glycogen concentration (Constable *et al.*, 1984; Kuipers *et al.*, 1987), although not always (Kuipers *et al.*, 1989). Therefore, it is possible that carbohydrate feedings given throughout prolonged exercise which varies from high to low intensity, or which includes rest periods, may result in less of a reduction in muscle glycogen concentration. Presumably this is due to glycogen resynthesis in fibres which are non-active during the low-intensity bouts of exercise.

Along these lines, in the laboratory simulation of the Tour de France, which utilized exercise of intermittent intensity, it was observed that the decline in muscle glycogen was reduced by ingesting large amounts of carbohydrate during exercise (Brouns *et al.*, 1989a). Although it is not clear if this is due to decreased glycogenolysis or increased resynthesis during exercise, there seems to be a good rationale for ingesting carbohydrate during intermittent exercise to reduce glycogen depletion. This may be particularly important when racing repeatedly with little time for recovery and possibly inadequate time for full glycogen resynthesis.

Carbohydrate feedings are also beneficial during sports involving high-intensity intermittent exercise such as soccer and ice hockey which causes fatigue due to glycogen depletion (Foster *et al.*, 1986; Muckle, 1973; Simard *et al.*, 1988). The ingestion of carbohydrate throughout the game, and during the half-time rest period, results in higher muscle glycogen and increased sprinting ability towards the end of the game compared to when no carbohydrate is ingested and muscle glycogen remains low. The sporting situations during which carbohydrate feedings appear to be of little benefit are those which are non-fatiguing (i.e. sprinting 100 m; baseball; easy basketball; weightlifting) and/or are not limited by carbohydrate availability.

3.6.4 Type of carbohydrate

Glucose, sucrose and maltodextrins appear to be equally effective in maintaining blood glucose concentration, carbohydrate oxidation and in improving performance (Massicotte *et al.*, 1989; Murray *et al.*, 1989; Owen *et al.*, 1986). In fact, it is likely that all of the liquid and solid high-glycaemic carbohydrates listed in Table 3.1 are equally effective. Therefore, the selection of carbohydrate for ingestion during exercise should be based upon what is best tolerated under the conditions. Liquids are obviously easier to ingest than solids and they also provide for fluid replacement. Maltodextrins have become a popular form of carbohydrate for inclusion in sports drinks because they are not very sweet tasting and therefore solution in concentrations of 10 g per 100 ml or more are more palatable for most people. That is the major benefit of maltodextrins or concentrated corn syrups compared to sugars because gastric emptying rates and metabolic responses are not appreciably different (Guezennec *et al.* 1989; Neufer *et al.*, 1986; Owen *et al.*, 1986).

The osmolality of maltodextrins is less than glucose and gastric secretions are sometimes less (Foster *et al.*, 1980). Since maltodextrins are not as sweet tasting, athletes who must supplement their diet with liquid carbohydrate in an attempt to maintain carbohydrate and energy balance during severe training and competition, will ingest more maltodextrins compared to sugars (Brouns *et al.*, 1989a). Simply, it is a more palatable way to consume a lot of carbohydrate.

Fructose feedings have not been observed to be effective for improving performance compared to glucose or sucrose because its conversion to and oxidation as glucose is not rapid enough to supply the carbohydrate energy requirements late in exercise (Bjorkman *et al.*, 1984; Murray *et al.*, 1989). For the same reason, the low-glycaemic fruits and other foods listed in Table 3.3 would probably be of little benefit if ingested during exercise.

3.6.5 Rate of carbohydrate ingestion

Based upon the rate of intravenous glucose infusion required to restore and maintain blood glucose availability and carbohydrate oxidation late in exercise, sufficient carbohydrate should be ingested to supply the blood with exogenous glucose at approximately 1 g min^{-1}, late in exercise. Therefore, approximately 60 g of exogenous glucose must be readily available within the body. To ensure this, it seems that larger amounts of carbohydrate must be ingested.

The majority of studies which have observed carbohydrate ingestion throughout exercise to improve performance have fed subjects at a rate of 30–60 g h^{-1}, beginning early in exercise. This generally agrees with the expected needs and glucose distribution within the body, although it should be recognized that the fate of the ingested glucose that is not oxidized is unclear. It should also be recognized that optimal rates of carbohydrate ingestion will differ according to the activity and from individual to individual. Therefore the recommendation that 30–60 g h^{-1} of carbohydrate should be ingested during exercise is a general one which should be adapted more specifically to the situation using trial and error and common sense.

The volume of fluid ingested during each hour of exercise to obtain a given amount of carbohydrate (i.e. 30–60 g h^{-1}) will of course depend upon the concentration of carbohydrate in that solution as indicated by Table 3.7. Contrary to previous thinking, the addition of carbohydrate to athletic drinks does not have to be at the expense of fluid replacement. People can empty carbohydrate solutions from the stomach at a rate of approximately 1000 ml h^{-1} when the carbohydrate concentration remains below 10 g per 100 ml (Neufer *et al.*, 1986; Mitchell *et al.*, 1989a). As indicated below, this will provide them with sufficient carbohydrate. Additionally, these 6–10% solutions will be equally as effective in minimizing hyperthermia as drinking only water (Neufer *et al.*, 1986; Owen *et al.*, 1986; Mitchell *et al.*, 1989b; Murray *et al.*, 1989a). Athletes rarely attempt to drink more than 1000 ml h^{-1} of fluid. It should also be noted that when attempting to maximize the rate at which carbohydrates are emptied from the stomach into the intestines for absorption (>1 g min^{-1}) that more concentrated solutions (>20 g per 100 ml) should be ingested (Mitchell *et al.*, 1989b).

Table 3.7 The desired rate of carbohydrate ingestion which can be obtained by ingesting the listed volume of fluids which range in concentration from 6 to 75 g/100 ml

Concentration of solution (%)	Fluid volume for given rate of CHO ingestion			
	30 g h^{-1} (ml)	40 g h^{-1} (ml)	50 g h^{-1} (ml)	60 g h^{-1} (ml)
6	500	667	833	1000
7.5	400	533	667	800
10	300	400	500	600
20	150	200	250	300
50	60	80	100	120
75	40	53	67	80

3.6.6 Specific recommendations

It is generally recommended that during athletic events which cause fatigue due to carbohydrate depletion, that approximately 30–60 g of high-glycaemic carbohydrates be ingested each hour beginning early in exercise. Since liquid feeding is most common, the appropriate volume and concentration of glucose, sucrose, maltodextrin or corn syrup solutions should be made available depending upon the circumstances, preference and need for fluid replacement. If circumstances do not allow carbohydrate ingestion throughout continuous exercise, performance can also be improved by ingesting a large amount (i.e. 100 g) of concentrated carbohydrate (i.e. 20–75%) at least 30 min prior to fatigue.

(Since recommendations in this chapter are made for a person weighing 70 kg (154 lbs), the application to persons weighing less or more than 70 kg should be calculated as stated in the introduction.)

REFERENCES

Ahlborg, G. and Bjorkman, O. (1987). Carbohydrate utilization by exercising muscle following preexercise glucose ingestion. *Clinical Physiology*, **7**, 181–95.

Ahlborg, G. and Felig, P. (1976). Influence of glucose ingestion on the fuel-hormone responses during prolonged exercise. *Journal of Applied Physiology*, **41**, 683–8.

Behall, K.M., Scholfield, D.J. and Canary, J. (1988). Effect of starch structure on glucose and insulin responses in adults. *American Journal of Clinical Nutrition*, **47**, 428–32.

Bergstrom, J. and Hultman, E. (1966). The effect of exercise on muscle glycogen and electrolytes in normals. *Scandinavian Journal of Clinical and Laboratory Investigation*, **18**, 16–20.

Bjorkman, O., Sahling, K., Hagenfeldt, L. and Wahren, J. (1984). Influence of glucose and fructose ingestion on the capacity for long-term exercise in well trained men. *Clinical Physiology*, **4**, 483–94.

Blom, P.C., Hostmark, A.T., Vaage, O., Vardal, K.R. and Maehlum, S. (1987). Effect of different post-exercise sugar diets on the rate of muscle glycogen synthesis. *Medicine and Science in Sports and Exercise*, **19**, 491–6.

Bourey, R.E., Coggan, A.R., Kohrt, W.M., Kirwan, J.P., King, D.S. and Holloszy, J.O. (1990). Of exercise on glucose disposal: response to a maximal insulin stimulus. *Journal of Applied Physiology*, **69**, 1689–94.

Brewer, J., Williams, C. and Patton, H. (1988). The influence of high carbohydrate diets on endurance running performance. *European Journal of Applied Physiology*, **57**, 698–706.

Brouns, F., Saris, W.H.M. and Beckers, E. (1989a). Metabolic changes induced by sustained exhaustive cycling and diet manipulation. *International Journal of Sports Medicine*, **10**, S49–S62.

Brouns, F., Rehrer, N.J., Saris, W.H.M., Beckers, E., Menheere, E. and ten Hoor, F. (1989b). Effect of carbohydrate intake during warming up on the regulation of blood glucose during exercise. *International Journal of Sports Medicine*, **10**, 568–75.

Coggan, A.R. (1991). Plasma glucose metabolism during exercise in humans. *Sports Medicine* (in press).

Coggan, A.R. and Coyle, E.F. (1987). Reversal of fatigue during prolonged exercise by carbohydrate infusion or ingestion. *Journal of Applied Physiology*, **63**, 2388–95.

Coggan, A.R. and Coyle, E.F. (1988). Effect of carbohydrate feedings during high-intensity exercise. *Journal of Applied Physiology*, **65**, 1703–9.

Coggan, A.R. and Coyle, E.F. (1989). Metabolism and performance following carbohydrate ingestion late in exercise. *Medicine and Science in Sports and Exercise*, **21**, 59–65.

Constable, S.H., Young, J.C., Higuchi, M. and Holloszy, J.O. (1984). Glycogen resynthesis in leg muscles of rats during exercise. *American Journal of Physiology*, **247**, R880–R883.

Costill, D.L., Coyle, E.F., Dalsky, G., Evans, W., Fink, W. and Hoopes, D. (1977). Effects of elevated plasma FFA and insulin on muscle glycogen usage during exercise. *Journal of Applied Physiology*, **43**, 695–9.

Costill, D.L., Sherman, W.M., Fink, W.J., Maresh, C., Witten, M. and Miller, J.M. (1981). The role of dietary carbohydrates in muscle glycogen resynthesis after strenuous running. *American Journal of Clinical Nutrition*, **34**, 1831–6.

Costill, D.L., Flynn, M.G., Kirwan, J.P., Houmard, J.A., Mitchell, J.B., Thomas, R. and Park, S.H. (1988). Effects of repeated days of intensified training on muscle glycogen and swimming performance. *Medicine and Science in Sports and Exercise*, **20**, 249–54.

Coyle, E.F., Hagberg, J.M., Hurley, B.F., Martin, W.H., Ehsani, A.A. and Holloszy, J.O. (1983). Carbohydrate feedings during prolonged strenuous exercise can delay fatigue. *Journal of Applied Physiology*, **55**, 230–5.

Coyle, E.F., Coggan, A.R., Hemmert, M.K., Lowe, R.C. and Walters, T.J. (1985). Substrate usage during prolonged exercise following a pre-exercise meal. *Journal of Applied Physiology*, **59**, 429–33.

Coyle, E.F., Coggan, A.R., Hemmert, M.K. and Ivy, J.L. (1986). Muscle glycogen utilization during prolonged strenuous exercise when fed carbohydrate. *Journal of Applied Physiology*, **61**, 165–72.

Crapo, P.A., Reavan, G. and Olefsky, J. (1977). Postprandial plasma glucose and insulin responses to different complex carbohydrates. *Diabetes*, **26** (12), 1178–83.

Davis, J.M., Burgess, W.A., Slentz, C.A., Barroli, W.P. and Pate, R.R. (1988). Effects of ingesting 6% and 12% glucose-electrolytes beverages during prolonged intermittent cycling exercise in the heat. *European Journal of Applied Physiology*, **57**, 563–9.

Devlin, J.T., Calles-Escandon, J. and Horton, E.S. (1986). Effects of pre-exercise snack feeding on endurance cycle exercise. *Journal of Applied Physiology*, **60**, 980–5.

Ericksson, E., Hygaard, E. and Saltin, B. (1977). Physiological demands in downhill skiing. *The Physician and Sportsmedicine*, **12**, 39–45.

Fielding, R.A., Costill, D.L., Fink, W.J., King, D.S., Hargreaves, M. and Kovaleski, J.E. (1985). Effect of carbohydrate feeding frequency and dosage on muscle glycogen use during exercise. *Medicine and Science in Sports and Exercise*, **17**, 472–6.

Fielding, R.A., Costill, D.L., Fink, W.J., King, D.S., Kovaleski, J.E. and Kirwan, J.P. (1987). Effects of pre-exercise carbohydrate feedings on muscle glycogen use during exercise in well-trained runners. *European Journal of Applied Physiology*, **56**, 225–9.

Flynn, M.G., Costill, D.L., Hawley, J.A. *et al.* (1987). Influence of selected carbohydrate drinks on cycling performance and glycogen use. *Medicine and Science in Sports and Exercise*, **19**, 37–40.

Foster, C., Costill, D.L. and Fink, W.J. (1979). Effects of pre-exercise feedings on endurance performance. *Medicine and Science in Sports and Exercise*, **11**, 1–5.

Foster, C., Costill, D.L. and Fink, W.J. (1980). Gastric emptying characteristics of glucose and glucose polymer solutions. *Research Quarterly for Exercise and Sport*, **51**, 299–305.

Foster, C., Thompson, N., Dean, J. and Kirkendall, D. (1986). Carbohydrate supplementation and performance in soccer players. *Medicine and Science in Sports and Exercise*, **18**, S12.

Gatti, E., Testolin, G., Noe, D., Brighenti, F., Buzzetti, G.P., Porrino, M. and Sirtori, C.R. (1987). Plasma glucose and insulin responses to carbohydrate food (rice) with different thermal processing. *Annals of Nutrition and Metabolism*, **31**, 296–303.

Gleeson, M., Maughan, R.J. and Greenhaff, P.L. (1986). Comparison of the effects of pre-exercise feedings of glucose, glycerol and placebo on endurance and fuel homeostatis in man. *European Journal of Applied Physiology*, **55**, 645–53.

Goddard, M.S., Young, G. and Marcus, R. (1984). The effect of amylose content on insulin and glucose responses to ingested rice. *American Journal of Clinical Nutrition*, **39**, 388–92.

Guezennec, C.Y., Satabin, P., Duforez, F., Merino, D., Peronnet, F. and Koziet, J. (1989). Oxidation of corn starch, glucose, and fructose ingested before exercise. *Medicine and Science in Sports and Exercises*, **21**, 45–50.

Hargreaves, M. and Briggs, C.A. (1988). Effect of carbohydrate ingestion on exercise metabolism. *Journal of Applied Physiology*, **65**, 1553–5.

Hargreaves, M., Costill, D.L., Katz, A. and Fink, W.J. (1985). Effect of fructose ingestion on muscle glycogen usage during exercise. *Medicine and Science in Sports and Exercise*, **17**, 360–3.

Hargreaves, M., Costill, D.L., Fink, W.J., King, D.S. and Fielding, R.A. (1987). Effect of pre-exercise carbohydrate feedings on endurance cycling performance. *Medicine and Science in Sports and Exercise*, **19**, 33–6.

Ivy, J.L., Lee, M.C. Brozinick Jr, J.T. and Reed, M.J. (1988a). Muscle glycogen storage after different amounts of carbohydrate ingestion. *Journal of Applied Physiology*, **65**, 2018–23.

Ivy, J.L., Katz, A.L., Cutler, C.L., Sherman, W.M. and Coyle, E.F. (1988b). Muscle glycogen synthesis after exercise: effect of time on carbohydrate ingestion. *Journal of Applied Physiology*, **65**, 1480–5.

Jenkins, D.J.A., Wolever, T.M.S., Jenkins, A.L., Josse, R.G., and Wong, G.S. (1984). The glycaemic response to carbohydrate foods. *Lancet*, **2**, 388–91.

Jenkins, D.J.A., Wolever, T.M.S., Buckley, G., Lam, K.Y., Giudici, S., Kalmusky, J., Jenkins, A.L., Patten, R.L., Bird, J., Wong, G.S. and Josse, R.G. (1988). Low glycemic index starchy foods in the diabetic diet. *American Journal of Clinical Nutrition*, **48**, 248–54.

Kiens, B., Raben, A.B., Valeur, A.K. and Richter, E.A. (1990). Benefit of dietary simple carbohydrates on the early postexercise muscle glycogen repletion in male athletes. *Medicine and Science in Sports and Exercise*, **22**, 588.

Keizer, H., Kuipers, A.H., van Kranenburg, G. and Geurten, P. (1986). Influence of liquid and solid meals on muscle glycogen resynthesis, plasma fuel hormone response, and maximal physical working capacity. *International Journal of Sports Medicine*, **8**, 99–104.

Keller, K.R. and Schwarzkopf, A. (1984). Pre-exercise snacks may decrease exercise performance. *Physician and Sportsmedicine*, **12**, 89–91.

Kirwan, J.P., Costill, D.L., Mitchell, J.B., Houmard, J.A., Glynn, M.G., Fink, W.J. and Beltz, J.D. (1988). Carbohydrate balance in competitive runners during successive days of intense training. *Journal of Applied Physiology*, **65**, 2601–6.

Koivisto, V.A., Harkonen, M., Karonen, S., Groop, P.H., Elovainio, R.A., Ferrannini, E. and DeFronzo, R.A. (1985). Glycogen depletion during prolonged exercise: influence of glucose, fructose or placebo. *Journal of Applied Physiology*, **58**, 7341–737.

Kuipers, H., Keizer, H.A., Brouns, F. and Saris, W.H.M. (1987). Carbohydrate feeding and glycogen synthesis during exercise in man. *Pfluegers Archives (European Journal of Physiology)*, **410**, 652–6.

Kuipers, H., Saris, W.H.M., Brouns, F. and ten Bosch, C. (1989). Glycogen synthesis during exercise and rest with carbohydrate feeding in males and females. *International Journal of Sports Medicine*, **10**, S63–S67.

Levine, L., Evans, W.J., Cadarette, B.S., Fisher, E.C. and Bullen, B.A. (1983). Fructose and glucose ingestion and muscle glycogen use during submaximal exercise. *Journal of Applied Physiology*, **55**, 1767–71.

Maughan, R. (1990). Effects of diet composition on the performance of high intensity exercises. In *Nutrition et Sport* (ed. H. Monod) pp. 200–11. Masson, Paris.

Maughan, R.J., Fenn, C.E. and Leiper, L.B. (1989). Effects of fluid, electrolyte and substrate ingestion on endurance capacity. *European Journal of Applied Physiology*, **58**, 481–6.

Massicotte, D., Peronnet, F., Brisson, G., Bakkouch, K. and Killiare-Marcel, C. (1989). Oxidation of a glucose polymer during exercise: comparison of glucose and fructose. *Journal of Applied Physiology*, **66**, 179–83.

McMurray, R.G., Wilson, J.R., Kitchell, B.S. (1983). The effects of fructose and glucose on high intensity endurance performance. *Research Quarterly*, **54**, 156–62.

Mitchell, J.B., Costill, D.L., Houmard, J.A., Fink, W.J., Pascoe, D.D. and Pearson, D.R. (1989a). Influence of carbohydrate dosage on exercise performance and glycogen metabolism. *Journal of Applied Physiology*, **67**, 1843–9.

Mitchell, J.B., Costill, D.L., Houmard, J.A., Fink, W.J., Robergs, R.A. and Davis, J.A. (1989b). Gastric emptying: influence of prolonged exercise and carbohydrate concentration. *Medicine and Science in Sports and Exercise*, **21**, 269–74.

Montain, S.J., Hopper, M.K., Coggan, A.R. and Coyle, E.F. (1991). Exercise metabolism at different time intervals following a meal. *Journal of Applied Physiology*, **70** (in press).

Maurot, J., Thouvenot, P., Couet, C., Antoine, J.M., Krobicka, A. and Debry, G. (1988). Relationship between the rate of gastric emptying and glucose and insulin responses to starchy foods in young healthy adults. *American Journal of Clinical Nutrition*, **48**, 1035–40.

Murray, R., Eddy, D.E., Murray, T.W., Seifert, J.G., Paul, G.L. and Halaby, G.A. (1987). The effect of fluid and carbohydrate feedings during intermittent cycling exercise, *Medicine and Science in Sports and Exercise*, **19**, 597–604.

Murray, R., Siefert, J.G., Eddy, D.E., Paul, G.L. and Halaby, G.A. (1989a). Carbohydrate feeding and exercise: effect of beverage carbohydrate content. *European Journal of Applied Physiology*, **59**, 152–8.

Murray, R., Paul, G.L., Seifert, J.G., Eddy, D.E. and Halaby, G.A. (1989b). The effects of glucose, fructose, and sucrose ingestion during exercise. *Medicine and Science in Sports and Exercise*, **21**, 275–82.

Muckle, D.S. (1973). Glucose syrup ingestion and team performance in soccer. *British Journal of Sports Medicine*, **7**, 340–3.

Neufer, P.D., Costill, D.L., Fink, W.J,. Kirwan, J.P., Fielding, R.A. and Flynn, M.G. (1986). Effects of exercise and carbohydrate composition on gastric emptying. *Medicine and Science in Sports and Exercise*, **18**, 658–62.

Neufer, P.D., Costill, D.L., Flynn, M.G., Kirwan, J.P., Mitchell, J.B. and Houmard, J. (1987). Improvements in exercise performance: effects of carbohydrate feedings and diet. *Journal of Applied Physiology*, **63**, 983–8.

Noakes, T.F., Lambert, E.V., Lambert, M.I., McArthur, P.S., Myburgh, K.H. and Benade, A.J.S. (1988). Carbohydrate ingestion and muscle glycogen depletion during marathon and ultramarathon racing. *European Journal of Applied Physiology*, **57**, 482–9.

O'Dea, K., Nestel, P.J. and Antonoff, L. (1980). Physical factors influencing postprandial glucose and insulin responses to starch. *American Journal of Clinical Nutrition*, **33**, 760–5.

Okano, G., Takeda, H., Morita, I., Katoh, M., Mu, Z. and Miyake, S. (1988). Effect of pre-exercise fructose ingestion on endurance performance in fed men. *Medicine and Science in Sports and Exercise*, **20**, 105–9.

Owen, M.D., Kregel, K.C., Wall, P.T. and Gisolfi, C.V. (1986). Effects of ingesting carbohydrate beverages during exercise in the heat. *Medicine and Science in Sports and Exercise*, **18**, 568–75.

Peden, C., Sherman, W.M., D'Aquisto, L. and Wright, D.A. (1989). 1 h preexercise carbohydrate meals enhance performance. *Medicine and Science in Sports and Exercise*, **21**, S59.

Reed, M.J., Brozlnick, J.T. Jr, Lee, M.C. and Ivy, J.L. (1989). Muscle glycogen storage post exercise: Effect on mode of carbohydrate administration. *Journal of Applied Physiology*, **66**, 720–6.

Sherman, W.M., Costill, D.L., Fink, W.J. and Miller, J.M. (1981). The effect of exercise and diet manipulation on muscle glycogen and its subsequent utilization during performance. *International Journal of Sports Medicine*, 2, 114–18.

Sherman, W.M., Brodowicz, G., Wright, D.A., Allen, W.K., Simonsen, J. and Dernbach, A. (1989). Effects of 4 h preexercise carbohydrate feedings on cycling performance. *Medicine and Science in Sports and Exercise*, 21, 598–604.

Simard, C., Tremblay, A. and Jobin, J. (1988). Effects of carbohydrate intake before and during an ice hockey match on blood, and muscle energy substrates. *Research Quarterly in Exercise and Sport*, 59, 144–7.

Slentz, C.A., Davis, J.M., Settles, D.L. Pate, R.R. and Settles, S.J. (1990). Glucose feedings and exercise in rats: glycogen use, hormone responses, and performance. *Journal of Applied Physiology*, 69, 989–94.

Williams, C., Nute, M.G., Broadbank, L. and Vinall, S. (1990). Influence of fluid intake on endurance running performance. A comparison between water, glucose and fructose solutions. *European Journal of Applied Physiology*, 60, 112–19.

Wright, D.A. and Sherman, W.M. (1989). Carbohydrate feedings 3 h before and during exercise improve cycling performance. *Medicine and Science in Sports and Exercise*, 21, S58.

Wursch, P., Del Vedovo, S. and Koellreutter, B. (1986). Cell structure and starch nature as key determinants of the digestion rate of starch in legume. *American Journal of Clinical Nutrition*, 433, 25–9.

COMMENTARY BY KIENS, RODRIGUEZ AND HAMM

Vegetarian diets

There are three forms of vegetarian diets: vegan, lactovegetarian and ovo-lactovegetarian.

The recommendation of a diet rich in carbohydrate may lead many athletes to one form of the above mentioned diets. Whilst a lactovegetarian and ovo-lactovegetarian diet may cover all nutritional needs there may be a shortage of iron, calcium, iodine, zinc and vitamin B12 in a strictly vegetarian diet.

Iron may be also short in a lactovegetarian diet because of the lack of haeme-iron, which is more absorbable and improves the absorption of iron from vegetable sources. Also a higher dietary content of vitamin C is very useful to enhance iron absorption. Large amounts of tea and coffee may reduce the iron availability. Foods like green vegetables, some legumes and cereals have a relatively high content of non-haeme iron.

Concerning the protein quality there are complete combinations for example:

beans and rice

peas and corn
lentils and bread
cereals with milk or egg
potatoes with egg or milk

In any case an athlete must have a good knowledge about the composition of food if he/she decides to become a vegetarian. It may also be convenient to monitor the iron status and blood profile (including serum ferritin), in order to prevent iron-deficiency anaemia, leading to performance impairment and also to possible health hazards.

COMMENTARY BY BROUNS

Carbohydrate availability and injury proneness

There is some good evidence that a low glycogen level is associated with increased injury risk in alpine downhill skiing, especially in recreational skiers.

The explanation is that glycogen depletion of the fast twitch fibres will limit the ability to develop a high muscle tension in a short period of time (needed to correct false turns or inadequate timing). Physical inability to correct movements in time will lead to increased injury risks. Along the same line it seems reasonable to assume that glycogen depletion of the dominant muscle in contact sports (rugby, ice hockey, soccer, etc.) will not only limit performance but will also influence injury occurrence, especially during the second half of the game. Research is needed to verify this assumption.

4

Effect of exercise on protein requirements

Peter W.R. Lemon

4.1 INTRODUCTION

The question of how much dietary protein is necessary for optimal athletic performance has been debated in the scientific literature for over 100 years (Butterfield, 1991; Cathcart, 1925; Dunlop *et al.*, 1897; Lemon, 1991a; von Liebig, 1842) and probably among athletes since the time of the ancient Greeks. Despite this long history surprisingly little information is available and no consensus exists. Due in part to the complexity of protein metabolism and the associated methodological difficulties, exercise protein metabolism has received relatively little attention in comparison to carbohydrate and fat metabolism. Current recommended protein intakes from a number of expert committees on nutrition throughout the world range from 0.8 (Canadian Department of National Health and Welfare, 1983; US Food and Nutrition Board, 1989; Food and Agricultural Organization, 1985) to 1.0 (Australian National Health and Medical Research Council, 1987; Dutch Nutrition Board, 1988 – for women) or 1.2 g/kg·d^{-1} (Dutch Nutrition Board, 1988 – for men). These recommendations are based primarily on nitrogen balance data (nitrogen intake minus nitrogen excretion) from individuals who were essentially sedentary. Although several of these committees acknowledged that exercise may increase protein need, especially when attempts are made to increase muscle mass (strength exercise), only one suggested an increased intake (1.5 g/kg·d^{-1}) for active individuals (Dutch Nutrition Board, 1988).

Food, Nutrition and Sports Performance
Edited by Clyde Williams and John T. Devlin
Published in 1992 by E & F N Spon, London. ISBN 0 419 17890 2

Despite this general lack of agreement regarding protein recommendations for those involved in regular, strenuous exercise a substantial amount of information exists indicating that protein needs are higher for these individuals. This chapter summarizes some of this information in an attempt to (a) identify the key factors responsible for any increased protein need associated with exercise and (b) provide dietary recommendations for different types of athletes. The benefits/hazards of individual amino acid supplementation have been reviewed recently (Lemon, 1991b) and will not be repeated here.

4.2 IMPORTANCE OF PROTEIN

Protein is essential for all life. It comprises about 15% of the bodyweight of a human and is found primarily in muscle. Although many different proteins exist each is made up of amino acids. Our bodies can synthesize protein from amino acids but they can only produce some of the necessary amino acids. Those that cannot be produced are called indispensable (or essential) amino acids (Table 4.1) because they must be obtained from our diet. This means that our actual requirement is not for protein but rather for select amino acids. Only some foods (called complete protein foods – Table 4.2) contain all the indispensable amino acids.

Table 4.1 Indispensable or essential amino acids

Histidine (at least for infants)
Isoleucine
Leucine
Lysine
Methionine/cysteine
Phenylalanine/tyrosine
Threonine
Tryptophan
Valine

When an inadequate amount of these foods is included in one's diet an appropriate combination of incomplete foods must be consumed or protein synthesis will be impaired. As a result, protein degradation increases and body protein content decreases (Fig. 4.1). If continued, this scenario leads to decreases in strength/endurance and eventually to impaired health. The protein and energy content of foods is highly variable (Table 4.3) so care must be taken to ensure adequate protein intake, especially if one is a vegetarian.

Table 4.2 Complete protein foods

Dairy products
Eggs
Fish
Meat
Poultry
Corn/rice plus beans
Corn plus peas
Lentils plus bread

Table 4.3 Protein and energy content of select foods (from Watt and Merrill, 1963)

Food group	Protein (% by weight)	Energy (kcal/100 g)
1. *Meat/Fish*		
Blue fish	26	159
Haddock	20	165
Salmon	28	168
Shrimp	25	118
Beef (hamburger)	25	288
(steak)	24	388
Chicken	24	135
Egg	12	160
Ham	21	237
Lamb	22	276
2. *Dairy products*		
Cheese (blue)	21	375
(cottage)	13	106
(swiss)	28	375
Ice cream	4	190
Milk (skim)	4	37
Yogurt (plain)	3	51
3. *Vegetables/Fruits*		
Apple	trace	47
Beans (lima)	8	135
Bananas	trace	57
Broccoli	4	26
Cauliflower	3	22
Potatoes	3	91
Peanuts	25	583
Almonds	19	592
4. *Grains*		
Bread (white)	8	280
(wheat)	12	240
Cereal (unsweetened)	9	377
Rice	2	107

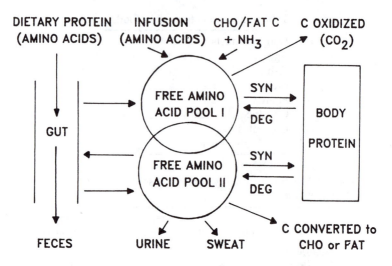

Fig. 4.1 Schematic representation of protein metabolism.

4.3 FACTORS THAT AFFECT PROTEIN NEED

4.3.1 Diet

There are a number of considerations related to diet that can influence exercise protein need including: energy balance, composition of overall diet, adaptation to any diet change, and the timing and composition of the meal preceding the exercise session. As a result, all these factors must be carefully controlled or experimental data will vary. Obviously, this is difficult especially with human subjects.

As a result data in the literature must be interpreted carefully. For example, it has been known for about 40 years that there is an interaction between total energy intake and protein need, i.e. insufficient energy intake can lead to negative nitrogen balance at protein intakes that promote positive nitrogen balance when energy intake is adequate (Munro, 1951). Numerous subsequent investigations have observed this effect (Butterfield and Calloway, 1984; Calloway and Spector, 1954; Goranzon and Forsum, 1985; Walberg *et al.*, 1988). Therefore, before it is possible to assess protein need one must be certain that overall energy requirements are adequate. This is not always the case especially with an exercise treatment.

Composition of the diet can also influence the exercise response in at least two ways. First, inadequate carbohydrate (CHO) intake causes more rapid depletion of muscle and liver glycogen during exercise and this contributes to a greater protein utilization (Anderson and Sharp, 1990; Lemon and Mullin, 1980; MacLean *et al.*, 1989). This may be due to an activation of the limiting enzyme in the oxidation pathway of the branched chain amino acids (branched chain oxoacid dehydrogenase) when CHO stores are low (Wagenmakers *et al.*, 1990). Second, high protein intakes can promote more positive nitrogen balance (Oddoye and Margen, 1979) which may enhance conditions for protein synthesis.

Whenever composition of the diet is changed a period of adaptation (approximately 8–18 days depending on the direction and magnitude of the change (Oddoye and Margen, 1979; Pivarnik *et al.*, 1989; Scrimshaw *et al.*, 1972)) is necessary before protein requirements can be assessed. This factor has been overlooked in many published studies.

Both the timing and the composition of the meal preceding the exercise can affect exercise fuel use (Cuthbertson *et al.*, 1937; Elia *et al.*, 1989; Lemon *et al.*, 1985). The results of many studies are difficult to interpret because this factor has been loosely controlled. More study is necessary to assess the importance of this factor.

4.3.2 Type and frequency of exercise

There are a great many different kinds of exercise ranging from high-intensity, short-duration activity (strength or speed exercise) to moderate-intensity, long-duration activity (endurance exercise). Although the acute response to exercise at either extreme of this exercise continuum follows a similar pattern (decreased protein synthesis and increased protein degradation during and immediately following exercise (Booth and Watson, 1985)), the time course and absolute magnitude of these component responses clearly differ. As a result, the overall effect of chronic exercise at one end of this exercise continuum is vastly different from the other. With endurance exercise, there are dramatic increases in mitochondrial (enzymatic) protein with minimal effects on muscle mass and strength (myofibrillar protein) while with strength or speed exercise, there is little change in mitochondrial protein but the gains in muscle mass and strength are truly phenomenal (Fig. 4.2). For this reason, the underlying rationale for increased protein need with different types of exercise may be substantially different. For example, in situations where energy demands are high and especially when prolonged, protein may provide a significant quantity of amino acids for use as an auxiliary exercise fuel (Fig. 4.1). If so, inadequate dietary protein and/or too frequent training (overtraining) could lead to losses of endogenous protein (probably both liver and muscle) and eventually to impaired exercise performance. In contrast, when an attempt is made to increase cell mass (hypertrophy) additional dietary protein may be necessary to provide sufficient amino acids to maximize protein synthesis (Fig. 4.1). As with endurance training, strength or speed training can also be done too frequently. In this case, the exercise catabolic response exceeds the subsequent anabolic response and the overall result is either reduced gains or even decreases in muscle mass and strength. Perhaps additional dietary protein can minimize this effect and, therefore, produce greater exercise-induced hypertrophy. In addition, some degree of muscle soreness is frequently present following exercise, especially with eccentric exercise, and both structural changes in muscle (mitochondrial swelling, degenerating fibres, contractile protein disorientation, etc.) and efflux of muscle-specific enzymes into the vascular system have been reported (Berg and Haralambie, 1978; Janssen *et al.*, 1989; Kuipers *et al.*, 1989). Additional dietary protein might help promote the recovery/repair process and as a result improve exercise performance.

Type of exercise	Muscle size (myofibrillar content)	Myofibrillar concentration	Cytochrome C content	Cytochrome C concentration
Run	→	→	↑	↑
Swim	↑	→	↑	↑
Weight-lifting	↑	→	↑	→

Fig. 4.2 Adaptive changes in skeletal muscle with regular bouts of exercise (from Booth and Watson, 1985).

Although the issue of exercise effects on protein need has been considered unimportant for most of the twentieth century, conflicting data began to appear in the literature in the mid-1970s. Utilizing the nitrogen balance technique, Gontzea *et al.* (1974, 1975) observed that, at least for the first 20 days of an endurance training programme, daily protein needs were elevated to about 1.5 g/kg·d^{-1} (approximately 125–188%* of current recommendations). In agreement with these data are a number of Japanese studies which found that a protein intake of about 2 g/kg·d^{-1} (approximately 167–250% of current recommendations) could reduce the observed loss of blood proteins during the first week or two of daily exercise (Yoshimura *et al.*, 1980). Moreover, recent data from experiments with experienced endurance athletes (2–40 years of training) from several different laboratories agree that the increased protein need continues long after the first few weeks of training. In one study, Tarnopolsky *et al.* (1988) reported that a protein intake of 1.37 g/kg·d^{-1} (approximately

*Range calculated using highest (1.5/1.2 × 100 = 125%) and lowest (1.5/0.8 × 100 = 188%) current protein intake recommendation from various countries.

114–171% of current recommendations) was necessary to maintain nitrogen balance with trained endurance men in their early twenties. Based on data from a similar study, Meredith *et al.* (1989) suggested a protein intake of 1.26 g/kg·d^{-1} (approximately 105–158% of current recommendations) for men (23–59 years) who participated in regular endurance exercise (Fig. 4.3). In male runners (24–29 years) who trained regularly for years, Friedman and Lemon (1989) calculated protein requirements to be between 1.14 and 1.39 g/kg·d^{-1} (approximately 95–174% of current recommendations). Brouns *et al.* (1989a, 1989b) observed that well-trained long distance cyclists (simulated Tour de France study) needed a protein intake in the range of 1.5–1.8 g/kg·d^{-1} (approximately 125–225% of current recommendations).

In addition to these nitrogen balance studies several other lines of evidence indicate that dietary protein needs are increased with regular exercise. For example, during the past 10 years a number of studies have reported substantial increases in whole body oxidation of the branched chain amino acid leucine with exercise (Babij *et al.*, 1983; Evans *et al.*, 1983; Hagg *et al.*, 1982; Lemon *et al.*, 1982, 1985; Rennie *et al.*, 1981; White and Brooks, 1981). It appears that in terms of oxidation the branched chain amino acids are quantitatively most important because they are taken up by active muscle during exercise while most other amino acids are released (Ahlborg *et al.*, 1974; Gelfand *et al.*, 1986). Although these oxidation data are consistent with the nitrogen balance results, more study is necessary because most of these investigations have been conducted over a relatively short time period associated with an exercise session (it is possible that compensatory decreases occur later in the day) and oxidation of at least one indispensable amino acid (lysine) is affected to a much lesser extent (Wolfe, 1984). Finally, numerous studies have measured an increased concentration (body fluids and/or tissues) or excretion (urine and/or sweat) of nitrogen (waste product of protein utilization) associated with prolonged exercise (Decombaz *et al.*, 1979; Dohm *et al.*, 1982; Haralambie and Berg, 1976; Lemon and Dolny, 1986; Lemon and Mullin, 1980; Refsum and Stromme, 1974; Van Zant and Lemon, 1990).

With strength or speed exercise, the nitrogen balance data are somewhat more variable; however, a considerable amount of data has been published suggesting that this type of exercise also increases protein need. Celejowa and Homa (1970) reported a negative nitrogen balance in at least 40% of male weight-lifters consuming protein equal to about 2 g/kg·d^{-1} (approximately 167–250% of current recommendations). Laritcheva *et al.* (1978) found that protein intakes of 1.3–1.6 g/kg·d^{-1} (approximately 108–200% of current recommendations) were necessary to avoid negative nitrogen balance. Torun *et al.* (1977) observed a decreased cell mass (based on ^{40}K measures) over 6 weeks of strength training when protein intake was about

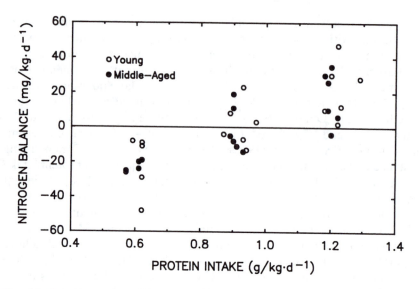

Fig. 4.3 Relationship between protein intake and nitrogen balance in young (○) and middle-aged (●) endurance-trained men. Data are for individual subjects (from Meredith *et al.*, 1989).

70 to 100% of current recommendations. More recent data indicate that protein needs of male body builders are about 1.2 to 1.7 g/kg·d^{-1} (Lemon *et al.*, 1990; Tarnopolsky *et al.*, 1988, 1990b). Although these studies clearly suggest that protein needs of strength or speed athletes exceed current recommendations the absolute values (1.2–2.0 g/kg·d^{-1}) fall considerably below the intakes reported by many strength athletes, especially body builders.

This discrepancy could be explained if nitrogen balance measures are insufficient to completely assess the value of high-protein diets. These athletes are not concerned with nitrogen balance but rather on their absolute gains in muscle mass and strength. Oddoye and Margen (1979) have demonstrated (Fig. 4.4) that it is possible to maintain a highly positive nitrogen balance for long periods of time (at least 50 days) when protein intake is very high (about 300% of current recommendations). Perhaps a highly positive nitrogen balance when combined with the powerful anabolic stimulus of heavy resistance exercise can enhance protein synthesis and/or reduce protein degradation resulting in greater gains in mass and strength. Although far from conclusive some experimental data are consistent with this hypothesis. For example, Consolazio *et al.* (1975) observed greater nitrogen retention (32.4 *vs* 7.1 g) and greater gains in lean body mass (3.28 *vs* 1.21 kg) over 40 days of training when protein intake was 2.8 *vs* 1.4 g/kg·d^{-1} (approximately 233–350 *vs* 116–175% of current recommendations). Marable *et al.* (1979) reported a greater nitrogen retention

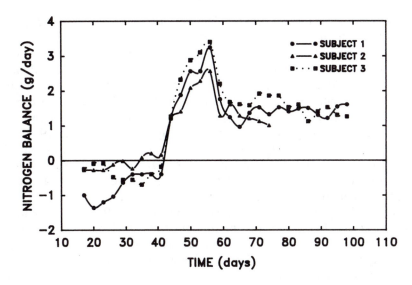

Fig. 4.4 Nitrogen balance during prolonged high protein intake. Data of individual subjects are shown (from Oddoye and Margen, 1979).

in men during a strength programme while consuming protein equal to approximately 200–300 *vs* 67–100% of current recommendations. In Romanian weight-lifters, Dragan *et al.* (1985) found gains in strength (5%) and lean body mass (6%) with several months of strength training when protein intake was increased from 2.2 to 3.5 g/kg·d^{-1} (approximately 183–275 to 292–438% of current recommendations). Frontera *et al.* (1988) reported that a daily supplement (2345 kJ) containing 23 g protein produced greater gains in thigh muscle mass (measured by computerized axial tomography) and urinary creatinine (an index of whole body muscle mass) over 12 weeks of training. Finally Lemon *et al.* (1990), Tarnopolsky *et al.* (1990b) also observed a greater nitrogen retention (Table 4.4) on a protein intake of 2.67 *vs* 0.99 g/kg·d^{-1} (223–334 *vs* 82–124% of current recommendations) in novice body builders during intensive training (6 d/wk, 3 d split routine, 4 × 8 repetitions to failure).

4.3.3 Exercise duration

Combining data from several laboratories Haralambie and Berg (1976) noted that a dramatic increase in blood urea (waste produce of protein utilization) concentration during prolonged exercise (approximately 60–70% VO$_2$ max) beginning at about 60–70 min. They hypothesized that this represented an increased protein utilization at this time because the increase was substantially greater than could be attributed to a reduced removal due to altered kidney function.

Similar observations have been made repeatedly since this paper was published (Dohm, 1986; Hood and Terjung, 1990; Lemon, 1991a; Poortmans, 1984). As already mentioned, this appears to be more related to availability of alternative substrate (especially CHO) than to exercise duration *per se.* This point is supported by the fact that starvation (i.e. low CHO availability) either activates (Wagenmakers *et al.*, 1984) or potentiates (Kasperek and Snider, 1987) the exercise activation of branched chain oxoacid dehydrogenase. Apparently neither species nor mode of exercise is important because this duration effect has been observed in humans running (Dohm *et al.*, 1982; Janssen *et al.*, 1989; Lemon *et al.*, 1983), cycling (Van Zant and Lemon, 1990), or swimming (Lemon *et al.*, 1989) and also in running rodents (Dohm *et al.*, 1982; Lemon and Dolny, 1986). Finally, in addition to this fuel use effect, long-duration exercise also causes degenerative and inflammatory responses in muscle as well as muscle enzyme efflux (Berg and Haralambie, 1978; Janssen *et al.*, 1989; Kuipers *et al.*, 1989). These data suggests that overall protein catabolism and/or muscle damage becomes greater as exercise is prolonged.

Table 4.4 Nitrogen balance during one month of strength training with variable protein intake (from Lemon *et al.*, 1990; Tarnopolsky *et al.*, 1990)

Nitrogen balance[a]	Group 1	Group 2
Intake (g/d)	12.8±0.9	34.8±1.3[b]
Excretion (g/d)		
Urine	12.5±0.3	21.1±1.6[b]
Faeces	2.0±0.3	2.2±0.3
Sweat	1.6±0.1	2.5±0.1[b]
Balance (g/d)	−3.4±0.5	8.9±1.2[b]

[a]Values are means ± s.e. for 12 subjects/group.
[b]$P < 0.01$ between groups.

4.3.4 Exercise intensity

It appears that exercise intensity is a critical factor in protein needs because the studies that have observed increased requirements have involved high-intensity exercise (Brouns *et al.*, 1989a, 1989b; Friedman and Lemon, 1989; Lemon *et al.*, 1990; Meredith *et al.*, 1989; Tarnopolsky *et al.*, 1988, 1990b). In contrast, those that have not have involved more moderate exercise (Butterfield and Calloway, 1984; Gontzea *et al.*, 1975; Todd *et al.*, 1984). This may be so because increased amino acid oxidation appears to be directly related to relative exercise intensity (Babij *et al.*, 1983; Lemon *et al.*, 1982; White and Brooks, 1981). Several pieces of evidence indicate that the underlying mechanism responsible for this increase is the exercise intensity-dependent activation (Fig. 4.5) of the branched chain oxoacid dehydrogenase (Hood and Terjung, 1987; Kasperek and Snider, 1987). However, high-intensity exercise alone is not sufficient because amino acid oxidation does not seem to increase significantly during or for 2 h following a rigorous strength training session (Tarnopolsky *et al.*, 1991). Apparently, some minimal exercise duration is necessary before the intensity effect becomes significant.

4.3.5 Exercise training

In vitro (Dohm *et al.*, 1977) and *in vivo* (Dohm *et al.*, 1977; Henderson *et al.*, 1985) experiments indicate that endurance training causes an adaptation which leads to an increased amino acid oxidation both at rest and during exercise. This is not surprising given the known effects of endurance training on both CHO and fat metabolism (Holloszy and Coyle, 1984); however, *in situ* muscle amino acid oxidation rates do not seem to increase with training (Hood and Terjung, 1987). If so, the observed whole body oxidation increases must be due to increases in tissues other than active muscle. This explanation is surprising and requires further confirmation.

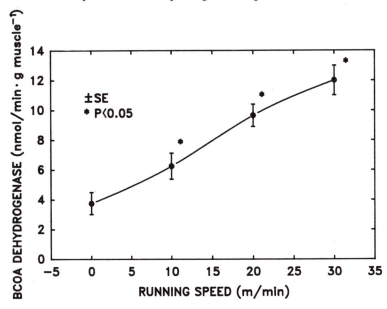

Fig. 4.5 Effect of exercise intensity on branched-chain oxoacid (BCOA) dehydrogenase activity. Values are for six animals/time point; each ran for 120 min (from Kasperek and Snider, 1987).

Alternatively, acute exercise changes in both protein synthesis and degradation (Fig. 4.1) would increase the body's free amino acid pool and this, by itself, would cause increased amino acid oxidation (Harper, 1974; Motil *et al.*, 1981).

The magnitude of this exercise-induced amino acid oxidation (Table 4.5) has been reported to be as high as 86–90% of daily requirements (Evans *et al.*, 1983; Young and Torun, 1981). These data suggest that the daily needs of at least some amino acids, especially the indispensable amino acids, are increased with regular endurance exercise. Some studies (Butterfield and Calloway, 1984; Gontzea *et al.*, 1975; Todd *et al.*, 1984) suggest that protein requirements are actually reduced as one becomes endurance-trained. The reasons for these discrepant results are not entirely clear; however, these later studies described the response to a standard training bout and therefore may not represent the same situation as with athletes who are continually increasing their training load. Further, the lower exercise intensity and/or lower total energy expenditure may also be responsible.

The effects of exercise training on exercise-induced muscle damage are also somewhat unclear. On one hand, a single exercise bout can reduce muscle soreness and enzyme efflux especially following eccentric exercise (Byrnes *et al.*, 1985; Schwane and Armstrong, 1983) indicating some protective effect of repeated exercise on muscle damage. However, data on the response of muscle proteases to training are contradictory. In some species regular exercise causes an increase while in others a decrease (Dahlmann *et al.*, 1981; Salminen and Vihko, 1984; Seene and Viru, 1982; Tapscott *et al.*, 1982).

Table 4.5 Oxidation of the amino acid leucine during 2 h exercise at 55% VO_2 max (from Evans *et al.*, 1983)[a]

Treatment	Rate (μmol kg^{-1} h^{-1})	Total (μmol)	Percentage of daily requirement
Rest[a]	14.8 ±1.3	2087 ±183	28 ±2
Exercise[a]	46.1[b] ±9.7	6500[b] ±1368	86[b] ±8

[a]Values are means ± s.e. for 8 subjects/treatment.
[b]$P < 0.01$ between treatments.

With strength exercise training, our recent data suggest that protein needs of novice body builders may be about 40% higher than experienced body builders (1.7 *vs* 1.2 g/kg·d^{-1} (Lemon *et al.*, 1990; Tarnopolsky *et al.*, 1988, 1990b). More study is necessary to determine whether this higher requirement is caused by a greater protein synthetic rate or by a greater protein catabolic rate during the early stages of an intensive strength programme.

Table 4.6 Effect of endurance training on protein synthesis and degradation in perfused muscle of male and female rodents (from Tapscott *et al.*, 1982)[a]

Gender	Protein synthesis (nmol tyrosine/h mg^{-1} protein)	Protein degradation (nmol tyrosine/h g^{-1} hemicorpus)
Male		
Untrained[a]	0.19±0.01	85±6
Trained[a]	0.20±0.02	111±8[b]
Female		
Untrained[a]	0.27±0.02	158±11
Trained[a]	0.27±0.02	160±12

[a]Values are means ± s.e. of at least 10 observations/group.
[b]$P<0.05$ between trained and untrained groups.

4.3.6 Gender

It is well known that the anabolic effect of strength training, although present in both genders, is greater in males due, at least in part, to a greater anabolic hormonal profile. Although a gender-specific response is less clear with endurance exercise some data are of interest. For example, Dohm and Louis (1978) noted that male rats produce more nitrogen during prolonged exercise than female rats. Tapscott *et al.* (1982) reported that protein degradation was increased in male rats with exercise training but not with females (Table 4.6). Tarnopolsky *et al.* (1990a) measured greater muscle glycogen utilization (by 25%) and greater nitrogen production (by 30%) in men *vs* women during a 15.5 km run at 65% VO_2 max. Amelink *et al.* (1988) observed a much greater (2–15 fold) skeletal muscle efflux in male *vs* female rats. Several types of evidence suggest that the mechanism of action is related to a gender-specific hormonal pattern and/or response to exercise. First, in the study by Tarnopolsky *et al.* (1990a) the men experienced a significantly lower insulin and higher adrenaline and growth hormone response to the run. Second, Bar *et al.* (1988) have shown that ovariectomized females show a similar muscle enzyme efflux as males and oestradiol treatment to either ovariectomized females or intact males reduces the enzyme efflux. Apparently, at least in the rat, oestradiol exerts a protective effect on the muscle membrane (Shumate *et al.*, 1979); however, this may not be the case in the human (Buckley-Bleiler *et al.*, 1990). Furthermore, as a result of hormonal changes it may be that the protein metabolic response to exercise can be substantially different (Fig. 4.6) over the menstrual cycle (Calloway and Kurzer, 1982; Lamont *et al.*, 1987).

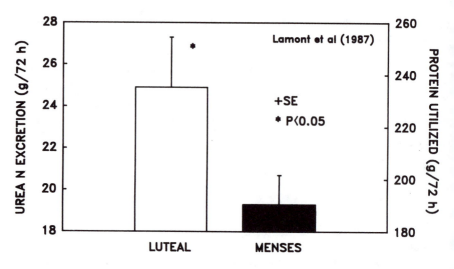

Fig. 4.6 Urea nitrogen (N) excretion and calculated protein utilization as a result of 60 min bicycle exercise at 70% VO_2 max ($n = 9$) either during the luteal phase or during menses (from Lamont *et al.*, 1987).

Finally, it is known that protein needs are greater during pregnancy but the interaction of exercise and pregnancy on protein metabolism is largely unstudied (Dolny and Lemon, 1986). Due to potential adverse effects on either the foetus or the mother this topic merits further study.

4.3.7 Ambient temperature

Ambient temperature can alter substrate utilization both at rest and during exercise. Low ambient temperatures tend to increase fat (Dolny and Lemon, 1988; Fink *et al.*, 1975) and protein utilization (Goodenough *et al.*, 1982; Dolny and Lemon, 1988), while high ambient temperatures increase glycogen utilization and lactic acid production (Claremont *et al.*, 1975; Dolny and Lemon, 1988; Fink *et al.*, 1975; MacDougall *et al.*, 1974). The mechanism(s) of these effects is (are) unclear but may involve the interaction of several factors including: differences in muscle blood flow, circulating hormones and lactic acid production. These temperature effects also require further study.

4.3.8 Age

Surprisingly few data exist regarding protein requirements of either the young (children/adolescents) or the elderly who engage in regular exercise (US Food and Nutrition Board, 1989; Food and Agricultural Organization, 1985). This is extremely unfortunate because in recent years significant numbers of individuals in both of these groups have begun to engage in vigorous athletic training. For the young, whose dietary protein needs are known to be evaluated anyway, inadequate protein intake could at the very least adversely affect the training response and might even reduce rates of growth. Although increased protein needs have not been established in the elderly, some studies indicate that protein requirements may be elevated despite a reduced active cell mass (Gersovitz *et al.*, 1982; Uauy *et al.*, 1978). Furthermore, because energy intake is frequently inadequate and several other factors may exist (i.e. fever, bed rest or surgery) which are known to increase protein need it is quite possible that protein requirements are in fact higher at least for some elderly people. Whether regular exercise superimposed on these conditions further increases protein need must await the completion of future investigations.

4.4 SUMMARY AND CONCLUSIONS

Despite the renewed interest in the effects of exercise on protein requirements this area of study is still in its infancy. Many methodological problems remain to be solved before definitive answers to many of the questions are possible. However, taken together the weight of the existing evidence strongly indicates that daily protein needs are increased as a result of either regular strength–speed or endurance exercise. Several factors including diet composition, total energy intake, exercise intensity, duration and training, ambient temperature, gender and perhaps even age can influence how exercise affects protein requirements. Future studies utilizing rigorous control (both diet and exercise conditions), direct measures, and large sample sizes are needed before exact recommendations are possible. This is especially true for activities that do not reside at either extreme of the exercise duration–intensity continuum but rather lie somewhere in between. Moreover, studies utilizing performance measures are desperately needed because laboratory measures may not be sensitive enough to detect differences between athletic performances that frequently differ by 1% or less. Based on available data it appears that protein intakes should be about $1.2–1.4$ g/kg·d^{-1} for most endurance athletes, perhaps slightly greater for those involved in extreme energy expenditures such as events like the Tour de France bicycle race. For strength–speed athletes protein intakes of $1.2–1.7$ g/kg·d^{-1} should be sufficient to maintain positive nitrogen balance. While higher intakes may enhance muscle mass and strength gains, a recommendation for higher protein intakes would, at this time, be premature. Although it is frequently stated that high protein intakes are harmful there is no reason to suspect intake at these levels will cause any problems (Lemon, 1991b).

Finally, despite the fact that these protein intakes exceed most current recommendations for sedentary individuals, it is not necessary for all athletes to increase their protein intake because as a result of very high energy intakes many athletes routinely consume 1.2–2.0 g/kg·d⁻¹. Therefore, before deciding to increase protein intake a complete dietary evaluation should be performed to determine if additional protein is necessary.

REFERENCES

Ahlborg, G., Felig, P., Hagenfeldt, L., Hendler, R. and Wahren, J. (1974). Substrate turnover during prolonged exercise in man. Splanchnic and leg metabolism of glucose, free fatty acids and amino acids. *Journal of Clinical Investigation*, **53**, 1080–90.

Amelink, G.J., Kamp, H.H. and Bar, P.R. (1988). Creatine kinase isoenzyme profiles after exercise in the rat: sex-linked differences in leakage of CK–MM. *Pflugers Archives*, **412**, 417–21.

Anderson, D.E. and Sharp, R.L. (1990). Effects of muscle glycogen depletion on protein catabolism during exercise. *Medicine and Science in Sports and Exercise*, **22** (2, suppl), S59.

Australian National Health and Medical Research Council. (1987). *Dietary Intakes for Use in Australia*. Australian Government Publishing Service, Canberra.

Babij, P., Matthews, S.M. and Rennie, M.F. (1983). Changes in blood ammonia, lactate and amino acids in relation to workload during bicycle ergometer exercise in man. *European Journal of Applied Physiology*, **50**, 405–11.

Bar, P.R., Amelink, G.J. Oldenburg, B., Blankenstein, M.A. (1988). Prevention of exercise-induced muscle membrane damage by oestradiol. *Life Sciences*, **42**, 2677–81.

Berg, A. and Haralambie, G. (1978). Changes in serum creatine kinase and hexose phosphate isomerase activity with exercise duration. *European Journal of Applied Physiology*, **39**, 191–201.

Booth, F.W. and Watson, P.A. (1985). Control of adaptations in protein levels in response to exercise. *Federation Proceedings*, **44**, 2293–300.

Brouns, F., Saris, W.H.M., Stroecken, J., Beckers, E., Thijssen, R., Rehrer, N.J. and ten Hoor, F. (1989a). Eating, drinking, and cycling. A controlled Tour de France simulation study, part I. *International Journal of Sports Medicine*, **10** (suppl I), S32–S40.

Brouns, F., Saris, W.H.M., Stroecken, J., Beckers, E., Thijssen, R., Rehrer, N.J. and ten Hoor, F. (1989b). Eating, drinking, and cycling. A controlled Tour de France simulation study, part II. Effect of diet manipulation. *International Journal of Sports Medicine*, **10** (suppl I), S41–S48.

Buckley-Bleiler, R.L., Maughan, R.J., Clarkson, P.M., Bleiler, T.L. and Whiting, P.H. (1990). The effect of menopause on serum creatine kinase activity following isometric exercise. *Experimental Ageing Research*, **15**, 195–8.

Butterfield, G.E. (1991). Amino acids and high protein diets. In: *Perspectives in Exercise Science and Sports Medicine*, Vol. 4, *Ergogenics – The Enhancement of Exercise and Sport Performance* (eds. M. Williams and D. Lamb). Benchmark Press, Indianapolis.

Butterfield, G.E. and Calloway, D.H. (1984). Physical activity improves protein utilization in young men. *British Journal of Nutrition*, **51**, 171–84.

Byrnes, W.G., Clarkson, P.M., White, J.S., Hsieth, S.S., Frykman, P.N. and Maughan, R.J. (1985). Delayed onset muscle soreness following repeated bouts of downhill running. *Journal of Applied Physiology*, **59**, 710–15.

Calloway, D.H. and Kurzer, M.S. (1982). Menstrual cycle and protein requirements of women. *Journal of Nutrition*, **112**, 356–66.

Calloway, D.H. and Spector, H. (1954). Nitrogen balance as related to caloric and protein intake of active young men. *American Journal of Clinical Nutrition*, **2**, 405–11.

Canadian Department of National Health and Welfare (1983). Committee for the Revision of Dietary Standards for Canada, Bureau of Nutritional Sciences, Food Directorate. *Recommended Intakes for Canadians*, Ottawa.

Cathcart, E.P. (1925). Influence of muscle work on protein metabolism. *Physiological Reviews*, **5**, 225–43.

Celejowa, I. and Homa, M. (1970). Food intake, nitrogen and energy balance in Polish weight lifters during a training camp. *Nutrition and Metabolism*, **12**, 259–74.

Claremont, A.D., Nagle, F.J., Redden, W.D. and Brooks, G.A. (1975). Comparison of metabolic temperature, heart rate and ventilatory response to exercise at extreme ambient temperatures (0 and 35°C). *Medicine and Science in Sports*, **7**, 150–4.

Consolazio, G.F., Johnson, H.L., Nelson, R.A., Dramise, J.G. and Skala, J.H. (1975). Protein metabolism during intensive physical training in the young adult. *American Journal of Clinical Nutrition*, **28**, 29–35.

Cuthbertson, D.P., McGirr, J.L. and Munro, H.N. (1937). A study of the effect of overfeeding on the protein metabolism of men, the effect of muscular work at different levels of energy intake with particular reference to the timing of work in relation to taking food. *Biochemical Journal*, **31**, 2293–305.

Dahlmann, B., Widjaja, A. and Reinauer, H. (1981). Antagonistic effects of endurance training and testosterone on alkaline proteolytic activity in rat skeletal muscles. *European Journal of Applied Physiology*, **46**, 229–35.

Decombaz, J., Reinhardt, P., Anantharaman, K., von Glutz, G. and Poortmans, J.R. (1979). Biochemical changes in a 100 km run: free amino acids, urea and creatinine. *European Journal of Applied Physiology*, **41**, 61–72.

Dohm, G.L. (1986). Protein as a fuel for exercise. In: *Exercise and Sport Science Reviews* (ed. Pandolf), pp. 143–73. Macmillan, New York.

Dohm, G.L. and Louis, T.M. (1978). Changes in androstenedione, testosterone, and protein metabolism as a result of exercise. *Proceedings of the Society for Experimental Biological Medicine*, **158**, 622–5.

Dohm, G.L., Hecker, A.L., Brown, W.E., Klain, G.J., Puente, F.R., Askew, E.W. and Beecher, G.R. (1977). Adaptation of protein metabolism to endurance training. Increased amino acid oxidation in response to training. *Biochemical Journal*, **164**, 705–8.

Dohm, G.L., Williams, R.T., Kasperek, G.J. and van Rij, A.M. (1982). Increased excretion of urea and N^+-methylhistidine by rats and humans after a bout of exercise. *Journal of Applied Physiology*, **52**, 27–33.

Dolny, D.G. and Lemon, P.W.R. (1986). Effect of exercise on protein utilization during pregnancy. *Canadian Journal of Applied Sport Sciences*, **11** (3), 11P.

Dolny, D.G. and Lemon, P.W.R. (1988). Effect of ambient temperature on protein breakdown during prolonged exercise. *Journal of Applied Physiology*, **64**, 550–5.

Dragan, C.I., Vasiliu, A. and Georgescu, E. (1985). Effects of increased supply of protein on elite weight lifters. In *Milk Proteins '84* (eds. T.E. Galesloot and B.J. Tinbergen) pp. 99–103. Pudoc, Wageningen, The Netherlands.

Dutch Nutrition Board. (1988). *Recommended Daily Allowances for Energy and Nutrients* (Dutch), The Hague.

Dunlop, J.C., Paton, D.N., Stockman, R. and MacCadam, I. (1897). On the influence of muscular exercise, sweating, and massage, on the metabolism. *Journal of Physiology*, **22**, 68–91.

Elia, M., Folmer, P., Schlatmann, A., Goren, A. and Austin, S. (1989). Amino acid metabolism in the muscle and in the whole body of man before and after ingestion of a single mixed meal. *American Journal of Clinical Nutrition*, **49**, 1203–10.

Evans, W.J., Fisher, E.C., Hoerr, R.A. and Young, V.R. (1983). Protein metabolism and endurance exercise. *Physician and Sportsmedicine*, **11**, 63–72.

Fink, W.J., Costill, D.L. and Van Handel, P.J. (1975). Leg muscle metabolism during exercise in the heat and cold. *European Journal of Applied Physiology*, **34**, 183–90.

Food and Agricultural Organization, World Health Organization, and United Nations University. (1985). *Energy and Protein Requirements*. World Health Organization Technical Report Series 724, Geneva.

Friedman, J.E. and Lemon, P.W.R. (1989). Effect of chronic endurance exercise on retention of dietary protein. *International Journal of Sports Medicine*, **10**, 118–23.

Frontera, W.R., Meredith, C.N. and Evans, W.J. (1988). Dietary effects on muscle strength gain and hypertrophy during heavy resistance training in older men. *Canadian Journal of Sport Sciences*, **13** (2), 13P.

Gelfand, R.A., Glickman, M.C., Jacob, R., Sherwin, R.S. and DeFronzo, R.A. (1986). Removal of infused amino acids by splanchnic and leg tissues in humans. *American Journal of Physiology*, **250**, E407–E413.

Gersovitz, M., Motil, K., Munro, H.N., Scrimshaw, N.S. and Young, V.R. (1982). Human protein requirements: assessment of the adequacy of the current recommended dietary allowance for protein in elderly men and women. *American Journal of Clinical Nutrition*, **35**, 6–14.

Gontzea, I., Sutzescu, P. and Dumitrache, S. (1974). The influence of muscular activity on the nitrogen balance and on the need of man for proteins. *Nutrition Reports International*, **10**, 35–43.

Gontzea, I., Sutzescu, P. and Dumitrache, S. (1975). The influence of adaptation to physical effort on nitrogen balance in man. *Nutrition Reports International*, **11**, 231–4.

Goodenough, R.D., Royle, C.T., Nadel, E.R., Wolfe, M.M. and Wolfe, R.R. (1982). Leucine and urea metabolism in acute human cold exposure. *Journal of Applied Physiology*, **53**, 367–72.

Goranzon, H. and Forsum, E. (1985). Effect of reduced energy intake versus increased physical activity on the outcome of nitrogen balance experiments in man. *American Journal of Clinical Nutrition*, **41**, 919–28.

Hagg, S.A., Morse, E.L. and Adibi, S.A. (1982). Effect of exercise on rates of oxidation, turnover and plasma clearance of leucine in human subjects. *American Journal of Physiology*, **242**, E407–E410.

Haralambie, G. and Berg, A. (1976). Serum urea and amino nitrogen changes with exercise duration. *European Journal of Applied Physiology*, **36**, 39–48.

Harper, A.E. (1974). Control mechanisms in amino acid metabolism. In *Control of Metabolism* (ed. J.D. Sink) pp. 49–74. University Park, Pennsylvania State University.

Henderson, S.A., Black, A.L. and Brooks, G.A. (1985). Leucine turnover and oxidation in trained rats during exercise. *American Journal of Physiology*, **249**, E137–E144.

Holloszy, J.O. and Coyle, E.F. (1984). Adaptations of skeletal muscle to endurance exercise and their metabolic consequences. *Journal of Applied Physiology*, **56**, 831–8.

Hood, D.A. and Terjung, R.L. (1987). Effect of endurance training on leucine in perfused rat skeletal muscle. *American Journal of Physiology*, **253**, E648–E656.

Hood, D.A. and Terjung, R.L. (1990). Amino acid metabolism during exercise and following endurance training. *Sports Medicine*, **9**, 23–35.

Janssen, G.M.E., Kuipers, H., Willems, G.M., Does, R.J.M.M., Janssen, M.P.E. and Geurten, P. (1989). Plasma activity of muscle enzymes: quantification of skeletal muscle damage and relationship with metabolic variables. *International Journal of Sports Medicine*, **10** (suppl 3), S160–S168.

Kasperek, G.J. and Snider, R.D. (1987). Effect of exercise intensity and starvation on activation of branched-chain keto acid dehydrogenase by exercise. *American Journal of Physiology*, **252**, E33–E37.

Kuipers, H., Janssen, G.M.E., Bosman, F., Frederik, P.M. and Geurten, P. (1989). Structural and ultrastructural changes in skeletal muscle associated with long-distance training and running. *International Journal of Sports Medicine*, **10** (suppl 3), S156–S159.

Lamont, L.S., Lemon, P.W.R. and Brout, B.C. (1987). Menstrual cycle and exercise effects on protein catabolism. *Medicine and Science in Sports and Exercise*, **19**, 106–10.

Laritcheva, H.A., Yalovaya, N.I., Shubin, V.I. and Smirnow, P.V. (1978). Study of energy expenditure and protein needs of top weight lifters. In *Nutrition, Physical Fitness, and Health* (eds. J. Parizkova and J. Rogozkin) pp. 155–63. University Park Press, Baltimore.

Lemon, P.W.R. (1991a). Does exercise alter dietary protein requirements? In *Advances in Nutrition and Topsport* (eds. F. Brouns, W.H.M. Saris and E.A. Newsholme). Karger, Basel.

Lemon, P.W.R. (1991b). Protein and amino acid needs of the strength athlete. *International Journal of Sports Nutrition*, 1 (in press).

Lemon, P.W.R. and Dolny, D.G. (1986). Role of individual body tissues in urea production. *Canadian Journal of Applied Sports Sciences*, 11 (3), 26P.

Lemon, P.W.R. and Mullin, J.P. (1980). Effect of initial muscle glycogen levels on protein catabolism during exercise. *Journal of Applied Physiology*, 48, 624–9.

Lemon, P.W.R., Nagle, F.J., Mullin, J.P. and Benevenga, N.J. (1982). *In vivo* leucine oxidation at rest and during two intensities of exercise. *Journal of Applied Physiology*, 53, 947–54.

Lemon, P.W.R., Dolny, D.G. and Sherman, B.A. (1983). Effect of intense prolonged running on protein catabolism. In *Biochemistry of Exercise* (eds. H.G. Knuttgen, J.A.Vogel and J. Poortmans) pp. 367–72. Human Kinetics, Champaign.

Lemon, P.W.R., Benevenga, N.J., Mullin, J.P. and Nagle, F.J. (1985). Effect of daily exercise and food intake on leucine oxidation. *Biochemical Medicine*, 33, 67–76.

Lemon, P.W.R., Deutsch, D.T. and Payne, W.R. (1989). Urea production during prolonged swimming. *Journal of Sports Sciences*, 7, 241–6.

Lemon, P.W.R., MacDougall, J.D., Tarnopolsky, M.A. and Atkinson, S.A. (1990). Effect of dietary protein and body building exercise on muscle mass and strength gains. *Canadian Journal of Sport Sciences*, 15 (4), 14S.

MacDougall, J.D., Redden, W.G., Layton, G.R. and Dempsey, J.A. (1974). Effects of metabolic hyperthermia on performance during heavy prolonged exercise. *Journal of Applied Physiology*, 36, 538–44.

MacLean, D.A., Graham, T.E. and Spriet, L.L. (1989). Carbohydrate supply and amino acid and ammonia metabolism during prolonged exercise. *Medicine and Science in Sports and Exercise*, 21 (2 suppl), S106.

Marable, N.L., Hickson, J.F., Korslund, M.K., Herbert, W.G., Desjardins, R.F. and Thye, F.W. (1979). Urinary nitrogen excretion as influenced by a muscle-building exercise program and protein intake variation. *Nutrition Reports International*, 19, 795–805.

Meredith, C.N., Zackin, M.J., Frontera, W.R. and Evans, W.J. (1989). Dietary protein requirements and body protein metabolism in endurance-trained men. *Journal of Applied Physiology*, 66, 2850–6.

Motil, K.J., Matthews, D.E., Bier, D.M., Burke, J.F. and Young, V.R. (1981). Whole body leucine and lysine metabolism studied with [1-^{13}C] leucine and [alpha-^{15}N] lysine; response in healthy young men given excess energy intake. *Metabolism*, 30, 783–91.

Munro, H.N. (1951). Carbohydrate and fat as factors in protein utilization and metabolism. *Physiological Reviews*, 31, 449–88.

Oddoye, E.B. and Margen, S. (1979). Nitrogen balance studies in humans: long-term effect of high nitrogen intake on nitrogen accretion. *Journal of Nutrition*, 109, 363–77.

Pivarnik, J.M., Hickson, J.F. and Wolinsky, I. (1989). Urinary 3-methylhistidine excretion increases with repeated weight training exercise. *Medicine and Science in Sports and Exercise*, **21**, 283–7.

Poortsmans, J. (1984). Protein turnover and amino acid oxidation during and after exercise. In *Medicine and Sport Science*, Vol. 17 (eds. E. Jokl and E. Hebbelinck) pp. 130–47. Karger, Basel.

Refsum, H.E. and Stromme, S.B. (1974). Urea and creatinine production and excretion in urine during and following prolonged heavy exercise. *Scandinavian Journal of Clinical and Laboratory Investigation*, **33**, 247–54.

Rennie, M.J., Edwards, R.H.T., Krywawych, S., Davies, C.T.M., Halliday, D. and Millward, D.J. (1981). Effect of exercise on protein turnover in man. *Clinical Science*, **61**, 627–39.

Salminen, A. and Vihko, V. (1984). Autophagic response to strenuous exercise in mouse skeletal muscle fibers. *Virchows Archives* [Cell Pathology], **45**, 97–106.

Schwane, J.A. and Armstrong, R.B. (1983). Effect of training on skeletal muscle injury from downhill running. *Journal of Applied Physiology*, **55**, 969–75.

Scrimshaw, N.S., Hussein, M.A., Murray, E., Rand, W.M. and Young, V.R. (1972). Protein requirements of man: variations in obligatory and fecal nitrogen losses in young men. *Journal of Nutrition*, **102**, 1595–604.

Shumate, J.B., Brooke, M.H., Carrol, J.E. and Davis, J.E. (1979). Increased serum creatine kinase after exercise – a sex linked phenomenon. *Neurology*, **29**, 902–4.

Seene, T. and Viru, A. (1982). The catabolic effect of glucocorticoids on different types of skeletal muscle fibers and its dependence upon muscle activity and interaction with anabolic steroids. *Journal of Steroid Biochemistry*, **16**, 349–52.

Tapscott, E.B., Kasperek, G.J. and Dohm, G.L. (1982). Effect of training on muscle protein turnover in male and female rats. *Biochemical Medicine*, **27**, 254–9.

Tarnopolsky, M.A., MacDougall, J.D. and Atkinson, S.A. (1988). Influence of protein intake and training status on nitrogen balance and lean body mass. *Journal of Applied Physiology*, **64**, 187–93.

Tarnopolsky, L.J., MacDougall, J.D., Atkinson, S.A., Tarnopolsky, M.A. and Sutton, J.R. (1990a). Gender differences in substrate for endurance exercise. *Journal of Applied Physiology*, **68**, 302–8.

Tarnopolsky, M.A., Lemon, P.W.R., MacDougall, J.D. and Atkinson, S.A. (1990b). Effect of body building exercise on protein requirements. *Canadian Journal of Sport Sciences*, **15** (4), 22S.

Tarnopolsky, M.A., Atkinson, S.A., MacDougall, J.D., Senor, B.B., Lemon, P.W.R. and Schwarcz, H. (1991). Whole body leucine metabolism during and after resistance exercise in fed humans. *Medicine and Science in Sports and Exercise*, **23**, 326–33.

Todd, K.S., Butterfield, G.E. and Galloway, D.H. (1984). Nitrogen balance in men with adequate and deficient energy intake at three levels of work. *Journal of Nutrition*, **114**, 2107–18.

Torun, B., Scrimshaw, N.S. and Young, V.R. (1977). Effect of isometric exercises on body potassium and dietary protein requirements of young men. *American Journal of Clinical Nutrition*, **30**, 1983–93.

Uauy, R., Scrimshaw, N.S. and Young, V.R. (1978). Human protein require-ments: nitrogen balance response to graded levels of egg protein in elderly men and women. *American Journal of Clinical Nutrition*, **31**, 779–85.

US Food and Nutrition Board. (1989). *Recommended Dietary Allowances*, Vol. 10, pp. 52–77. National Academy Press, Washington DC.

Van Zant, R.S. and Lemon, P.W.R. (1990). Effect of fructose and glucose pre-exercise feedings on muscle glycogen and protein catabolism during exercise. *Medicine and Science in Sports and Exercise*, **22** (2 suppl), S59.

von Liebig, J. (1842). *Animal Chemistry or Organic Chemistry in its Application to Physiology and Pathology* (trans. W. Gregory). Taylor and Walton, London.

Wagenmakers, A.J.M., Schepens, J.T.G., Veldhuizen, J.A.M. and Veerkamp, J.G. (1984). The activity state of the branched-chain 2-oxo acid dehydrogenase complex in rat tissue. *Biochemical Journal*, **220**, 273–81.

Wagenmakers, A.J.M., Coakley, J.H. and Edwards, R.H.T. (1990). Metabolism of branched-chain amino acids and ammonia during exercise: clues from McArdle's disease. *International Journal of Sports Medicine*, **11** (suppl 2), S101–S113.

Walberg, J.L., Leidy, M.K., Sturgill, D.J., Hinkle, D.E., Ritchey, S.J. and Sebolt, D.R. (1988). Macronutrient content of a hypoenergy diet affects nitrogen retention and muscle function in weight lifters. *International Journal of Sports Medicine*, **9**, 261–6.

Watt, B.K. and Merrill, A.L. (1963). *Composition of Foods – Raw, Processed, and Prepared*. US Department of Agriculture, Washington DC.

White, T.P. and Brooks, G.A. (1981). [U-14C] glucose, -alanine, -leucine oxidation in rats at rest and during two intensities of running. *American Journal of Physiology*, **240**, E155–E165.

Wolfe, R.R. (1984). *Tracers in Metabolic Research: Radioisotope and Stable Iso-tope/Mass Spectrometry Methods*. AR Liss, New York.

Yoshimura, H., Inoue, T., Yamada, T. and Shiraki, K. (1980). Anemia during hard physical training (sports anemia) and its casual mechanism with special reference to protein nutrition. *World Review of Nutrition and Dietetics*, **35**, 1–86.

Young, V.R. and Torun, B. (1981). Physical activity: impact on protein and amino acid metabolism and implications for nutritional requirements. In *Nutrition in Health and Disease and International Development* (eds. A.E. Harper and G.K. Davis) pp. 57–85. Liss, New York.

5

Importance of fat as a support nutrient for energy: metabolism of athletes

Per Bjorntorp

5.1 INTRODUCTION

Exercise needs energy substrate. The two main energy sources during exercise are carbohydrate and fat. In principle, the bodily reserves of these substrates are limited for carbohydrate, but for all practical purposes unlimited for fat. The carbohydrate stores in the human body consist of the glycogen stores in muscle and liver. Muscle glycogen can be used directly by the contractile process. Liver glycogen is utilized after being transported from the liver to the contracting muscle as blood glucose. Gluconeogenetic substrate in the form of lactate, glycerol and alanine are transformed to glucose in the liver, which can then be utilized also. In addition, exogenous glucose can be furnished and utilized during exercise.

In contrast to the limited carbohydrate stores, the lipid stores in the human body are, from a practical standpoint, unlimited. To take some examples to illustrate this point, jogging at about two-thirds of maximal aerobic power requires in the order of 1.2 to 2 MJ (3–500 kcal/h). This means that 1 kg adipose tissue is sufficient to supply energy for approximately 10–20 h. Similarly, a marathon run of 4–5 h duration would require less than 1 kg of body fat, provided only fat was utilized for combustion. Cross-country ski-racing has been considered to be particularly energy-demanding, employing almost all the major muscle groups in the body, including the legs, the back and the arms. One of the classical long-distance races, the Vasaloppet, with a racing distance of over 90 km, has

Food, Nutrition and Sports Performance
Edited by Clyde Williams and John T. Devlin
Published in 1992 by E & F N Spon, London. ISBN 0 419 17890 2

been estimated to require about 1 kg body fat, again provided that only fat is burned.

These figures can be compared with the amount of depot fat stored in the human body. An average middle-aged man in Göteborg, Sweden, has approximately 10 kg of body fat. Elite endurance athletes usually have several kg of body fat, and thus a 'gasoline tank' sufficient for several marathon races or triathlons; in other words sufficient lipid stores to provide energy even for athletic performances of extremely long duration. Needless to say, the average man or woman has a large excess of energy for these purposes.

The large fat store in humans and some other mammals has most likely not developed to furnish extra energy for exercise purposes, but to be used for survival in periods of famine. With this large fat depot there is thus no need to supplement an athlete with exogenous fat during exercise, even during extremely demanding competitions of long duration.

5.2 UTILIZATION OF THE FAT DEPOTS

The problem with lipid utilization during exercise is not the physical availability of fat as an energy source, but to bring the lipid to the site of oxidation in the muscles, and actually have it used in the oxidative processes to furnish energy. If this can be brought about efficiently, then the limited carbohydrate stores, which are essential for the needs of the brain, can be spared, and exercise prolonged. This is accomplished by several processes adapted during the process of physical conditioning. Since supplementation of fat during exercise is neither needed, nor desired, the mobilization process and peripheral adaptation of the lipid oxidation processes will be reviewed here. There is also a question of replenishing fat stores between series of demanding, long-lasting athletic events. For example, if someone is running a marathon each week he or she would need to replenish about 1 kg of fat in adipose tissue. From a practical purpose this is not a problem and occurs automatically. However, after long periods of increased carbohydrate feeding, attention should be paid to providing sufficient amounts of fatty acids essential for specific body functions.

Exercise during low carbohydrate intake poses particular problems and seems to be followed by other types of adaptations. Apparently, low-intensity exercise is possible on these diets if a sufficiently long period of adaptation is allowed before work. During such conditions with ketosis, work can be performed with lipid becoming the major fuel, and net carbohydrate utilization is markedly reduced during moderate but ultimately exhausting exercise. This has been observed in a group of moderately obese, untrained subjects (Phinney *et al.*, 1980).

These findings seem to be relevant also for well-trained athletes, who after 4 weeks on a ketogenic, low carbohydrate diet still were able to perform aerobic endurance exercise at 62–64% of maximal aerobic capacity equally well as when consuming ordinary amounts of carbohydrates. In this ketotic, adapted situation the glucose and muscle glycogen stores were conserved (Phinney *et al.*, 1984). These observations indicate that given a sufficient period of adaptation, muscles are able to change their preferred substrate for energy requirements from carbohydrate to lipid, at least to some extent. In this particular situation then the importance of lipid as an energy substrate for working muscle becomes more important than on a normal type of diet. This, however, probably only allows relatively low-intensity work.

5.2.1 Triglyceride stores

Lipid for utilization during exercise is present in three forms: triglycerides in adipose tissue (the main store), triglycerides within the muscle and circulating triglycerides, primarily in very low-density lipoproteins, produced by the liver, as well as chylomicrons, transporting exogenous, absorbed lipids. Since the latter appear only post-prandially, they will not be dealt with further here. This area has been recently reviewed and for detailed information the reader is referred to these reviews (Oscai and Palmer, 1983; Bjorntorp, 1983; Newsholme, 1990; Bjorntorp, 1990; Oscai and Palmer, 1990).

The intermediate triglyceride stores in muscle, which are limited in size to about 10–40 mol/kg/w.w (Essen *et al.*, 1977; Hurley *et al.*, 1986; Brouns *et al.*, 1989), are utilized during work, because they decrease in mass under appropriate exercise conditions. There is evidence that fatty acid re-esterification is also going on in muscle during exercise. The latter probably occurs during conditions of excess mobilization of adipose tissue triglycerides. It seems most likely that the local, muscular stores are taxed of their energy during exercise and that the net mass of these depots is dependent on the balance between influx from circulating free fatty acids (FFA) from adipose tissue, and efflux to the machinery from transforming fat to utilizable energy in the muscle. The regulatory controls are poorly known. For example, are circulating fatty acids oxidized directly, or by going totally or partially through the local muscle depots before oxidation? The reason for the limited knowledge here is probably due to difficulties in studying these depots from a methodological point of view.

5.2.2 Adipose tissue

From a quantitative aspect, the main source of lipid energy comes from adipose tissue, which contains almost 400 MJ (100 000 kcal) in a sedentary person. This lipid is stored as triglyceride, which first has to be hydrolysed to FFA and glycerol before being mobilized. It is important to realize the difference in lipid mobilization potential between different adipose tissue regions, as well as topography in relation to circulation. The fat depots drained by the portal vein have a specific topographic position insofar as the FFA produced here will reach the liver directly and in high concentrations. The liver will transform the excess of these FFA, which are not needed for oxidation purposes in the liver, to very low-density lipoproteins (VLDL).

These VLDL are then utilized in the periphery, for example for energy purposes in muscle during exercise. These circulating triglycerides also have to be hydrolysed before they enter the muscle tissue. This is catalysed by lipoprotein lipase, localized at the level of the capillary endothelium, where circulating VLDL are captured for hydrolysis of their triglyceride. This enzyme has an increased activity in muscle and heart during fasting conditions, while the adipose tissue enzyme is activated in the post-prandial state to facilitate uptake of circulating, exogenous lipid by adipose tissue. This may have significance for the situation where carbohydrate is furnished during exercise, because carbohydrate feeding might theoretically direct VLDL from muscle to adipose tissue, particularly during low-intensity exercise if high insulin concentrations are produced by feeding. In this situation FFA mobilization may also be hampered as will be seen in a following section.

The main mobilizer of fat for exercise purposes is the sympathetic nervous system (SNS), with varying capacity to stimulate the lipase system. The beta-adrenergic receptors have been found in three different forms (BAR 1, BAR 2 and BAR 3) and it is still not clear which of whose activity is already increasing in anticipation of physical exercise. The nerve endings release the lipolytic hormone norepinephrine, which stimulates triglyceride hydrolysis by activation of a specific, hormone-sensitive lipase. The immediate fate of the norepinephrine released is to bind to specific hormonal adrenergic receptors. These occur in several forms, the most efficient of which are involved in the stimulation of lipolysis in human adipose tissue. All seem to have some activity in this direction. In addition, there are alpha-adrenergic receptors, also of different kinds (AAR 1 and AAR 2), where clearly the AAR 2 inhibit lipolysis. The end result in terms of net lipolysis is dependent on which of these receptors are stimulated. This is most likely dependent on local factors, modifying the balance between receptors. Such factors also probably exert different actions in different regions. For example, starvation seems to increase the AAR 2 activity in gluteal-femoral regions of women, apparently protecting these depots from depletion at least during early phases of starvation. In contrast, the visceral depots have a low density of AAR's and are therefore easy to mobilize during negative energy balance, actually diminishing most rapidly during such conditions. The regulation of the net balance of the density of the lipolytic BAR's and the antilipolytic AAR's is poorly known, but it seems likely that steroid hormones might be involved in these processes. This area needs more research to better elucidate these control mechanisms.

After stimulation of the adrenergic receptors, signals are sent through a system of stimulatory (Gs) or inhibitory (Gi) proteins which activate or inhibit a cyclase enzyme in the adipocyte membrane. Through a protein kinase system the hormone-sensitive lipase protein is phosphorylated and becomes active to facilitate triglyceride cleavage in the 1,3-(outer) positions of the triglyceride. The 2-(middle) position is then hydrolysed by a monoglyceride lipase which is apparently not rate-limiting for triglyceride hydrolysis.

Once liberated by these hydrolytic processes the glycerol moiety diffuses out of adipose tissue and is used mainly for gluconeogenetic purposes in the liver. The fatty acids also diffuse out, and are then bound to albumin and transported to various end organs. Some of them are re-esterified within the adipocyte to form new triglycerides. This process is dependent on the availability of glucose transported into the adipocyte by the action of insulin. During exercise this process is not very active, and presumably the majority of the fatty acids hydrolysed are mobilized from the adipocyte and transported as FFA, bound to albumin, to be used by the contracting muscle.

5.3 FFA FLUXES IN CIRCULATION DURING EXERCISE

These are the main cellular events at the level of the adipocyte. The balance between these processes and the uptake by the periphery are reflected by the concentrations and turn-over of FFA in plasma at the commencement of, during and after exercise. The circulating FFA concentration curve is the end-result of FFA flux into the circulation and the efflux into various tissues. Immediately upon the start of exercise, muscle capillaries are opened up, facilitating FFA uptake, and this process is revised at the end of the exercise. The lipolytic process is stimulated by exercise, but this occurs gradually and does not cease when exercise has ended. The resulting concentrations of FFA during exercise are often decreasing at the start of exercise and then gradually increase. After the end of exercise, when lipolysis stimulation continues, but the efflux is suddenly diminishing, there is usually an overshoot of plasma FFA concentration reaching rather high levels.

In man the main stimulator of FFA mobilization by lipolysis is the SNS. There are also inhibitory factors which keep the system in balance. We have already seen that there is a balance at the level of the adrenergic receptors between BAR's and AAR's. Insulin is probably the most important counter-regulatory hormone for this process, and acts mainly by stimulating the phosphodiesterase, which breaks down cAMP to AMP, thereby preventing the stimulation by cAMP of the hormone-sensitive lipase. Insulin concentrations are suppressed during exercise, with the SNS inhibiting the release of insulin, facilitating lipid mobilization by diminishing the inhibitory effect of insulin. Lactate may also directly inhibit the lipolytic process. It should be observed that various drugs (beta-adrenergic blocking drugs and nicotinic acid derivatives, for example) which inhibit the lipolytic process, and thereby the availability of FFA for working muscle, might be hazardous when the glycogen stores and circulating glucose are limited.

5.4 ADAPTATIONS BY PHYSICAL TRAINING

The main importance and impact on the organism of endurance physical training are the gradual build-up of the capacity to transport oxygen efficiently to the working muscles. This occurs by a number of useful adaptations. The circulatory system more efficiently directs blood-flow to the working muscles, and both the oxygen transporter, haemoglobin and the heart are adapted to facilitate oxygen transport. The muscle is adapted towards more efficient extraction of available oxygen and therefore can perform the same submaximal work with less blood flow. The morphology changes towards more red, oxygen-consuming, muscle fibres and more capillaries.

In addition, the enzymic equipment of muscle adapts by increasing the activity of the lipid oxidizing enzymes, including those involved in the beta-oxidation of fatty acids, as well as the activity of the electron transport chain. Lipoprotein lipase activity is also increased, making uptake of circulating VLDL for oxidation more efficient. These adaptations are paralleled by a more efficient system for energy delivery in the form of lipid. Measures other than physical training attempting to increase fat availability (coffee, heparin, carnitine) have failed to show clear beneficial effects (Wagenmakers, 1991).

The fat depot decreases with physical training to facilitate bodily movement. An unnecessarily large adipose tissue is a burden which prevents rapid long-term physical activities in the form of running or skiing. It should be noted that there is no reliable evidence to suggest a local effect of training to deplete selectively regional adipose tissue stores (e.g. sit-ups to decrease abdominal fat).

With training the lipolytic process becomes more sensitive to stimuli by adaptations at the level of the adrenergic receptors. The BAR's increase in density, and the cyclase system is also more active. Insulin levels are lower than in the unconditioned state, and lactate production lower, both shifting metabolism towards a more efficient delivery of lipid substrate to the oxidative processes in the muscle. Finally, the signals from the SNS for lipid mobilization are less pronounced at the same submaximal work load. In other words, the whole system has adapted towards more econ-omy and efficiency than before physical training.

Physical training thus has the effects that the limited carbohydrate stores can be spared, and the fat stores utilized in their place. This means that in a long-distance race, for example a marathon, lipid substrate not only is able to replace carbohydrate as an oxidative fuel, but also can be oxidized at higher absolute levels of work intensity. In practical terms this means that such a race can be performed at a higher speed, utilizing the large 'gasoline' tank of lipid in adipose tissue. However, losses of fluid and electrolytes will have to be continuously replaced. Furthermore, in such races carbohydrate is usually furnished from various sources to pro-vide additional substrate for use by the brain, which cannot function on lipid substrate, and for contracting muscle tissue which cannot function without glycogen. There is also evidence that local muscle triglycerides are utilized to a greater extent after physical training (Hurley *et al.*, 1986; Brouns *et al.*, 1989).

REFERENCES

Bjorntorp, P. (1983). Physiological and clinical aspects of exercise in obese per-sons. *Exercise and Sports Sciences Reviews*, **11**, 159–80.

Bjorntorp, P. (1990). Adipose tissue adaptation to exercise. In *Exercise, Fitness and Health. A Consensus of Current Knowledge* (eds. C. Bouchard *et al.*) pp. 315–24. Human Kinetic Books, Illinois.

Brouns, F., Saris, W.H.M., Adlercreutz, H., van der Vurre, G.J., Keizer, H.A., Kuipers, M., Menheere, P., Wagenmakers, A.J.M. and ten Hoor, F. (1989). Metabolic changes induced by sustained exhaustive cycling and diet manipu-lation. *International Journal of Sports Medicine*, **10** (suppl 1) S49–S62.

Essen, B., Hagenfehdt, L. and Kaijser, L. (1977). Utilization of blood-borne and intramuscular substrates during continuous and intermittent exercise in man. *Journal of Physiology*, **265**, 489–506.

Hurley, B.F., Nemeth, P.M., Martin, W.M., Hagberg, J., Dalsky, G. and Hollozy, J.O. (1986). Muscle triglyceride utilization during exercise: effect of training. *Journal of Applied Physiology*, **60**, 582–67.

Newsholme, E.A. (1990). Effects of exercise on aspects of carbohydrate, fat, and amino acid metabolism. In C. Bouchard *et al.*, op. cit., pp. 293–308.

Oscai, L.B. and Palmer, W.K. (1983). Cellular control of triacylglycerol metabolism. *Exercise and Sports Sciences Reviews*, **11**, 1–23.

Oscai, L.B. and Palmer, W.K. (1990). Adipose tissue adaptation to exercise. In C. Bouchard *et al.*, op. cit., pp. 325–30.

Phinney, S.D., Horton, E.S., Sims, E.A.H., Hanson, J.S., Danforth, E. Jr and La Grange, B.M. (1980). Capacity for moderate exercise in obese subjects after adaptation to a hypocaloric diet. *Journal of Clinical Investigation*, **66**, 1152–61.

Phinney, S.D., Bistrian, B.R., Evans, W.J., Gervion, E. and Blackburn, G.L. (1984). The human metabolic response to chronic ketosis without caloric restriction. Prevention of submaximal exercise capability with reduced carbohydrate oxidation. *Metabolism*, **32**, 769–76.

Wagenmakers, A.J.M. (1991). L-carnitine supplementation and performance in man (Review). In *Advances in Topsport and Nutrition, Medicine and Sport Science* (eds. F. Brouns, W.H.M. Saris and E.A. Newsholme). Karger, Basel.

6

Vitamin supplementation and physical exercise performance

Eric J. van der Beek

6.1 INTRODUCTION

Vitamins, minerals and trace elements are of great interest in the world of sports because of their supposed role in enhancing physical performance during training and competition.

Thirteen different compounds are now considered as vitamins. Other compounds used by athletes, however, are not considered as vitamins (i.e. vitamin B-15 or pangamic acid, and carnitine) and will not be discussed. Vitamins are classified into two large groups, water-soluble and fat-soluble compounds. To meet dietary recommendations vitamins have to be consumed as part of the daily food intake. The adequacy of vitamin supply depends on the vitamin content of the food. Vitamin-rich food product groups are listed in Table 6.1.

The water-soluble vitamins thiamin, riboflavin, vitamin B-6, niacin, pantothenic acid, biotin and vitamin C are involved in mitochondrial energy metabolism. Folate and vitamin B-12 are primarily involved in DNA synthesis and red blood cell development, however, vitamin B-12 is also involved in mitochondrial metabolism. Of the fat-soluble vitamins, only vitamin E probably plays such a role. In addition, vitamins C and E have antioxidant properties. These assumed functions in muscle cells have led to a wide use of vitamins by athletes in an attempt to 'supercharge' energy-producing reactions. However, the available information of the influence of vitamin supplementation on mitochondrial metabolism is

Food, Nutrition and Sports Performance
Edited by Clyde Williams and John T. Devlin
Published in 1992 by E & F N Spon, London. ISBN 0 419 17890 2

scarce. This chapter presents a review of the assumed increased vitamin requirements of athletes and of the effects of vitamin supplementation on physical performance in humans.

Table 6.1 Dietary sources of vitamins

Vitamin	Sources
Thiamin	Dark bread and other unrefined cereal products, pulses, pork, potatoes, vegetables, nuts, liver
Riboflavin	Milk and milk products, cheese, meat, liver, eggs, green leafy vegetables
Niacin	Meat, poultry, liver, fish, dark bread and other unrefined cereal products, pulses, green leafy vegetables, nuts
Pantothenic acid	Dark bread and other unrefined cereal products, potatoes, meat, liver, milk and milk products
Vitamin B-6	Dark bread and other unrefined cereal products, meat, poultry, liver, fish, potatoes, vegetables, milk and milk products, eggs, bananas, nuts
Folate	Meat, liver, green leafy vegetables, dark bread and other unrefined cereal products, potatoes, fruit
Vitamin B-12	Fish, shellfish, meat, poultry, liver, milk and milk products, eggs
Biotin	Liver, eggs, milk and milk products, fish, nuts
Vitamin C	Vegetables, fruit, potatoes
Vitamin A	Liver, fish, milk and milk products, eggs, margarine, butter
Provitamin A carotenoids	Carrots, dark green leafy vegetables, tomatoes, oranges
Vitamin E	Liver, eggs, dark bread and other unrefined cereal products, vegetable and seed oils, margarine, butter
Vitamin D	Fish, liver, eggs, milk and milk products, margarine
Vitamin K	Liver, green leafy vegetables, cheese, butter

6.2 PROLOGUE

The principal argument for supplementation is the assumption that athletes need an increased vitamin intake. This assumption looks plausible because marginal vitamin deficiency (van der Beek, 1985) has been observed in athletes (Haralambie and van Dam, 1977; van Dam, 1978; van der Beek *et al.*, 1981). Although (marginal) vitamin deficiency may affect exercise performance (van der Beek, 1986), some comments are, therefore, necessary. Theoretically, a marginal vitamin status can be caused by decreased absorption by the gastrointestinal tract, increased excretion in sweat, urine and faeces, increased turnover, and biochemical adaptation to training and/or acute physical exercise. Of course, a marginal vitamin status can simply be the consequence of a long-term inadequate vitamin intake. However, apart from extremes in energy intake there are, considering the recommended dietary allowances (RDAs), insufficient indications that the vitamin intake among athletes is inadequate (van der Beek, 1988; Saris *et al.*, 1989a; van Erp-Baart *et al.*, 1989). By definition RDAs are put forward by a country's nutrition experts to designate the level of intake of a micronutrient to meet the known nutritional needs of practically all healthy persons. They are derived from a statistical treatment of the minimum daily requirement of micronutrients, derived experimentally from depletion studies and epidemiological surveys. This minimum daily requirement (MDR) is the level of an essential nutrient from an exogenous source needed to prevent the occurrence of a deficiency state or biochemical hypofunction. Assuming a normal distribution, the RDA is set to cover 97.5% of the population, by covering the mean MDR plus two standard deviations (van der Beek, 1985). As such, the purpose of these recommendations is for assessment of the adequacy of dietary intake of groups or populations, and has limited use in the assessment of nutrient intake of individuals. The wide margin of safety does not mean that individuals who consume less than the RDA are necessarily deficient in this nutrient. However, the more the actual intake lies below the RDA, the greater the risk of developing a deficiency state.

Neither are there indications for a higher faecal and urinary vitamin excretion or vitamin turnover in athletes. Moreover, the vitamin loss via sweat during exercise is negligible (Consolazio, 1983; Sargent *et al.*, 1944; Tapar *et al.*, 1976). Nevertheless, it has been observed that physical training may increase riboflavin requirement (Belko *et al.*, 1983; Ohno *et al.*, 1988). The increase in erythrocyte glutathione reductase activity coefficients is not accompanied by a decrease in aerobic power (Belko *et al.*, 1984). Moreover, the increase in activation coefficients can be corrected by an increased riboflavin intake without a change in maximum aerobic power (Belko *et al.*, 1985). It is very likely that the putative increased riboflavin requirement is a consequence of biochemical adaptation due to long-term physical training. There are indications that physical training causes an increased retention of riboflavin in skeletal muscles (Hunter and Turkki, 1987). The same has been observed for vitamin B-6 (Dreon and Butterfield, 1986). Apparently the opposite holds for Vitamin E (Gohill *et al.*, 1987). It was observed that endurance training was associated with a substantial decrease in vitamin E concentration in muscle mitochondrial membranes in spite of a constant concentration of vitamin E in muscle tissue. However, endurance exercise is accompanied by an increased biogenesis of mitochondria in skeletal muscles as well as by a relatively smaller increase in skeletal muscle mass. Therefore, increased vitamin E retention during endurance training cannot be excluded. For vitamin B-6 the hypothesis of increased storage is that physically active individuals may have a labile pool of pyridoxine, possibly acquired under the stimulus of strenuous efforts, which is capable of redistribution under circumstances of increased need (Dreon and Butterfield, 1986). Indeed, an increase in plasma levels of pyridoxal 5'-phosphate was observed immediately after long-distance running (Leklem and Schultz, 1983). A comparable increase after acute exercise has been observed for vitamins C and E (Gleeson and Maughan, 1987; Pincemail *et al.*, 1988). Knowledge of these adaptive changes is essential for proper assessment of the vitamin status, that is, for selection and interpretation of indicators to be used in vitamin status assessment (Schrijver, 1991). In summary, the currently available information does not support the idea of an increased vitamin requirement of athletes. Nevertheless, there have been several reports on the potentially ergogenic role of vitamins, especially in connection with endurance exercise.

6.3   VITAMIN SUPPLEMENTATION STUDIES

In this review single-vitamin studies are discussed first. In subsequent sections multiple B-vitamin supplementation studies and other multivitamin studies are reviewed. Results of (older) studies, lacking a controlled design and/or proper statistical analysis are not included.

The studies reviewed were carried out mainly on men who were not well trained. Moreover, most studies have been performed in the laboratory. Therefore, there may be difficulties in extrapolating the results obtained to females, highly-trained individuals and to competitive (Olympic) events.

6.3.1   B-complex vitamins

Thiamin

Until now, no controlled research has been carried out on the role of thiamin alone in physical performance.

Riboflavin

Tremblay *et al.* (1984) studied the effect of riboflavin supplementation on performance in 14 top swimmers with a normal status for this vitamin and a consumption pattern in accordance with Canadian recommendations. The group of volunteers was divided into two subgroups which were matched for sex and for performance. One subgroup was supplemented with 60 mg/day of riboflavin for 16 to 20 days, whereas the other subgroup received a placebo. Performance was assessed by a swimming test consisting of six 50-m free-style bouts. In addition, a treadmill test was performed to determine maximum aerobic power and ventilatory 'anaerobic threshold'. Riboflavin supplementation did not affect the biochemical indices for this vitamin in blood nor the performance of the swimmers. It was concluded that swimmers subjected to a thorough training can maintain a normal riboflavin status without any supplementation.

Vitamin B-6

Marconi *et al.* (1982) observed in a double-blind, placebo-controlled experiment with 10 trained volunteers that daily administration of 30 mg/kg body weight of an alpha-ketoglutarate-pyridoxine complex over a period of 30 days increased maximum aerobic power by 6% and decreased lactate accumulation after a short supramaximal work load. No changes were observed in the control group of the same size. The increase in maximum aerobic power and the corresponding decrease in lactate accumulation were not found when the individual components of the complex were administered separately. That observation suggests a synergistic or additive effect of the metabolic intermediate alpha-ketoglutarate and vitamin B-6. The authors concluded that the alpha-ketoglutarate-pyridoxine complex stimulates aerobic metabolism, probably by enhancing the flow of reducing equivalents across the mitochondrial membrane. In addition, it has been observed recently that supplementation of the metabolic intermediates dihydroxyacetone and pyruvate may enhance endurance capacity (Stanko *et al.*, 1990a, 1990b).

Pantothenic acid

Nice *et al.* (1984) studied 18 highly trained runners who ran to exhaustion on a treadmill on two occasions 2 weeks apart. Diet and training were kept constant. Nine subjects consumed 1 g of pantothenic acid per day while the nine control runners took a placebo in a double-blind protocol. No significant differences were found between both groups in run time, pulse rate and blood biochemical parameters. It was concluded that pantothenic acid in pharmacological dosages has no significant influence on human exercise capacity.

Niacin

Hilsendrager and Karpovich (1964) studied in a double-blind experiment the acute ergogenic effect of niacin (75 mg), glycin (750 mg), a combination thereof and a placebo in 86 subjects. Performance assessment consisted of two all-out bouts of bicycle ergometer exercise with a 5-min rest between them. No significant effect of the treatments on performance could be observed.

In other studies on the acute effect of niacin supplementation (300 mg to 1 g), both at rest (Carlson and Orö, 1962; Carlson *et al.*, 1963) and during exercise (Carlson *et al.*, 1963; Jenkins, 1965; Bergstrøm *et al.*, 1969; Pernow and Saltin, 1971), a decrease of plasma free fatty acids (FFA) was observed owing to an inhibition of FFA mobilization from fatty tissue in the body. One can speculate that the depressed FFA levels will lead to the development of fatigue during endurance exercise, because muscle glycogen will be used at a faster rate (Costill, 1988).

Bergstrøm *et al.* (1969), studying the effect of nicotinic acid on endurance capacity, observed that the ability to perform either short-term near-maximal work or prolonged submaximal work remained unchanged after the administration of nicotinic acid. The subjects, however, experienced the work as heavier and more fatiguing after the administration of nicotinic acid. Thus, although glycogen was utilized to a greater degree during exercise and theoretically has a larger efficiency ratio than the oxidation of fats, the objective evidence was inconsistent with the subjective appraisal of the exercise intensity. In a subsequent study by Pernow (1971) it was shown that when the glycogen stores are reduced, prolonged work can still be performed at submaximal levels (less than 60% of maximum aerobic power) provided that the supply of FFA is adequate. However, a decrease of muscle glycogen by preceding exercise and a decrease of FFA availability induced by niacin seriously impairs subsequent endurance exercise performance.

Vitamin B-12

Montoye *et al.* (1955) conducted a 7-week study on the effect of vitamin B-12 supplementation upon performance in a half-mile run and the Harvard step test in 51 male adolescents, residents of a state correctional institute. Three groups were formed, the experimental group receiving one capsule containing 50 mg vitamin B-12 daily, a placebo group and a control group receiving no nutritional supplements. The capsules were distributed according to a double-blind procedure. The subjects in the B-12 and placebo groups were matched on the basis of preliminary tests of their ability to run the half mile.

During the study, the B-12 and placebo groups trained equally. In the 7 weeks of the study, there was no significant change in the step test score in either group, but there was a significant improvement in half-mile running time in both the B-12 and the placebo groups.

The effect of parenteral vitamin B-12 administration on aerobic power and physical fitness test scores in 36 male students was investigated by Tin-May Than *et al.* (1978). The subjects were matched for weight and age and randomly assigned to an experimental or placebo group. The experimental group received an injection containing 1 mg of cyanocobalamin three times a week over a 6-week period. The placebo group received a placebo injection in a similar schedule. There was no significant increase in any of the measurements in the subjects receiving cyanocobalamin injections compared with those receiving the placebo.

Folate

Until now, no controlled research has been carried out on the role of folate alone on physical performance.

Biotin

Until now, no controlled research has been carried out on the role of biotin alone on physical performance.

6.3.2 Vitamin C

In their excellent reviews Williams (1985), Consolazio (1983) and Gerster (1989) concluded that the results of studies on the relationship between the intakes of high doses of vitamin C and physical performance are very controversial.

During the past four decades numerous investigators have tried to detect a possible effect of vitamin C supplementation on physical performance. Aerobic power, blood lactate levels and heart rate after bicycle ergometer or treadmill exercise have frequently been used as criteria, or athletic performance has been assessed directly in competitive events. Analysis of the volunteer's initial vitamin C status or intake has not been consistent. Earlier trials, not based on a controlled design and/or proper statistical analysis, frequently indicated a positive effect of vitamin C. Most of the more recent studies were well controlled by a double-blind, placebo-controlled design and did not demonstrate vitamin C supplement-induced improvement of physical performance (Rasch, 1962; Margaria *et al.*, 1964; Kirchhoff *et al.*, 1969; Bailey *et al.*, 1970a; Gey *et al.*, 1970). Only two studies observed a small but significant positive effect (Hoogerwerf and Hoitink, 1963; Howald *et al.*, 1975). However, in the latter of these two studies placebo and vitamin C treatment were given in sequence. Therefore, effects of training cannot be excluded. There is some evidence that vitamin C supplementation may enhance heat acclimatization. This may have implications for athletes during training and competition in hot climates (Strydhom *et al.*, 1976).

6.3.3 Vitamin E

Although not all metabolic functions of vitamin E have been revealed, there are numerous investigations showing the influence of vitamin E on the electron flow within the mitochondrial respiratory chain and its radical-scavenging properties. Through these functions vitamin E may promote an economic energy metabolism and act as a stabilizer on membranous structures in the cell by preventing oxidation of polyunsaturated fatty acids in membranes. Both functions may be of importance for maintaining health and physical performance (Berg *et al.*, 1987). These suggested functions of vitamin E in muscle cells have led to a widespread use of the vitamin by athletes. Several reports are devoted to the use of the vitamin as an ergogenic aid, especially in connection with exercise of long duration. However, experimental results are conflicting.

Regarding the possible effect on energy metabolism, Williams (1985) and Consolazio (1983) mention that some studies reported significant effects of vitamin E, in wheat germ oil, on athletic performance. However, the actual benefits are doubtful since many of the experiments were not properly controlled.

In recent years there have been several well-controlled studies that show that supplemental vitamin E has no effect on physical performance. Interestingly, most of these studies have been done with swimmers.

For example, in a double-blind experiment, Sharman *et al.* (1971) studied two experimental groups, each of 15 boys: one group took 400 mg of alpha-tocopherol acetate a day and the other a placebo. Swimming and a series of physical performance tests were carried out by subjects during the 6-week study. The subjects were paired individually on the basis of age, ponderal index and the time needed for swimming 400 m. Significant differences were observed in both groups as a result of training, but no significant differences were found between the vitamin E and the placebo groups. In a subsequent study with 15 swimmers, Sharman *et al.* (1976) obtained results that were similar to his earlier study (Sharman *et al.*, 1971).

Shephard *et al.* (1974) subjected 20 male swimmers to an 85-day double-blind experiment on the effect of daily supplementation of 1200 IU of alpha-tocopherol acid succinate on physical performance. On the basis of results of preceding tests, subjects were paired for aerobic power, body weight and swimming event. The matched pairs were randomly assigned to an experimental or a placebo group. Of the original 20 athletes, only 14 completed the experiment, leaving 7 matched pairs. Despite substantial swimming training, neither the test nor the control group improved their aerobic power or muscle strength. It was concluded that the results provided little support for the view that vitamin E improves the performance of a well-trained athlete or his tolerance to a demanding training schedule.

In a double-blind study 20 physically active inter-collegiate ice-hockey players were matched in pairs, according to their maximum oxygen uptake, with one member of each pair randomly selected to receive 1200 IU of vitamin E daily for 50 days (Watt *et al.*, 1974). The other member of each pair was given a placebo. Their training regimen was controlled as well as one meal a day. At the end of the experimental period there was no significant difference in aerobic power between the groups.

Lawrence *et al.* (1975a) assigned 48 well-trained competitive swimmers into an experimental and a placebo group. The experimental group received 900 IU alpha-tocopherol acetate daily for 6 months, while the other group was given a placebo. A swimming endurance test was performed before the start of supplementation and after 1, 2, 5 and 6 months. No difference in swimmers' endurance was observed between the two groups during the 6-month period. In a comparable experiment, Lawrence *et al.* (1975b) assigned 72 swimmers to three groups matched for age, sex and swimming ability as judged by their coach. Daily supplementation with either vitamin E (900 IU alpha-tocopherol acetate), vitamin B-6 (51 mg pyridoxine-HCl) or a placebo, was assigned randomly to the groups in a double-blind design. Under the conditions used in this study, neither vitamin E nor B-6 appears to have had any effect on swimming endurance.

Regarding the antioxidant properties of vitamin E, it is well known that heavy exercise is followed by an increase in serum muscle enzyme concentrations, indicating that muscle damage has occurred. In two studies, using a double-blind design, it was concluded that supplementation of trained individuals with 300 or 800 mg of vitamin E, respectively did not limit the extent of muscle damage after endurance exercise (Helgheim *et al.*, 1979; Robertson *et al.*, 1990), but that it did cause a reduction in endogenous lipid peroxidation (Robertson *et al.*, 1990; Sumida *et al.*, 1989).

Contrary to the studies mentioned above, all of which were carried out at sea level, a few studies (Nagawa *et al.*, 1968; Simon-Schnass *et al.*, 1987, Simon-Schnass and Pabst, 1988) have shown that vitamin E has a beneficial effect on physical performance (i.e. maximum aerobic power) and a partially protective effect on cell membranes at high altitudes.

6.3.4 Vitamins A, D and K

Like vitamins E and C, vitamin A and β-carotene have antioxidant properties. As yet, however, no controlled research has been conducted on the role of the other fat-soluble vitamins A, D and K alone in physical performance.

6.3.5 Multiple B-vitamin supplementation studies

Early and Carlson (1969) attempted to examine the acute effects of B-vitamin supplementation on fatigue occurring in natural work in hot environmental conditions, on the assumption that there are significant vitamin losses in sweat. Eighteen high school boys were matched to form experimental and control groups. To ensure consistent heavy sweating, all subjects in both the experimental and the control group took part in a 40-min general outdoor running programme every day of the experiment. On days 9 and 15 and on another day halfway between these two days, the experimental group received a liquid supplement including 100 mg of thiamin, 8 mg of riboflavin, 5 mg of pyridoxine, 25 mg of cyanocobalamin, 100 mg of nicotinic acid and 30 mg of pantothenic acid, and performed test sessions. Each of the test sessions consisted of ten 50-yard runs with 30 s rest after each sprint. Using analysis of variance, they concluded that the degree of fatigue of the experimental groups was less than that of the placebo group on the days of vitamin supplementation. They hypothesized that thiamin and pantothenic acid could be the active substances in delaying fatigue, due primarily to their roles in oxidative metabolism. This result may have implications for athletes during training and competing in hot climates.

Read and McGuffin (1983) performed a double-blind experiment to investigate the relationship between B-complex vitamin supplementation and endurance capacity. The experimental group received daily a supplement containing 5 mg of thiamin, 5 mg of riboflavin, 25 mg of nicotinic acid, 2 mg of pyridoxine, 0.5 mg of vitamin B-12 and 12.5 mg of pantothenic acid; the control group received a placebo. Both groups were tested for endurance three times during the 6-week period of supplementation. No beneficial effect of vitamin supplementation on endurance was observed.

In two experiments Bonke and Nickel (1986) studied the effect of large daily intakes of a combination of thiamin (90 mg and 600 mg), vitamin B-6 (90 mg and 600 mg) and vitamin B-12 (120 mg and 600 mg) on shooting performance. Both experiments lasted 8 weeks. The first study was performed in an open-controlled design, whereas in the second study the group treated with the B-vitamins was compared in a double-blind fashion with a placebo and a control group including 8 by 8 and 10 by 9 volunteers, respectively. The volunteers were randomly assigned to each of the groups. In both studies, firing accuracy improved considerably in the vitamin-treated groups, whereas the placebo group did not show any prominent change. They concluded that elevated dosages of the B-vitamins tested do improve sensory motor control.

6.3.6 Other multiple vitamin supplementation studies

Keul *et al.* (1974) and Haralambie *et al.* (1975) subjected 14 male subjects to a 2-h bicycle ergometer test at an intensity of 60% of maximum working capacity to measure the influence of a multivitamin-electrolyte granulate product ('Beneroc') on physical performance. The ratio of work load to heart rate reached an average increase of 3.3%; the difference became significant in the last 50 min of the exercise. Because there was a fixed sequence of trials, namely placebo and then supplementation, the effects of training cannot be excluded. In a comparable double-blind study with 'Beneroc' in 14 adolescents, Keul *et al.* (1979) observed a 4.3% increase in speed during a cross-country ski run lasting 1 h. As the supplements contained minerals too, the small effects cannot be attributed exclusively to one or more vitamins.

A study of 4 months' duration was performed to evaluate the effect of daily multivitamin and iron supplementation on aerobic power (van der Beek, *et al.*, 1981, unpublished observations). In this double-blind, placebo-controlled experiment, 77 healthy male and female sports students participated. The supplement, which contained almost all vitamins as well as iron, contained twice the Dutch RDA for vitamins A and D and 10 times the RDA for the B vitamins, vitamin C, vitamin E and iron. An effect of training on aerobic power in both the supplement and the placebo group was demonstrated at the end of the experimental period. This result is in agreement with all other controlled studies of this kind.

Barnett and Conlee (1984) investigated whether a commercially available supplement, comprising vitamins, minerals, trace elements, amino acids and fatty acids, improved endurance. The daily supplement provided all vitamins except vitamin K in amounts equivalent to 100 to 1000% of the American RDA. Twenty male runners received either a placebo or the supplement over a 4-week period in a double-blind design. The supplement had no beneficial effect on aerobic power nor on performance in a 60-min treadmill run (65 to 75% of maximum aerobic power).

Weight *et al.* (1988a) studied the effect of vitamin, mineral and trace element supplementation on running performance of trained athletes. The daily supplement provided up to 43 times the RDA for all vitamins except folate and vitamin K. In this 9-month double-blind cross-over, placebo-controlled study design, 30 well-trained male runners randomly received the supplement or a placebo for 3 months. After a 3-month washout period the two treatments were crossed over and used for another 3-month period. At 0, 3, 6 and 9 months the runners performed a progressive treadmill test to volitional exhaustion for measurement of aerobic power, peak running speed, blood lactate turning point and peak post-exercise blood lactate concentration. Running time in a 15-km trial was also measured. None of the variables examined was influenced by 3 months of vitamin supplementation. On the four occasions mentioned all blood variables were normal. Except for riboflavin and vitamin B-6, there were no significant changes in the blood concentrations of any micronutrient. As regards the daily intake of the micronutrients studied, the diet of all volunteers was adequate during the 9-month period. It was concluded that vitamin, mineral and trace element supplementation is not needed for athletes who eat a normal diet.

6.4 EPILOGUE

It can be concluded that most of the more recent well-controlled experiments have demonstrated that for individuals eating a well-balanced diet supplementation with one or more vitamins does not result in increased physical performance. Possibly, exceptions have to be made for the use of vitamin E at high altitude, and for the use of vitamin C and multiple B-vitamin supplements in hot climates. Nevertheless, there continue to be claims that vitamin supplements, especially B-complex vitamins, vitamin C and vitamin E, may improve physical working capacity. Older studies, lacking a double-blind experimental design and/or proper statistical analysis, frequently indicated a positive effect of vitamin supplementation.

However, in the absence of adequate controls, it is impossible to discriminate the effects of time, training and of a placebo effect from an effect of the (multi)vitamin supplement. Although vitamin supplementation has no effect when the diet is adequate, it remains possible that vitamin supplementation might be appropriate in sports associated with either extremely high or extremely low energy intakes. There is a linear relationship between energy intake and vitamin intake (see Fig. 6.1). Therefore, taking the high energy intakes expected of the majority of athletes, vitamin intakes should be well in excess of the RDAs provided that an adequately varied diet is chosen. However, if energy intake surpasses 21 MJ/day (or 5000 kcal/day) consumption of additional food products with a low nutrient density may be inevitable. It is unlikely, however, that this has an impact on vitamin status. However, no controlled research has been carried out on the consequences of such diets (Saris *et al.*, 1989). As vitamin intake is the result of both food quality and food quantity, an extremely low energy intake (<4.2 MJ/day or <1000 kcal/day) may also result in a vitamin intake below the RDAs. It is also important to bear in mind those clinical situations in which vitamin intake and/or absorption might be impaired – e.g. gastrointestinal problems, malabsorption, eating disorders, infectious diseases, etc. – and so vitamin intake or availability might be reduced below the RDAs. Again, no controlled research has been carried out on the consequences of such diets. In both extremes of energy intake

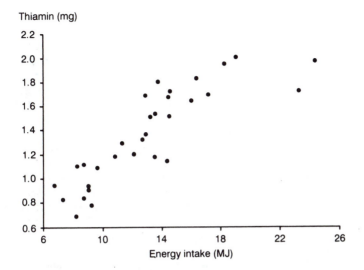

Fig. 6.1 Relationship between daily mean energy intake and mean thiamin intake in various groups of elite athletes (endurance, strength and team sport groups). (Van Erp-Baart *et al.*, 1989).

it might be advisable to consider the use of vitamin supplements providing the RDA (but no 'megadosing'). In conclusion, there is no justification for 'food fads' and advertising claims, especially when sportsmen stick to an adequate diet.

Besides the fact that vitamin supplementation has no effect on physical working capacity, there have been suggestions in recent years that large doses of water-soluble vitamins are not fully innocuous (Aldaheff *et al.*, 1984). It has long been known that excessive consumption of fat-soluble vitamins can have toxic effects. In addition, it is now known that high doses of niacin, vitamin C, thiamin, vitamin B-6, folate and pantothenic acid, may also be toxic. For instance, large doses of vitamin C have been associated with urinary stone formation and impaired copper absorption while large doses of vitamin B-6 can cause sensory neuropathy (Finley and Cerklewski, 1983).

REFERENCES

Alhadeff, L., Gualtiery, C.T. and Lipton, M. (1984). Toxic effects of water-soluble vitamins. *Nutrition Reviews*, **42**, 33–40.
Bailey, D.A., Carron, A.V., Teece, R.G. and Wehner, H.J. (1970a). Effect of vitamin C supplementation upon the physiological response to exercise in

trained and untrained subjects. *International Journal for Vitamin and Nutrition Research*, **40**, 435–41.

Bailey, D.A., Carron, A.V., Teece, R.G. and Wehner, H.J. (1970b). Vitamin C supplementation related to physiological response to exercise in smoking and non-smoking subjects. *American Journal of Clinical Nutrition*, **23**, 905–12.

Barnett, D.W. and Conlee, R.K. (1984). The effect of a commercial dietary supplement on human performance. *American Journal of Clinical Nutrition*, **40**, 586–90.

Beek, E.J. van der (1981) unpublished observations.

Beek, E.J. van der (1985). Vitamins and endurance training – food for running or faddish claims? *Sports Medicine*, **2**, 175–97.

Beek, E.J. van der (1986). Restricted vitamin intake and physical performance of military personnel. In *Predicting decrements in military performance due to inadequate nutrition*, Proceedings of a workshop (presented by the Committee on Military Nutrition Research, Food and Nutrition Board, Commission on Life Sciences, National Research Council), pp. 139–69. National Academy Press, Washington DC.

Beek, E.J. van der, Bovens, M.F., Kistemaker, C., van Eck, I. and Weimar, M. (1988). De voeding van triatleten. *Geneeskunde en Sport*, **21**, 40–7.

Belko, A.Z., Miller, D., Haas, J.D. and Roe, D.A. (1983). Effects of exercise on riboflavin requirements of young women. *American Journal of Clinical Nutrition*, **37**, 509–17.

Belko, A.Z., Obarzanek, E., Roach, R., Rotter, M.A., Urban, G., Weinberg, S. and Roe, D.A. (1984). Effects of aerobic exercise and weight loss on riboflavin requirements of moderately obese, marginally deficient women. *American Journal of Clinical Nutrition*, **40**, 553–61.

Belko, A.Z., Meredith, M.P., Kalkwarf, H.J., Obarzanek, E., Weinberg, S., Roach, R., McKeon, G. and Roe, D.A. (1985). Effects of exercise on riboflavin requirements: biological validation in weight reducing women. *American Journal of Clinical Nutrition*, **41**, 270–7.

Berg, A., Simon-Schnass, I., Rokitzki, L. and Keul, J. (1987). Die Bedeutung des Vitamin E für den Sportler. *Deutsche Zeitschrift für Sportmedzin*, **38**, 416–24.

Bergström, J., Hultman, E., Jorfeldt, L., Pernow, B. and Wahren, J. (1969). Effect of nicotinic acid on physical working capacity and on metabolism of muscle glycogen in man. *Journal of Applied Physiology*, **26**, 170–6.

Bonke, D. and Nickel, B. (1986). Improvement of fine motoric movement control by elevated dosages of vitamin B1, B6 and B12 in target shooting. In J.J. Himberg, W. Tackmann, D. Bonke and H.O. Karppanen, *B vitamins in medicine*, pp. 198–204. F. Vieweg u. Sohn, F. Braunschweig.

Carlson, L.A. and Orö, L. (1962). The effect of nicotinic acid on plasma free fatty acids – demonstration of a metabolic type of sympathicolysis. *Acta Medica Scandinavica*, **172** (suppl), 641–5.

Carlson, L.A., Havel, R.J., Ekelund, L.G. and Holmgren, A. (1963). Effect of nicotinic acid on the turnover rate and oxidation of the free fatty acids of plasma in man during exercise. *Metabolism*, **12**, 837–45.

Consolazio, C.F. (1983). Nutrition and performance. *Progress in Food and Nutrition Science*, **7**, 1–187.

Costill, D.L. (1988). Carbohydrates for exercise: dietary demands for optimal performance. *International Journal of Sports Medicine*, **9**, 1–18.

Dam, B. van (1978). Vitamins and sport. *British Journal of Sports Medicine*, **12**, 74–9.

Dreon, D.M. and Butterfield, G.E. (1986). Vitamin B6 utilization in active and inactive young men. *American Journal of Clinical Nutrition*, **43**, 816–24.

Early, R.G. and Carlson, B.R. (1969). Water-soluble vitamin therapy in the delay of fatigue from physical activity in hot climatic conditions. *Internationale Zeitschrift für Angewandte Physiologie*, **27**, 43–50.

Erp-Baart, A.M.J. van, Saris, W.H.M., Binkhorst, R.A., Vos, J.A. and Elvers, J.W.H. (1989). Nationwide survey on nutritional habits in elite athletes, part II. Mineral and vitamin intake. *International Journal of Sports Medicine*, **10**, S11–S16.

Finley, E.B. and Cerklewski, F.L. (1983). Influence of ascorbic acid supplementation on copper status in young adult men. *American Journal of Clinical Nutrition*, **37**, 533–6.

Gerster, H. (1989). The role of vitamin C in athletic performance. *Journal of the American College of Nutrition*, **8**, 636–43.

Gey, G.O., Cooper, K.H. and Bottenberg, R.A. (1970). Effect of ascorbic acid on endurance performance and athletic injury. *Journal of the American Medical Association*, **211**, 105.

Gleeson, M. and Maughan, R.J. (1987). Changes in ascorbic acid content of plasma and lymphocytes following exercise in man. *Journal of Physiology*, **386**, 98 p.

Gohill, K., Rothfuss, L., Lang, J. and Packer, L. (1987). Effect of exercise training on tissue vitamin E and ubiquinone content. *Journal of Applied Physiology*, **63**, 1638–41.

Haralambie, G. and van Dam, B. (1977). Untersuchungen über den Vitamin-Elektrolyt-Status bei Spitzenfechterinnen. *Leistungssport*, **7**, 214–19.

Haralambie, G., Keul, J., Baumgartner, A., Winkler, K.H. and Bauer, G. (1975). Die Wirkung eines Multivitamin-Elektrolytgranulats auf Elektrodermal reflex und neuromuskuläre Erregbarkeit bei langwährender Körperarbeit. *Schweizerische Zeitschrift für Sportmedizin*, **23**, 113–28.

Helgheim, I., Hetland, Ø., Nilsson, S., Ingjer, F. and Strømme, S.B. (1979). The effects of vitamin E on serum enzyme levels following heavy exercise. *European Journal of Applied Physiology*, **40**, 283–9.

Hilsendrager, D. and Karpovich, P.V. (1964). Ergogenic effect of glycine and niacin separately and in combination. *Research Quarterly*, **35** (suppl), 389–92.

Hoogerwerf, A. and Hoitink, A.W.J.H. (1963). The influence of vitamin C administration on the mechanical efficiency of the human organism. *Internationale Zeitschrift für Angewandte Physiologie*, **20**, 164–72.

Howald, H., Segesser, B. and Körner, W.F. (1975). Ascorbic acid and athletic performance. *Annals of the New York Academy Science*, **258**, 458–64.

Hunter, K.L. and Turkki, P.R. (1987). Effect of exercise on riboflavin status of rats. *Journal of Nutrition*, **117**, 298–304.

Jenkins, D.J.A. (1965). Effects of nicotinic acid on carbohydrate and fat metabolism during exercise. *Lancet*, **i**, 1307–8.

Keul, J., Haralambie, G., Winkler, K.H., Baumgartner, A. and Bauer, G. (1974). Die Wirkung eines Multivitamin-Elektrolyt-Granulats auf Kreislauf und Stoffwechsel bei langwährender Körperarbeit. *Schweizerische Zeitschrift für Sportmedizin*, **22**, 169–84.

Keul, J., Huber, G., Schmitt, M., Spielberger, B. and Zöllner, G. (1979). Die Veränderungen von Kreislauf- und Stoffwechselgrössen während eines Skilanglaufes unter einem Multivitamin-Elektrolyt-Granulat. *Deutscher Zeitschrift für Sportsmedicine*, **30**, 65–72.

Kirchhoff, H.W. (1969). Uber den Einfluss von Vitamin C auf Energieverbrauch, Kreislauf- und Ventilationsgrüssen im Belastungsversuch. *Nutritio de Dieta*, **11**, 184–92.

Lawrence, J.D., Bower, R.C., Riehl, W.P. and Smith, J.L. (1975a). Effect of alpha-tocopherol acetate on the swimming endurance of trained swimmers. *American Journal of Clinical Nutrition*, **28**, 205–8.

Lawrence, J.D., Smith, J.L., Bower, R.C. and Riehl, W.P. (1975b). The effect of alpha-tocopherol (vitamin E) and pyridoxine-HCl (vitamin B6) on the swimming endurance of trained swimmers. *Journal of the American College of Health Associations*, **23**, 219–22.

Leklem, J. and Schultz, T.D. (1983). Increased plasma pyridoxal 5′-phosphate and vitamin B6 in male adolescents after a 4500-meter run. *American Journal of Clinical Nutrition*, **38**, 541–8.

Marconi, C., Sassi, G. and Ceretelli, P. (1982). The effect of an alpha-ketoglutarate-pyridoxine complex on human maximal aerobic performance. *European Journal of Applied Physiology*, **49**, 307–17.

Margaria, R., Aghemo, P. and Rovelli, E. (1964). The effect of some drugs on the maximal capacity of athletic performance in man. *International Zeitschrifte für Angewandte Physiologie*, **20**, 281–7.

Montoye, H.J., Spata, P.J., Pinckney, V. and Barron, L. (1955). Effect of vitamin B12 supplementation of physical fitness and growth of young boys. *Journal of Applied Physiology*, **7**, 589–92.

Nagawa, T., Kita, H., Aoki, J., Maeshima, T. and Shiozawa, K. (1968). The effect of vitamin E on endurance. *Asian Medical Journal*, **11**, 619–23.

Nice, C., Reeves, A.G., Brinck-Johnson, T. and Noll, W. (1984). The effect of pantothenic acid on human exercise capacity. *Journal of Sports Medicine and Physical Fitness*, **24**, 26–9.

Ohno, H., Yahata, T., Sato, Y., Yamamura, K. and Taniguchi, N. (1988). Physical training and fasting erythrocyte activities of free radical scavenging systems in sedentary men. *European Journal of Applied Physiology*, **57**, 173–6.

Pernow, B. and Saltin, B. (1971). Availability of substrates and capacity for prolonged heavy exercise in man. *Journal of Applied Physiology*, **31**, 416–22.

Pincemail, J., Deby, C., Camus, G., Pirnay, F., Bouchez, R., Massaux, L. and Goutier, R. (1988). Tocopherol mobilization during intensive exercise. *European Journal of Applied Physiology*, **57**, 189–91.

Rasch, P.J. (1962). Effect of vitamin C supplementation on cross country runners. *Sportärzliche Praxis*, **5**, 1013.

Read, M.H. and McGuffin, S.L. (1983). The effect of B-complex supplementation on endurance performance. *Journal of Sports Medicine and Physical Fitness*, **23**, 178–84.

Robertson, J.D., Crosbie, L., Maughan, R.J., Leiper, J.B. and Duthie, G.G. (1990). Influence of vitamin E supplementation on muscle damage following endurance exercise. *International Journal for Vitamin and Nutrition Research*, **60**, 171–2.

Sargent, F., Robinson, P. and Johnson, R.E. (1944). Water-soluble vitamins in sweat. *Journal of Biological Chemistry*, **153**, 285–94.

Saris, W.H.M., Schrijver, J., van Erp-Baart, A.M.J. and Brouns, F. (1989a). Adequacy of vitamin supply under maximal sustained workloads: the Tour de France. In: P. Walter, G. Brubacher and H. Stöhelin, *Elevated dosages of vitamins, benefits and hazards*. (*International Journal for Vitamin and Nutrition Research*, suppl. 30), pp. 205–12. Hans Huber, Toronto.

Saris, W.H.M., van Erp-Baart, A.M.J., Brouns, F., Westerterp, K.R. and ten Hoor, F. (1989b). Study on food intake and energy expenditure during extreme sustained exercise: the Tour de France. *International Journal of Sports Medicine*, **10**, S26–S31.

Schaumburg, H., Kaplan, J., Windebank, A., Vick, N., Rasmus, S., Pleasure, D. and Brown, M.J. (1983). Sensory neuropathy from pyridoxine abuse. *New England Journal of Medicine*, **309**, 445–8.

Schrijver, J. (1991). Indices of vitamin status in man: an urgent need of functional markers. *Food Review International*, **7**, 1–31.

Sharman, I.M., Down, M.G. and Sen, R.N. (1971). The effect of vitamin E and training on physiological function and athletic performance in adolescent swimmers. *British Journal of Nutrition*, **26**, 265–76.

Sharman, I.M., Down, M.G. and Norgan, N.G. (1976). The effect of vitamin E on physiological function and athletic performance of trained swimmers. *Journal of Sports Medicine and Physical Fitness*, **16**, 215–25.

Shephard, R.J., Campbell, R., Pimm, P., Stuart, D. and Wright, G.R. (1974). Vitamin E, exercise, and the recovery from physical activity. *European Journal of Applied Physiology*, **33**, 119–26.

Simon-Schnass, I. and Pabst, H. (1988). Influence of vitamin E on physical performance. *International Journal of Vitamin Nutrition Research*, **58**, 49–54.

Simon-Schnass, I., Pabst, H. and Herrlighoffer, K.M. (1987). Der Einfluss von vitamin E auf der leistungsabhängige Parameter beim Höhenbergsteigen. *Deutscher Zeitschrift für Sportsmedicine*, **38**, 199–206.

Stanko, R.T., Robertson, R.J., Spina, R.J., Reilly, J.J., Greenawalt, K.D. and Goss, F.L. (1990a). Enhancement of arm exercise endurance capacity with dihydroxyacetone and pyruvate. *Journal of Applied Physiology*, **68**, 119–24.

Stanko, R.T., Robertson, R.J., Galbreath, R.W., Reilly, J.J., Greenawalt, K.D. and Goss, F.L. (1990b). Enhanced leg exercise endurance with a high-carbohydrate diet and dihydroxyacetone and pyruvate. *Journal of Applied Physiology*, **69**, 1651–6.

Strydhom, N.B., Kotze, M.E., van der Walt, W.H. and Rogers, G.G. (1976). Effect of ascorbic acid on rate of heat acclimation. *Journal of Applied Physiology*, **41**, 202–5.

Sumida, S., Tanaka, K., Kitao, H. and Nakadomo, F. (1989). Exercise-induced lipid peroxidation and leakage of enzymes before and after vitamin E supplementation. *International Journal of Biochemistry*, **21**, 835–8.

Tapar, G.S., Shenolikar, I.S. and Tulpe, P.G. (1976). Sweat loss of nitrogen and other nutrients during heavy physical activity. *Indian Journal of Medical Research*, **64**, 590–6.

Tin-May-Than, Ma-Win-May, Khin-Sann-Aung and Mya-Tu, M. (1978). The effect of vitamin B12 on physical performance capacity. *British Journal of Nutrition*, **40**, 269–73.

Tremblay, A., Boilard, F., Breton, M.F., Bessette, H. and Roberge, A.F. (1984). The effect of a riboflavin supplementation on the nutritional status and performance of elite swimmers. *Nutrition Research*, **4**, 201–8.

Watt, T., Romet, T.T., McFarlane, I., McGuey, D., Allen, C. and Goode, R.C. (1974). Vitamin E and oxygen consumption. *Lancet*, **i**, 354–5.

Weight, L.M., Myburgh, K.H. and Noakes, T.D. (1988a). Vitamin and mineral supplementation: effect on the running performance of trained athletes. *American Journal of Clinical Nutrition*, **47**, 192–5.

Weight, L.M., Noakes, T.D., Labdarios, D., Graves, J., Jacobs, P. and Berman, P.A. (1988b). Vitamin and mineral status of trained athletes including the effects of supplementation. *American Journal of Clinical Nutrition*, **47**, 186–91.

Williams, M.H. (1985). *Nutritional aspects of human physical and athletic performance*. 2nd edition, pp. 147–85. Charles C. Thomas, Springfield, Illinois.

7

Minerals: exercise performance and supplementation in athletes

Priscilla M. Clarkson

7.1 INTRODUCTION

Each year many new products catering to athletes appear in the health food section of grocery stores and nutrition centres. While most of the shelf space is allotted to amino acid, protein and vitamin supplements, minerals are gaining prominence. Mineral supplements purporting to increase energy production, decrease fatigue, and enhance muscle mass are widely advertised in popular sports magazines. These claims stem from the importance of minerals to a wide variety of body functions, such as imparting hardness to bones, serving as co-factors to many enzyme systems, and, in the case of iron, maintaining the oxygen-carrying capacity of the blood. Whether mineral supplements will also enhance exercise performance is the focus of this chapter.

Minerals could be effective as performance enhancers under two conditions. First, if an athlete is deficient in a certain mineral, the deficiency could detrimentally affect performance. Supplementation in this case would restore any performance decrements incurred by the deficiency. Second, an increased level of a mineral could boost its natural effect in the body and thereby enhance performance. With these considerations in mind, the mineral status of athletes will be discussed before examining the effects of supplementation.

Food, Nutrition and Sports Performance
Edited by Clyde Williams and John T. Devlin
Published in 1992 by E & F N Spon, London. ISBN 0 419 17890 2

7.2   GENERAL DESCRIPTION OF MINERALS

Minerals are categorized as macrominerals or microminerals (trace minerals) based upon the extent of their occurrence in the body (Hunt and Groff, 1990). The macrominerals, calcium, magnesium and phosphorus, each constitute at least 0.01% of total body weight. (Other macrominerals, potassium, sulphur, sodium and chloride will not be discussed in this chapter as they are either not thought to enhance performance or they function as electrolytes and are described elsewhere.) Trace minerals each comprise less than 0.001% of total body weight. Fourteen trace minerals have been identified as essential for body function, and these are iron, zinc, copper, selenium, chromium, iodine, fluorine, manganese, molybdenum, nickel, silicon, vanadium, arsenic and cobalt (Hunt and Groff, 1990). This review will focus on the five minerals that have been suggested to act as performance enhancers – iron, zinc, copper, selenium and chromium. Another review of trace minerals as ergogenic aids has appeared elsewhere (Clarkson, 1991). A summary of information on minerals and trace minerals is presented in Tables 7.1 and 7.2. Because many of the minerals are only needed in small amounts, a small change in intake can make a critical difference to health. Likewise, it is possible that a small change in status can alter performance capabilities.

7.3   DETERMINATION OF MINERAL STATUS

Mineral status can be assessed directly from samples of body tissues or body fluids, or indirectly from analysis of the diet. In the latter method, dietary intake of a given mineral is compared with the RDA (recommended dietary allowance). The RDAs are defined as 'the levels of intake of essential nutrients that, on the basis of scientific knowledge, are judged by the Food and Nutrition Board to be adequate to meet the known nutrient needs of practically all healthy persons' (National Research Council, 1989). The RDAs (presented in Table 7.3) are meant to provide general guidelines. It should be noted that the data used to determine the RDAs often did not include athletes or regularly exercising individuals in the studies or the exercise status of the subjects was not reported. Therefore, the RDAs may not be an accurate means of evaluating nutritional needs of athletes. However, if anything, athletes could require a greater amount of a given mineral than non-athletes, and therefore a problem could arise if athletes are not meeting the RDA.

Because the RDAs provide only a general guideline for an individual, deficiencies or excesses are commonly expressed as a percentage of the

Table 7.1 Minerals: function and location (Hunt and Groff, 1990; Marieb, 1989; National Research Council, 1989)

Minerals	Function	Location
Macrominerals		
Calcium	Required for hard bones; transmission of nerve impulses; activates certain enzymes; necessary for maintenance of membrane potential, muscle contraction	99% in skeleton, remainder in extracellular fluids, intracellular structures, cell membranes
Magnesium	Co-factor of enzymes in energy metabolism; maintenance of electrical potentials in muscles and nerves; component of bone	40% in muscles and soft tissue, 1% in extracellular fluid, remainder in skeleton
Phosphorus	Component of bone; buffer in body fluids, component of ATP, nucleotides and co-enzymes	85% in skeleton, remainder in soft tissue and blood
Trace minerals		
Zinc	Co-factor of several enzymes in energy metabolism, immune function, possible anti-oxidant, wound healing, taste and smell	Bones and muscle, liver, kidney, brain
Copper	Required for proper use of iron; role in development of connective tissue; co-factor to oxidases	Liver, heart, kidney, spleen, brain
Selenium	Anti-oxidant; co-factor of glutathione peroxidase	Stored in liver and kidneys; widely distributed
Chromium	Enhances effectiveness of insulin (no function as co-factor to enzymes)	Widely distributed
Iron	Necessary component of haemoglobin, myoglobin – transport of oxygen, facilitates transfer of electrons in electron transport system	60–70% in haemoglobin, remainder in bone marrow, muscle, liver, spleen

RDA. Two-thirds (66%) or three-quarters (75%) of the RDA is considered a poor mineral intake. For copper, chromium and selenium, inadequate data exist to establish a specific RDA. However, provisional recommendations entitled 'Estimated Safe and Adequate Daily Dietary Intakes' (ESADDI) have been developed as guidelines.

There are other problems with dietary information as an estimation of mineral status. In the case of calcium, it is uncertain if there are important differences in the absorption of calcium from different foods (National Research Council, 1989). Moreover, the levels of dietary protein and phosphorus can affect the requirement for calcium. Increased protein intakes can increase excretion, or loss of calcium, while increased phosphorus intake will increase the reabsorption of calcium and thereby retain it (National Research Council, 1989).

Table 7.2 Minerals: dietary source, excesses and deficiencies (Hunt and Groff, 1990; Marieb, 1989; National Research Council, 1989)

Minerals	Dietary source	Excesses	Deficiencies
Macrominerals			
Calcium	Dairy products, sardines, clams, oysters, turnip/ mustard greens, broccoli, legumes	Constipation, hypercalcaemia, kidney stones, high levels may inhibit intestinal absorption of iron, zinc, other nutrients	Risk of bone injury and osteoporosis especially in females
Magnesium	Nuts, legumes, unmilled grains, soybeans, chocolate, corn, peas, carrots, seafood, brown rice, lima beans	Nausea, vomiting	Rare: muscle weakness
Phosphorus	Protein-rich food, milk, meat, poultry, fish, eggs, nuts, legumes, cereals	Lowers blood calcium	Rare

Table 7.2 *continued*

Trace minerals

Zinc	Oysters, wheat germ, beef, calf liver, dark meat in poultry, whole grains	Gastro-intestinal irritation, impair copper absorption, decline in HDLs	Appetite loss, poor wound healing, abnormal taste, smell, changes in hair, skin
Copper	Organ meats, shellfish, whole grains, legumes, chocolate, nuts	Rare: potentially toxic	Rare: anaemia
Selenium	Grains, meat, poultry, fish, dairy products	Not known: hair loss, nausea, diarrhoea (possible)	Not known: myalgia, cardiac myopathy (possible)
Chromium	Mushrooms, prunes, nuts, asparagus, organ meats, whole grain bread and cereals	Not known	Not known: impaired glucose tolerance anaemia (possible)
Iron	Organ meats, black strap molasses, clams, oysters, dried legumes, nuts and seeds, red meats, dark green leafy vegetables	Rare: liver damage	Anaemia, fatigue

For the trace minerals, the National Research Council (1989) explain that not all foods have been analysed for their nutrient composition so that the databases used to assess diets are incomplete. Also processing of foods can alter the mineral composition, and the composition of the diet can affect the bioavailability, although the data have been equivocal. In the case of zinc, interactions with protein, fibre and other minerals can occur. In fact studies have shown that the percentage absorption of zinc supplements ranged from 2.4 to 38.2% of the supplements when added to meals of different composition. The bioavailability of copper can also be altered by the intake of vitamin C, zinc and the type of carbohydrate consumed.

Table 7.3 Recommended dietary allowances (RDA) and estimated safe and adequate daily dietary intakes (ESADDI) (National Research Council, 1989)

	Males (age in years)			Females (age in years)		
	15–18	19–24	25–50	15–18	19–24	25–50
Minerals						
Calcium (mg)	1200	1200	800	1200	1200	800
Phosphorus (mg)	1200	1200	800	1200	1200	800
Magnesium (mg)	400	350	350	300	280	280
Trace minerals						
Iron (mg)	12	10	10	15	15	15
Zinc (mg)	15	15	15	12	12	12
Selenium (μg)	50	70	70	50	55	55

Trace minerals		
	11 + years	adults
Copper (mg)	1.5–2.5	1.5–3.0
Chromium (μg)	50–200	50–200

In addition to the problems with the databases for food analysis, the bioavailability of the minerals, and the accuracy of the RDA for athletes, there is the added problem of collecting the diet information. Perhaps the most accurate means of collecting food intake data is through analysis of the food eaten. This is time-consuming and costly and therefore not commonly used. Diet records are generally used but this procedure is fraught with problems, especially for mineral assessment. For example, a recent study showed that for iron and zinc it may be more desirable to obtain diet records over a number of short separate days rather than a 3- or 7-day diet record (Nelson *et al.*, 1989). An obvious problem with diet records is the accuracy of the subjects' reports. Whether subjects may forget or actually be reluctant to report certain foods would clearly alter a correct assessment of their intake.

It should be noted that not all studies that examined diet records of athletes used the same recall procedures or the same databases. Another consideration when evaluating studies that compare nutrient intake to the RDA, is that RDAs are established independently in each country and in many cases are not the same as those in the US. Although information from diet records should be reviewed with some caution, these studies can provide an overall picture of diet practices for a group.

The RDAs were revised in 1989 (10th edition) and the changes in minerals from the prior RDAs (1980) are that: calcium is now set at 1200 mg day^{-1} up to 24 years of age, whereas in the 9th edition 1200 mg day^{-1} was recommended to age 18 and from 18 to 24 years, 800 mg day^{-1} was recommended; the RDA for iron is 15 mg day^{-1} for women (adolescent and adults) which is reduced from the value of 18 mg day^{-1} in the 9th edition; the RDA for zinc for adult women is now set at 12 mg day^{-1} compared with 15 mg day^{-1} in the 9th edition; RDAs for selenium have been established for the first time in the 10th edition. In the 9th edition the ESADDI was 50–200 μg day^{-1} for adults and the RDA now is 70 μg day^{-1} for men and 55 μg^{-1} for women; for copper the ESADDI is set at 1.5–3 mg day^{-1} compared with 2–3 mg day^{-1} in the 9th edition.

7.4 NUTRITIONAL ASSESSMENT OF ATHLETES

An excellent and complete review of nutritional assessment of athletes is that of Short (1989). However, a representative overview will be presented here.

Nutritional assessments of several groups of endurance athletes have been made. From examination of 3-day diet records, Deuster *et al.* (1986) studied highly trained women runners and found that out of the group of 51, 24 were taking some form of dietary supplement. The runners who were not taking any supplements had intakes of calcium and magnesium that were above the RDA (130%), but zinc, iron and copper intakes were less than 75%, 50% and 8% of the RDA, respectively. Subjects in this study who were taking supplements were well above the RDA for all five minerals. For male endurance runners during normal training, calcium, magnesium, zinc and iron intake exceeded or equalled the RDA (Peters *et al.*, 1986). These same runners were studied during a 20-day road race, and the magnesium, iron and calcium intake exceeded the RDA but zinc was slightly less than the RDA. Another study of endurance runners showed that the female runners had a zinc intake of less than two-thirds the RDA (Nieman *et al.*, 1989). Ultra-endurance athletes were found to have adequate iron intakes (O'Toole *et al.*, 1989). However, 91% of female endurance runners ingested less than 14 mg iron/day (Clement and Asmundson, 1982).

As a group, elite swimmers were found to have diets that exceeded the RDA for calcium and iron (Berning, 1986). However, a high percentage (about half) of the females in the group did not meet the RDAs. Adams *et al.* (1982) studied a group of collegiate female swimmers and found that most of the swimmers had above, or marginally below, the RDA for calcium, above the RDA for phosphorus, and significantly below (about 45% below) the RDA for iron. Between 50 and 79% of collegiate female athletes fell below an acceptable level of iron and calcium ingestion (Welch *et al.*, 1987).

Australian male triathletes (Burke and Read, 1987) and male Nordic skiers (Ellsworth *et al.*, 1985) exceeded the RDAs for calcium and iron. Female skiers exceeded the RDA for calcium, but were marginally below the RDA for iron (Ellsworth *et al.*, 1985). Of 77 male and female Australian Olympic athletes all but two females (of 14) exceeded the RDA for calcium and iron (Steel, 1970).

Van Erp-Baart *et al.* (1989) studied the nutrient intakes of several groups of Dutch athletes and found that all groups of athletes exceeded the Dutch RDA for calcium. However, the Dutch RDA (700–900 mg day^{-1} for adults and female adolescents for 900–1200 mg day^{-1} for adolescent boys) is lower than the US RDA. Compared to the US RDA, 5 (all female) of the 15 athletes would be ingesting less than 75% of the RDA for calcium. The male athletes exceeded the RDA for iron (>9 mg day^{-1}) as did the female runner, rower and cyclist (>15 mg day^{-1}). However, low iron intakes were found for other female athletes including a swimmer, 2 gymnasts and 3 team sport players.

Studies of athletes who are maintaining low body weights present a less favourable picture. Fifty-two per cent of college wrestlers during mid-season consumed less than two-thirds of the RDA for zinc, and 63% consumed less than two-thirds of the RDA for magnesium (Steen and McKinney, 1986). Even during the pre- and post-season, at least 30% were not consuming two-thirds of the RDA for magnesium or zinc. Less than 30% of the wrestlers did not consume two-thirds of the RDA for iron during their mid-season but this percentage dropped to less than 15% during the off season. An examination of diet patterns of female gymnasts showed that 53%, 41%, 40%, 15% and 78% of adolescent gymnasts were not consuming two-thirds of the RDAs for iron, magnesium, calcium, phosphorus, and zinc, respectively (Loosli *et al.*, 1986). A similar nutritional status was found for adolescent ballet dancers (Benson *et al.*, 1985). The percentage of dancers consuming less than two-thirds of the RDA for calcium, phosphorus, magnesium, iron and zinc were 40.2%, 17.3%, 43.4%, 48.9% and 75.0%, respectively.

In a study of adult classical ballet dancers, only one female of the 22 dancers studied ingested <75% of the RDA of iron and all other dancers ingested >75% of the RDA for iron, calcium and phosphorus (Cohen *et al.*, 1985). The favourable iron and calcium intake for adult dancers was largely due to the supplements that the dancers were taking. In contrast, another study of adult professional ballet dancers found that of the 25 female dancers studied, 24 ingested less than 85% of the RDA for iron, 17 ingested less than 85% of the RDA for calcium, and 9 ingested less than 85% of the RDA for phosphorus (Calabrese *et al.*, 1983). When supplements were taken into account, 19, 15 and 9 dancers were still deficient in iron, calcium and phosphorus, respectively.

Dietary intakes of chromium and selenium in athletes have not been assessed. However, for the general population results have shown that dietary intake of chromium is suboptimal (Anderson and Guttman, 1988) but the intake of selenium is adequate (Lane, 1989).

In summary, it seems that most male athletes are ingesting at least the RDA of minerals with the possible exception of zinc. Many female athletes are often ingesting less than the RDA for calcium and iron. The picture is different for those athletes who are attempted to maintain low body weights, i.e. dancers, gymnasts and wrestlers. These athletes are not ingesting adequate amounts of iron, magnesium, calcium and zinc, and to a smaller extent, phosphorus. This is likely due to poor dietary habits associated with the maintenance of the low body weights.

It is interesting to note that a high percentage of these athletes were taking a vitamin/mineral supplements, but the type of supplements was in many cases unrelated to a possible deficient intake. For example, although 40% of the adolescent gymnasts (Loosli *et al.*, 1986) and 60% of the adolescent ballet dancers (Benson *et al.*, 1985) were taking supplements, only 12% of the gymnasts and 7% of the ballet dancers took a supplement that was sufficient to raise their intake of at least one nutrient to more than two-thirds of the RDA. Moreover, of the 16 gymnasts who were taking a calcium supplement, 9 had already met the RDA through diet, another 5, even with the supplement, were not achieving the RDA (Loosli *et al.*, 1986). Calabrese *et al.* (1983) also noted that although 40% of the adult ballet dancers took vitamin/mineral supplements, the supplements were usually narrow ranged, often consisting of massive doses of one or two select nutrients. This clearly illustrated the necessity of nutritional counselling for athletes.

7.5 MINERAL STATUS OF ATHLETES

There are several means to assess mineral status and these include the examination of clinical signs (deficiencies and excesses), body fluids or tissue levels. Although tissue analysis may be an accurate reflection of a specific deficiency, as in the case of iron deficiency from the analysis of bone marrow (Wishnitzer *et al.*, 1983), these techniques are invasive, time-consuming and costly. Measurement of mineral content of hair samples can often provide an easily obtainable 'history' of mineral status. More common is the measurement of mineral levels in blood and urine.

An important consideration in evaluating blood levels of minerals is whether what is assessed in the blood is an accurate representation of what is present in the tissues. Since blood levels seem to be affected by several factors, including acute exercise, an accurate interpretation of the results may be difficult. Exercise may cause a redistribution of minerals between body compartments. For example, several of the minerals may be mobilized from tissues into the blood during or after exercise. Also, exercise may affect mineral levels in the blood by loss in sweat or altered excretion in the urine. While some of these changes after acute exercises are short-lived, others may take 24–48 h before returning to resting values. Therefore differences between trained and untrained individuals in resting levels of a certain mineral may simply reflect change incurred by performing an exercise up to 48 h earlier (McDonald and Keen, 1988).

7.5.1 Status assessment techniques

Measurement of bone density provides an accurate indication of calcium status (Hunt and Groff, 1990) and these measurements are made using radiographic techniques (Sanborn, 1990). Three common and safe techniques are single-photon absorptiometry (SPA), dual-photon absorptiometry (DPA) and dual-energy X-ray absorptiometry (DEXA), a recent modification of DPA (Sanborn, 1990). Serum levels of calcium are carefully regulated so that they may provide only a very general index of calcium status.

Although serum and urine levels of magnesium are commonly used to assess magnesium status, normal plasma and urine levels may occur despite a severe intracellular deficit (Hunt and Groff, 1990). An accurate means of determining magnesium status would be to measure renal magnesium excretion after administration of an intravenous magnesium load. In this case, a decreased excretion would indicate a deficiency.

The body can quickly adapt to fluctuations of phosphorus intake by adjusting plasma phosphate to the level at which absorbed phosphate and urine phosphate are equal. Therefore the measurement of phosphorus status from blood samples can only provide a very general indicator of status. Because all food contains phosphorus, deficiencies are considered rare, and there is little need to assess status.

Zinc status is commonly assessed from serum samples but the accuracy of this procedure has been questioned (Hunt and Groff, 1990; Lukaski *et al.*, 1983). The concentration of zinc in hair samples is affected by the rate of hair growth, the delivery of zinc to the root and environmental contamination (i.e. tap water and shampoo) (Hunt and Groff, 1990). Also zinc concentration in hair differs between males and females and colour of the hair (Allegri *et al.*, 1990). One functional test that may prove an effective assessment of status is the measurement of alkaline phosphatase activity in neutrophils before and after zinc supplementation (Hunt and Groff, 1990). Alkaline phosphatase is a metalloenzyme that is sensitive to zinc deficiency.

Copper can be assessed from serum samples by use of absorption spectrophotometry (Hunt and Groff, 1990), although this procedure is not considered unequivocal (Lukaski *et al.*, 1983). Copper status is also assessed by ceruloplasmin (a copper containing protein) activity in the blood and by the activity of erythrocyte Cu,Zn-superoxide dismutase (Fischer *et al.*, 1990). Much of the plasma copper is bound to ceruloplasmin. Analysis of copper in hair samples is considered unreliable since relatively low copper concentrations are present in hair.

Selenium from blood samples has traditionally been assessed using a graphite-furnace (flameless) atomic absorption spectroscopy technique (Hunt and Groff, 1990). A more promising technique involves the assessment of glutathione peroxidase activity in platelets before and after selenium supplementation. Selenium is an essential co-factor for the enzyme glutathione peroxidase.

Accurate assessment of chromium status from biological fluids is questionable (Anderson, 1988; Hunt and Groff, 1990), although at present there seems to be no more reliable method. Recent studies have assessed urinary chromium levels using an atomic-absorption spectrophotometric and graphite-furnace technique (Anderson *et al.*, 1990). When assessing chromium levels in urine, it may be necessary to take the diet into account, since carbohydrates that alter circulating insulin have been shown also to alter urinary chromium losses (Anderson *et al.*, 1990).

Although the most accurate means of assessing iron status is through bone marrow biopsy, this method is invasive and costly. Measurements of serum ferritin, transferrin saturation, amount of haemoglobin and red cell protoporphyrin also provide a good index of iron status (Haymes, 1987; Hunt and Groff, 1990). Poor iron status is indicated by low levels of serum ferritin, increased levels of red cell protoporphyrin, reduced haemoglobin levels, increased transferrin levels and the degree of transferrin saturation. These markers are useful in determining the degree of iron deficiency.

There are three stages if iron deficiency and, ranging from mild to severe, these are: (1) iron depletion, (2) iron deficiency erythropoiesis (deficiency in the production of red blood cells), and (3) iron deficiency anaemia. A reduction in serum ferritin and an increase in transferrin levels would indicate iron depletion. Ferritin is secreted from all ferritin-producing cells and serum levels parallel the concentration of body iron stores. Transferrin carries iron in the blood, and when iron is not available, levels of transferrin will increase. Continued iron deficiency results in an impairment in red blood cell formation, the second stage. This second stage is determined by a decrease in transferrin saturation and an increase in red cell protoporphyrin. When iron is not available to bind with the red cell protoporphyrin, which is used in the formation of the haeme molecule, the amount of red cell protoporphyrin will increase in the blood. If red cells are not being formed, haemoglobin levels begin to fall and this marks the final stage, iron deficiency anaemia.

7.5.2 Calcium status

Serum calcium levels were found to be similar in male runners and controls (Olha *et al.*, 1982) and were within normal ranges for professional ballet dancers (Cohen *et al.*, 1985). More recent studies have examined bone density as related to physical activity (Sanborn, 1990). Exercise, particularly load-bearing activities, were found positively to affect bone density (Lane *et al.*, 1986). Davee *et al.* (1990) studied three groups of women: sedentary, aerobic exercise participants, and muscle-building exercise participants. There was no significant difference among the groups in calcium intake but the group participating in muscle-building activity had significantly greater spinal bone density. Optimal changes in the skeleton in response to exercise are found in those women with adequate dietary calcium (Dalsky *et al.*, 1988). Adequate calcium intake is particularly important since stress fractures are more likely to occur in athletes with low bone density, menstrual irregularity and low calcium intake (Myburgh *et al.*, 1990). It should also be noted that calcium is lost in sweat (Costill and Miller, 1980) so that exercise may increase an athlete's calcium requirement.

With regard to menstrual irregularities, those athletes who are amenorrhoeic were found to have a 14% lower lumbar bone density compared with regularly menstruating women (Drinkwater *et al.*, 1984). Moreover, when amenorrhoeic athletes resumed their normal menstrual cycles for over 1 year, bone mineral density was increased by 6.3% (Drinkwater *et al.*, 1986). Thus oestrogen is implicated as a factor contributing to bone density. Several suggestions have been made as to the mechanism of oestrogen action and these include (1) oestrogen reduces urinary calcium, (2) oestrogen improves intestinal absorption of calcium, and (3) oestrogen increases the secretion of calcitonin and reduces bone resorption (Lindsay, 1987). However, the results of studies assessing the mechanism of oestrogen action on bone have been equivocal (Lindsay, 1987).

7.5.3 Magnesium status

Several studies showed that serum magnesium levels of athletes were similar to controls and within the normal range of the general population (Conn *et al.*, 1986; Olha *et al.*, 1982; Weight *et al.*, 1988). In contrast, Casoni *et al.* (1990) found significantly lower serum magnesium levels in 11 well-trained athletes compared with controls, but the serum magnesium values for the athletes (1.70 mEq l^{-1}) were within the normal range (1.3–2.1 mEq l^{-1}). It should be noted that athletes who were shown to have a less than adequate intake of magnesium, i.e. those maintaining low body weights, have not been examined for possible deficiencies.

Following the 1969 Boston Marathon, eight runners were found to have significantly lower serum magnesium levels compared with before the race (Rose *et al.*, 1970). This change could reflect a redistribution of serum magnesium into either muscle tissue, adipocytes or red blood cells (McDonald and Keen, 1988). In a case study of a marathon runner during a race, Franz *et al.* (1985) found that during the race serum magnesium increased followed by a decrease by the end of the race. Deuster *et al.* (1987) reported that a high-intensity anaerobic exercise produced a significant increase in urinary excretion of magnesium on the day of the exercise and then returned to normal. Increased urinary excretion of magnesium was also found 12 h after a marathon (Lijnen *et al.*, 1988). Costill and Miller (1980), based on several studies from their laboratory, suggest that a sizeable amount of magnesium could be lost in sweat during exercise. Whether the magnesium lost through sweating could induce a magnesium deficiency that could not be made up by dietary intake alone has been questioned (Brotherhood, 1984). Also, a loss of magnesium from muscle cells due to muscle damage incurred by very strenuous exercise has been suggested to produce a magnesium deficiency (Stendig-Lindberg *et al.*, 1988).

7.5.4 Phosphorus status

Phosphorus deficiencies are rare in the general population (National Research Council, 1989) and are assumed to be rare for athletes as well. However, Dale *et al.* (1986) found that runners who collapsed during a half marathon 'fun run' were clinically hypophosphataemic. Elite runners who completed the half marathon had high serum phosphate levels. Also serum phosphate levels were elevated after élite runners completed a 30 min treadmill test (Dale *et al.*, 1986). Increased serum phosphate levels may reflect a release of phosphate from storage to meet the cellular demands of exercise. The seemingly rare case of hypophosphataemia induced by exercise could indicate a depletion in the phosphate stores.

7.5.5 Zinc status

Two studies found that blood zinc levels were adequate in female triathletes and endurance athletes (Bazzarre *et al.*, 1986) and highly trained males (Weight *et al.*, 1988). However, many studies have reported that endurance athletes had relatively low resting blood levels of zinc (Couzy *et al.*, 1990; Deuster *et al.*, 1986; Dressendorfer and Sockolov, 1980; Dressendorfer *et al.*, 1982; Hackman and Keen, 1983; Haralambie, 1981; Marrella *et al.*, 1990). Singh *et al.* (1990) found that runners had a lower plasma zinc level than controls but they also had a higher erythrocyte zinc concentration. The authors suggested that chronic training produced a redistribution of zinc.

The relationship of zinc status and zinc intake has also been addressed. Bazzarre *et al.* (1986) found athletes to have lower than adequate intakes of zinc but blood levels were normal. Hackman and Keen (1983) and Deuster *et al.* (1986) did not find a strong correlation between dietary zinc intake and serum zinc, although Deuster *et al.* (1986) did find a relationship between zinc intake and red blood cell zinc.

Results of studies that have examined acute changes in blood levels of zinc after exercise are equivocal with regard to whether there is an increase or decrease in zinc levels (Anderson *et al.*, 1984; Dressendorfer *et al.*, 1982; Hetland *et al.*, 1975; Ohno *et al.*, 1985). Post-exercise changes in plasma zinc levels were found to be sensitive to the zinc status of the individual (Lukaski *et al.*, 1984). Aruoma *et al.* (1988) suggested that the lower plasma zinc concentrations immediately after exercise may simply reflect an acute phase response to exercise stress. The above studies are consistent in noting that whatever change occurred was temporary, and generally plasma zinc levels returned to baseline within a few hours to a day.

In a study of chronic exercise effects, Couzy *et al.* (1990) found that serum zinc was significantly decreased after 5 months of intensive training. Ohno *et al.* (1990) found that 10 weeks of training apparently reduced the circulating exchangeable zinc. Since zinc is lost from the body primarily through sweat and urine (Anderson and Guttmann, 1988), exercise training could induce a zinc deficiency via sweating. Also, Anderson and Guttmann (1988) found a 1.5-fold increase in urinary zinc excretion after a 6-mile run. Coupled with the information from diet records, there is reason to suspect that some athletes could be deficient in zinc.

7.5.6 Copper status

Fischer *et al.* (1990) examined copper status of 384 healthy adults; the subjects were separated into four activity levels ranging from sedentary to vigorous. There was no significant difference between groups for serum copper, ceruloplasmin activity or Cu,Zn-superoxide dismutase activity (Fischer *et al.*, 1990). The authors suggested that the activity level of subjects in the vigorous exercise group may be less than that for trained athletes, and results may differ if athletes were examined. Lukaski (1989a) examined copper status of collegiate swimmers before and after the competitive season and found no difference in plasma copper levels or ceruloplasmin activity. However, Cu,Zn-superoxide dismutase activity was increased in the swimmers which could reflect an adaptation of copper metabolism in response to aerobic training (Lukaski, 1989a). Lukaski (1989b) concluded that physical training does not adversely affect copper status. Also, runners (Conn *et al.*, 1986; Olha *et al.*, 1982) and a variety of college athletes (Lukaski *et al.*, 1983) were found to have higher resting blood levels of copper compared with sedentary controls.

Significant increases in blood levels of copper have been found immediately after graded cycle ergometry exercise to exhaustion (Olha *et al.*, 1982) and 30 min of cycle ergometry exercise at 70–80% VO_2 max (Ohno *et al.*, 1984). Dressendorfer *et al.* (1982) found that plasma copper concentration increased over the first 8 days of a 20-day road race and then remained elevated. These authors suggested that the elevation in plasma copper may be due to an increase in the liver's production of ceruloplasmin in response to exercise stress. Ceruloplasmin, a physiological antioxidant, acts as an acute phase protein to increase antioxidant defences (Aruoma *et al.*, 1988).

In contrast, Dressendorfer and Sockolov (1980) reported no difference in plasma copper levels between runners and controls, and Dowdy and Burt (1980) found that serum copper levels were significantly lower after 6 months of swim training. Marrella *et al.* (1990) also reported that resting copper concentrations were lower in triathletes compared to controls, but no differences were found for ceruloplasmin and total blood cell copper. Singh *et al.* (1990) found that plasma copper concentration in samples from runners was significantly higher than non-runners, but the reverse was true for erythrocyte concentration. The authors suggested that chronic exercise may induce a redistribution of copper. Marrella *et al.* (1990) also found that plasma copper concentration decreased significantly after exercise in triathletes but ceruloplasmin did not.

The results on changes in copper status due to exercise and training are equivocal and may reflect the inadequacy of the techniques to assess copper status or may reflect a redistribution of copper between body compartments. One study did find that copper was present in sweat collected after exercise (Gutteridge *et al.*, 1985) and this could contribute to a loss in body copper in athletes. However, at present there is no basis to suggest that athletes may be copper deficient.

7.5.7 Chromium status

Chromium status has not been examined in athletes. However, Anderson *et al.* (1984) found that immediately and at 2 h after a 6-mile run, serum chromium was increased, which probably reflects a mobilization of chromium from body tissues. Urinary concentration and excretion of chromium were also increased at 2 h after the run. This would produce a net loss of chromium after exercise. Possible losses of chromium in sweat after exercise have not been established.

Resting urinary chromium excretion is significantly less for trained subjects compared to untrained subjects either on a self-selected diet (Anderson and Kozlovsky, 1985) or a controlled diet (Anderson *et al.*, 1988).

However, after exercise there was a significant increase in chromium excretion for the trained subjects but not the untrained subjects. The reason for these findings is unclear. The lower resting levels of chromium excretion for the trained subjects may be due to either a deficiency of chromium or to an adaptive response to conserve chromium (Anderson *et al.*, 1988). Also, the untrained subjects may not have exercised to a sufficient intensity to alter chromium excretion (Campbell and Anderson, 1987).

7.5.8 Iron status

More studies have been done to assess iron status of athletes than for all other minerals combined. Discussion here is limited to a general overview of this topic since several excellent reviews on iron status of athletes are available (Clement and Sawchuk, 1984; Eichner, 1986; Haymes, 1987; Pate, 1983; Risser and Risser, 1990; Rowland, 1990; Sherman and Kramer, 1989).

Assessment of iron status is generally done from blood samples; however, two studies are available that assessed iron status in bone marrow aspirations from runners (Ehn *et al.*, 1980; Wishnitzer *et al.*, 1983). The 11 male and 1 female runner in one study (Wishnitzer *et al.*, 1983) and the 8 male runners in the other study (Ehn *et al.*, 1980) had insufficient iron stores. The former study found that serum iron levels, percentage iron saturation and haemoglobin concentrations were normal despite the insufficient level of stored iron (Wishnitzer *et al.*, 1983).

Several studies have shown that athletes are iron depleted. For example, low serum ferritin levels have been found for male middle- and long-distance runners (Dufaux *et al.*, 1981), female distance runners (Clement and Asmundson, 1982), female endurance athletes (Bazzarre *et al.*, 1986), and male and female endurance runners (Casoni *et al.*, 1985). However, the number of athletes who are iron-depleted is no more than that found for the general population (Balaban *et al.*, 1989; Risser *et al.*, 1988; Selby and Eichner, 1989). Serum ferritin levels in 35 male and 37 female élite runners were similar to levels found for the general population (Balaban *et al.*, 1989). In a sample of 100 female varsity athletes, Risser *et al.* (1988) found that 31% of the athletes were iron depleted compared with 45.5% of the controls, but this was not statistically significant. Based upon plasma ferritin data from 14 athletes, Selby and Eichner (1989) concluded that iron depletion in athletes seemed to be no greater than that for non-athletes. Plowman and McSwegin (1981) found that 33.3% of high school cross country runners and 28.6% of the controls were iron deficient, as assessed by serum iron levels and total iron binding capacity of the blood. A group of 47 cyclists and 81 rowers had similar or higher serum ferritin levels compared to the controls (Dufaux *et al.*, 1981).

In contrast, Mouton *et al.* (1990) found that, compared with controls, serum iron and ferritin levels were significantly lower in 44 male runners. Examination of serum ferritin levels of 61 male runners showed that they had significantly lower serum ferritin levels and serum iron levels compared with controls, although there was considerable overlap of the values (Dufaux *et al.*, 1981).

Since the degree of iron depletion is similar for some athlete groups as for the general population, then part of the reason for the low iron status may be unrelated to exercise. Therefore a poor diet as well as loss of iron during menstruation in women would be implicated (Rowland, 1990).

However, there is reason to believe that exercise could also contribute to an iron depleted state. Pattini *et al.* (1990) found that prolonged exercise increased the rate of iron metabolism. Another study showed that 7 weeks of intense physical exercise in untrained subjects significantly decreased iron status (Magazanik *et al.*, 1988). It should be noted that several of the athletes in this study had only modest falls in serum ferritin which could be due to plasma volume expansion. Recent attention has been given to the role of training-induced plasma volume expansion as an explanation for iron depletion since the increased plasma could dilute serum ferritin.

Ehn *et al.* (1980) suggested that a low absorption and an increased elimination of iron could explain the depleted iron stores in athletes and Lamanca *et al.* (1988) found a significant amount of iron was lost in sweat. The low bioavailability of iron in vegetarian diets can also contribute to lower serum ferritin levels for athletes following a modified vegetarian diet (Snyder *et al.*, 1989).

Not all studies found that exercise decreased iron status. No change in iron status was found after a more moderate training programme (Blum *et al.*, 1986) than the exercise programme used by Magazanik *et al.* (1988). Ricci *et al.* (1988) and Lampe *et al.* (1986) reported no change in serum ferritin levels during endurance training in male long-distance runners and in female marathon runners, respectively. However, after the marathon, serum ferritin was shown to be elevated for 3 days (Lampe *et al.*, 1986).

Although many athletes would be considered iron depleted, incidence of iron deficiency erythropoiesis and iron deficiency anaemia is small in the athlete population (Sherman and Kramer, 1989). Studies that have found marginal or low haemoglobin and low serum ferritin levels in athletes generally attribute these findings to an expansion in plasma volume. This condition has sometimes been termed pseudoanaemia (Eichner, 1986). There is no decrease in the number of red cells so oxygen-carrying capacity is not impaired. Furthermore, the increase in plasma volume may be beneficial for exercise since it could reduce viscosity and increase cardiac output. To determine if an individual has actual iron deficiency anaemia rather than pseudoanaemia, the effect of ingestion of iron supplements should be tested. An increase in haemoglobin after iron supplementation would indicate the presence of iron deficiency anaemia.

The haemolysis that occurs from foot strike, or pounding on the feet during running, could also result in low haemoglobin levels (Eichner, 1986). Dressendorfer *et al.* (1982) found that plasma levels of iron increased significantly over the first 2 days of a 20-day road race and then decreased. Since the increase was coincident with a fall in haemoglobin, increased iron was considered to be due to intravascular haemolysis. Mouton *et al.* (1990) and Dufaux *et al.* (1981) implicated haemolysis as a factor contributing to low haptoglobin values in a group of male runners. The contribution of haemolysis to decreased iron status is still questionable since other researchers have suggested that with normal training the degree of haemolysis is mild and transitory (McDonald and Keen, 1988).

7.6 THE RELATIONSHIP OF MINERAL STATUS AND PERFORMANCE

In the preceding sections, several athlete groups were shown to be deficient in certain minerals, especially calcium, zinc and iron. Moreover, blood levels and urinary excretion of several of the minerals are affected by performance of an acute bout of exercise. The following discussion will focus on the relationship of mineral status and performance and whether supplementation will alter performance measures.

7.6.1 Calcium

Effects of calcium supplementation on performance have not been adequately addressed (Bucci, 1989; Wilmore and Freund, 1984). Bucci (1989) referred to one early study showing that daily ingestion of calcium gluconate would aid recovery from exercise. More recently, calcium gluconate supplementation in solution was found to prevent the normal plasma volume increase after fluid ingestion during exercise in the heat (Greenleaf and Brock, 1980). Of interest, calcium supplementation has mostly been used as a placebo in the form of calcium carbonate or calcium phosphate (Bucci, 1989).

The major interest in calcium supplementation is to prevent bone loss. As discussed earlier, both exercise and adequate calcium intake have been shown to prevent bone loss in women (Birge and Dalsky, 1989). In a recent study (Myburgh *et al.*, 1990), bone mineral density as assessed by dual-energy X-ray absorptiometry and calcium intake as assessed from 7-day diet records were determined for 25 athletes (19 women) with confirmed stress fractures and 25 control athletes with no history of bone fractures. Compared to the athletes without fractures, a greater percentage of the athletes with fractures had menstrual irregularities and a lower calcium intake. The results suggest that calcium supplements may be important in reducing the likelihood of injury to bones in women with menstrual irregularities.

7.6.2 Magnesium

Lukaski *et al.* (1983) found that plasma magnesium levels were significantly correlated with VO_2 max in athletes but not in non-athletes. The authors suggested that magnesium may facilitate oxygen delivery to working muscle in the trained subjects. Conn *et al.* (1986) found a significant correlation between serum magnesium levels and VO_2 max in untrained subjects but not the trained runners. Taken together these studies suggest that magnesium status is related to aerobic capacity.

Lemon (1989) cited an earlier study showing that cycle ergometry exercise was enhanced after magnesium supplementation in subjects who had low magnesium levels in their blood. A case study of a female tennis player with low blood magnesium levels and muscle spasms showed that the spasms stopped after daily supplementation with 500 mg of magnesium gluconate (Bucci, 1989). Mader *et al.* (1990) examined the effects of magnesium supplementation (21 mmol day^{-1}) during high-altitude training for 3.5 weeks. Blood magnesium levels were normal before the supplementation and remained at the same level despite the supplementation. The authors suggested that intensive training can produce a negative magnesium balance such that supplementation is necessary to maintain normal status.

Magnesium supplementation (15 mmol magnesium-L-aspartate-hydro-chloride) taken daily for 14 days produced a change in hormonal response to a 1 h ergometric exercise (Golf *et al.*, 1984). Specifically, aldosterone and cortisol did not increase in response to the exercise after the supplementation period. Exercise performance was not assessed. This study showed that magnesium plays a role in aldosterone and cortisol function during exercise but the meaning and the implications of these findings are unclear.

7.6.3 Phosphorus

The use of phosphate as an ergogenic aid dates back to the First World War (Bucci, 1989). Embden (of the Embden–Meyerhof pathway) developed foods and drinks rich in phosphate to aid German soldiers in the field. A review of early studies can be found elsewhere (Bucci, 1989), and these studies, which were generally not well controlled, suggested that phosphate supplementation would delay fatigue. Several more recent studies have also examined the effect of phosphate supplementation (now called phosphate loading) to enhance aerobic performance, but the results are somewhat equivocal.

Cade *et al.* (1984), in a well-designed cross-over, placebo-controlled study, gave 10 male distance runners 1 g of neutral-buffered phosphate supplement four times a day for 3 days. Subjects completed an intermittent graded, treadmill run to exhaustion before and after the supplementation period. The phosphate supplement produced a significant increase in serum phosphate and erythrocyte 2,3-diphosphoglycerate (2,3-DPG) content. Moreover, the supplement resulted in a proportionate increase (6–12%) in VO_2 max. The increase in 2,3-DPG may have been responsible for the improvement in aerobic capacity. However, a submaximal exercise rest was also performed and lactate levels were found to be lower during the phosphate loading condition. These results may suggest that phosphate loading delays the onset of anaerobic metabolism.

Similar results were found by Kreider *et al.* (1990) in a well-controlled study that examined phosphate loading in seven competitive runners. One gram of tribasic sodium phosphate, taken 4 times per day for 6 days, resulted in a 7.9% increase in VO_2 max, a 10.5% increase in ventilatory anaerobic threshold and a trend towards improvement on 5-mile run performance. No change in red cell 2,3-DPG was found. Subjects performed more work during the phosphate-loaded trial, but lactate levels were only slightly higher than for the placebo condition. The authors suggested that the beneficial effects of the phosphate load was due to an enhanced metabolic efficiency.

In contrast, two studies from the same laboratory (Weatherwax *et al.*, 1986; Ahlberg *et al.*, 1986) found no beneficial effects of phosphate loading. Both studies administered 1 g four times a day for 4 days to nine subjects in a double-blind cross-over design. The phosphate loading did not alter anaerobic threshold or lactate levels significantly (Ahlberg *et al.*, 1986), nor did the loading alter bicycle time trial performance (Weatherwax *et al.*, 1986). Kreider *et al.* (1990) suggested that the lack of a beneficial effect from the phosphate load could be explained by the fact that subjects were tested up to 12 h after the loading and that the length of the washout period (9 days) may not have been sufficient.

Duffy and Conlee (1986), in a double-blind cross-over design, examined the effect of an acute (1.24 g given 1 h before the exercise) or chronic (3.73 g day^{-1} for 6 days before the exercise) ingestion of a commercially available product containing mono and dibasic sodium phosphate, tribasic potassium phosphate and vitamin C. No significant effect of the phosphate product was found on treadmill run time to exhaustion or leg power measured by an isokinetic dynamometer. Neither blood lactate nor 2,3-DPG were measured. It is difficult directly to compare the results of this study with those above since the supplement that was used contained a different phosphate composition.

Because of the positive changes observed in studies that were well controlled, further study of the effects of phosphate loading are warranted.

7.6.4 Zinc

Despite the incidence of hypozincaemia in athletes, few studies have examined the relationship between zinc status and performance or the effects of zinc supplementation. Lukaski *et al.* (1983) reported no correlation between blood zinc levels and VO_2 max. Krotkiewski *et al.* (1982) found that zinc supplementation of 135 mg daily for 14 days resulted in a significant increase in isokinetic strength at fast angular velocities (3.14 Rad s^{-1} or 180° s^{-1}) only and in isometric endurance. No change was found for dynamic endurance or isokinetic strength at 1.05 or 2.1 Rad s^{-1} (60 or 120° s^{-1}). Krotiewski *et al.* (1982) suggested that zinc may have an effect on anaerobic work with high lactate production. Since zinc acts as a co-factor to the enzyme lactate dehydrogenase, such a suggestion is plausible, but further study is warranted before any conclusions can be made.

Hackman and Keen (1986) found that supplementation with 22.5 mg zinc per day for 4 weeks resulted in a significant increase in serum zinc levels in male runners and controls, and that this increase was not measurable until the third week of supplementation. Zinc supplementation at levels in excess of the RDA has been shown to pose a health risk (Campbell and Anderson, 1987). Excessive zinc can inhibit copper absorption and decrease serum high-density lipoprotein levels. Therefore it is recommended that zinc intake remain close to the RDA.

Recent attention has focused on the effects of zinc deficiency on immunity (Keen and Gershwin, 1990). Humans with low serum zinc levels tend to be more susceptible to a variety of infectious diseases (Keen and Gershwin, 1990). This could suggest that athletes with zinc deficiencies may have an impaired immune response. Bray and Bettger (1990) have also presented evidence that zinc may play a physiological role as an antioxidant. Further study of the role of zinc during exercise and training is warranted.

7.6.5 Copper

Conn *et al.* (1986) reported that for trained athletes, there was no correlation between VO_2 max and plasma copper levels. Similar results were reported by Lukaski *et al.* (1983) for male university athletes and untrained men. The effects of copper supplementation on performance have not been examined.

7.6.6 Selenium

Selenium acts as an antioxidant in conjunction with vitamin E in reducing lipid peroxidation by cells. In this role selenium may be important in offsetting the known increases in lipid peroxidation induced by strenuous exercise (Kanter *et al.*, 1988; Maughan *et al.*, 1989). Although the effects of selenium supplementation on exercise have not been examined, Goldfarb *et al.* (1989) did find that vitamin E intake successfully reduced lipid peroxidation during exercise. One possible reason for a lack of data on selenium supplementation is that excessive selenium intake may be toxic, and levels for the general population, and most probably athletes, are considered to be adequate (Lane, 1989).

7.6.7 Chromium

Chromium has received much attention in recent years because of its role in the potentiation of insulin (Evans, 1989). In a study of non-insulin dependent diabetics, 6 weeks of chromium supplementation was shown to decrease blood glucose by 24%, decrease total cholesterol by 13% and decrease LDL cholesterol by 11% (Evans, 1989). Whether chromium supplementation in athletes will affect energy metabolism has not been investigated.

Insulin is important in the transport of not only blood sugar but also amino acids into cells, and it regulates protein metabolism as well as protein synthesis. On this basis, chromium has been suggested to be an alternative to steroids (Evans, 1989). In two studies involving young men participating in weight training programmes, Evans (1989) showed that chromium picolinate supplements (200 microgrammes (μg) of chromium a day) resulted in significant losses in body fat and increases in lean body mass. In the first study, 10 entrant college students were attending a weight-lifting class two times a week for 6 weeks. Subjects were placed into two groups. One group was given the chromium supplement and the other group took a placebo of calcium phosphate. After 6 weeks, a significant increase in lean body mass (2.2 kg) and no change in body fat were found in the chromium supplemented group. For the placebo group, an increase of only 0.4 kg in lean body mass was found, but body fat increased by 1.21 kg. Football players participating in a supervised weight-lifting programme for 6 weeks took part in the second study. The group given the chromium picolinate supplements lost 3.4 kg of fat and increased 2.6 kg lean body mass, whereas the placebo group lost 1 kg fat and gained only 1.8 kg lean body mass.

The results of the studies described above should be reviewed with some caution. The percentage body fat and lean body mass were estimated by skinfold measurements. The equations used to predict percentage body fat and lean mass from skinfold measures were based on data derived from an average population. These equations provide only an indirect estimate, and for football players the accuracy of this method is questionable. It is possible that the small differences reported in lean body mass between the chromium supplemented group and the placebo group may be due to errors in the estimation techniques. Also there was no attempt to assess the chromium status of the subjects, nor was any measure of muscle function assessed. No other published study has examined the effect of chromium picolinate on muscle development. Because of these interesting findings by Evans (1989), further study on the effects of chromium supplementation is warranted.

7.6.8 Iron

Many studies have documented that iron deficiency anaemia can compromise performance (Haymes, 1987). However, iron depletion, the early stage of iron deficiency, is not associated with performance decrements (Newhouse *et al.*, 1989). Matter *et al.* (1987) found no difference in maximal treadmill performance between female marathon runners with low serum ferritin levels and those with high levels. Celsing *et al.* (1986) induced iron deficiency in 9 healthy male subjects by repeated venesection over a 9-week period followed by a transfusion to re-establish normal haemoglobin levels. These venesections artificially induced iron deficiency. When the anaemia was corrected by transfusion, but not the iron deficiency, time to exhaustion on a treadmill test was unaltered. This study clearly demonstrated that iron deficiency, isolated from anaemia, did not affect exercise performance.

When iron supplements are given to subjects with iron deficiency anaemia, the iron status is improved and so is exercise and work performance (Haymes, 1987; Sherman and Kramer, 1989). Several studies have reported no change in exercise performance after iron supplementation in athletes who had mild iron deficiencies (Matter *et al.*, 1987; Newhouse *et al.*, 1989; Risser *et al.*, 1988; Schoene *et al.*, 1983). Although Rowland *et al.* (1988) found that adolescent non-anaemic iron-deficient runners did show improvements in endurance time when given iron supplements compared to those given a placebo, their data suggest that some subjects may have had an early stage of anaemia. Properly controlled studies seem to agree that 'non-anaemic iron deficiency' does not impair performance.

The iron deficiency observed in athletes, especially females, may result from a poor diet, iron lost in sweat and exercise stress. Minimal iron depletion does not seem to affect exercise performance but iron deficiency anaemia does. Although the data are equivocal, in adult athletes with minimal iron deficiency, performance is not improved by iron supplements.

7.7 SHOULD MINERAL SUPPLEMENTS BE RECOMMENDED?

The use of calcium supplements, although not thought to enhance performance, are important for the health of bones. Athletes tend to have enhanced calcium status as assessed by bone mineral density. The notable exception to this is female athletes who are amenorrheic, and these women should certainly be taking calcium supplements. Other female athletes could consider taking calcium supplements to ensure adequate calcium status. Moderately elevated intake does not appear to present a health hazard. Although no adverse effects have been found in adults consuming 2500 mg calcium per day, intakes much above the RDA are not recommended (National Research Council, 1989).

Magnesium status is generally adequate for athletes; however, athletes who may have a tendency for magnesium deficiency, i.e. those maintaining low body weights, have not been examined. Magnesium supplements may be important for those athletes who have poor diets and are maintaining low body weights, although this has not been fully established. Magnesium can be lost in sweat, and magnesium status may be compromised in some athletes. However, there is no evidence that magnesium supplements can enhance performance. Magnesium supplements do not appear to be harmful, but there seems to be no justification for their use at this time, especially in excess of the RDA.

There are little data to suggest that athletes are deficient in phosphorus. Phosphorus supplementation over an extended period of time is not recommended, since it can result in lowered blood calcium levels. Some well-controlled studies have shown that phosphate loading (phosphate ingestion for several days prior to an exercise) will enhance performance.

The majority of studies suggest that athletes have a less than adequate zinc status and may have a zinc deficiency. Since zinc is mainly lost from the body in sweat and urine, exercise training could create a deficiency through sweat loss. Also exercise has been shown to result in increased urinary excretion of zinc. However, only one study suggested zinc supplementation would enhance performance. The wisdom of taking excessive zinc is questionable, since excessive zinc consumption can produce several negative effects including an inhibition of copper absorption from the diet possibly leading to anaemia, and a reduction in circulation of high-density lipoproteins (McDonald and Keen, 1988). McDonald and Keen (1988) recommend that zinc supplementation should not exceed 15 mg day^{-1}.

Athletes' diets do not seem to be deficient in copper and widespread deficiencies in body status have not been documented. Copper status of athletes has been assessed by serum copper levels and the results are equivocal. There seems to be insufficient information to suggest that athletes may be copper deficient. Although it has been shown that copper is lost in sweat (Gutteridge *et al.*, 1985), this loss seems to be easily corrected by a well-balanced diet. Since copper status is unlikely to be compromised in athletes, and there are no data to suggest that copper supplementation will enhance performance, and excessive copper ingestion is potentially toxic, copper supplementation should be discouraged.

Selenium status of athletes has not been documented but there is no reason to suspect deficiencies. The relationship between selenium status and performance has also not been established, but selenium may play a role as an antioxidant during exercise. Since excessive selenium intake could be potentially harmful, at this time there is no basis to recommend selenium supplements for athletes.

Chromium status of athletes has not been documented, but because of the low intakes for the general population, there is reason to suspect that athletes may be deficient. Exercise may create a net loss in chromium because of increased excretion into the urine. Little data exist on the effects of chromium supplementation in athletes. However, one laboratory has shown that chromium may enhance muscle building during strength training (Evans, 1989). Other studies have shown that chromium potentiates the effects of insulin, and although not documented, in this way chromium may alter energy metabolism during exercise. Further studies on exercise/training and chromium are needed before any sound rationale can be made for recommending chromium supplements to enhance performance.

Numerous studies have shown that athletes, particularly females, are iron depleted, but true iron deficiencies are rare. Iron depletion does not affect exercise performance but iron deficiency anaemia does. Iron supplements have not been shown to enhance performance except where iron deficiency anaemia exists. There are two concerns over excessive iron intakes. First, excessive iron can inhibit the absorption of zinc (McDonald and Keen, 1988), and second, some individuals (2–3 persons per 10 000) have a genetic defect that leads to enhanced iron absorption. McDonald and Keen (1988) recommend that supplements of 15 mg day^{-1} be taken to reduce the potential negative effect on zinc absorption yet still correct possible iron depletion. There is little basis to suggest that iron supplementation for individuals without serious iron deficiency will have any effect on exercise performance.

7.8 CONCLUDING REMARKS

Poor diets are perhaps the main reason for any mineral deficiencies found in athletes, although in certain cases exercise could contribute to the deficiency. With the possible exceptions of calcium and iron, these deficiencies could easily be corrected by ingestion of a well-balanced diet. Few studies have definitively documented any beneficial effects of mineral supplementation on performance. Athletes who take mineral supplements or a vitamin/mineral supplement are, for the most part, not taking them to enhance performance, but rather to ensure good health.

Many athletes, however, are taking supplements without regard for specific deficiencies so that even after supplementation they remain deficient in certain nutrients. Most studies report that athletes do not have an adequate knowledge of proper dietary practices and have not received qualified dietary advice (Steel, 1970; Short, 1989). College wrestlers (Steen and McKinney, 1986) and adolescent gymnasts (Loosli *et al.*, 1986), groups who may have mineral deficiencies, were found to have serious misconceptions about diet. Parr *et al.* (1984) surveyed 2977 college and high school athletes concerning nutrition knowledge and practices and found approximately 67% were not familiar with dietary goals or guidelines, other than the basic food groups.

A significant and interesting finding in the study by Parr *et al.* (1984) was that those athletes who were familiar with dietary guidelines used them regularly. This suggests that if athletes become acquainted with proper nutritional practices, they will make use of them. It would seem then, that an important task for exercise and health professionals should be to provide athletes with sound information and counselling on sports nutrition so that they are not left to rely on some of the enticing, and sometimes misleading, information presented in the media.

REFERENCES

Adams, M.M., Porcello, L.P. and Vivian, V.M. (1982). Effect of a supplement on dietary intakes of female collegiate swimmers. *Physician and Sportsmedicine*, **10**, 122–34.

Ahlberg, A., Weatherwax, R.S., Deady, M., Perez, H.R., Otto, R.M., Cooperstein, D., Smith, T.K. and Wygand, J.W. (1986). Effect of phosphate loading on cycle ergometer performance. *Medicine and Science in Sports and Exercise*, **18**, S11 (abstract).

Allegri, G., Costa, C., Biasiolo, M., Arban, R., Bertazzo, A. and Cardin de Stefani, E.L. (1990). Tryptophan copper and zinc in hair of healthy subjects, correlation with differences in hair pigmentation. *Italian Journal of Biochemistry*, **39**, 209–15.

Anderson, R.A. (1988). Selenium, chromium and manganese. B. Chromium. In *Modern Nutrition in Health and Disease*, 7th edn (eds. M.E. Shils and V.R. Young), pp. 268–77. Lea and Febiger, Philadelphia.

Anderson, R.A. and Guttman, H.N. (1988). Trace minerals and exercise. In *Exercise, Nutrition and Energy Metabolsim* (eds. E.S. Horton and R.L. Terjung), pp. 180–95. Macmillan, New York.

Anderson, R.A. and Kozlovsky, A.S. (1985). Chromium intake, absorption and excretion of subjects consuming self selected diets. *American Journal of Clinical Nutrition*, **41**, 1177–83.

Anderson, R.A., Polansky, M.M. and Bryden, N.A. (1984). Strenuous running: Acute effects on chromium, copper, zinc, and selected clinical variables in urine and serum of male runners. *Biology Trace Element Research*, **6**, 327–36.

Anderson, R.A., Bryden, N.A., Polansky, M.M. and Deuster, P.A. (1988). Exercise effects on chromium excretion of trained and untrained men consuming a constant diet. *Journal of Applied Physiology*, **64**, 249–52.

Anderson, R.A., Bryden, N.A., Polansky, M.M. and Reiser, S. (1990). Urinary chromium excretion and insulinogenic properties of carbohydrates. *American Journal of Clinical Nutrition*, **51**, 864–8.

Aruoma, O.I., Reilly, T., MacLaren, D. and Halliwell, B. (1988). Iron, copper and zinc concentrations in human sweat and plasma; the effect of exercise. *Clinica Chimica Acta*, **177**, 81–8.

Balaban, E.P., Cox, J.V., Snell, P., Vaughan, R.H. and Frenkel, E.P. (1989). The frequency of anemia and iron deficiency in the runner. *Medicine and Science in Sports and Exercise*, **21**, 643–8.

Bazzarre, T.L., Marquart, L.F., Izurieta, M. and Jones, A. (1986). Incidence of poor nutritional status among triathletes, endurance athletes and control subjects. *Medicine and Science in Sports and Exercise*, **18**, S90 (abstract).

Benson, J., Gillien, D.M., Bourdet, K. and Loosli, A.R. (1985). Inadequate nutrition and chronic calorie restriction in adolescent ballerinas. *Physician and Sportsmedicine*, **13**, 79–90.

Berning, J. (1986). Swimmers' nutrition, knowledge and practice. *Sports Nutrition News*, **4**, 1–4.

Birge, S.J. and Dalsky, G. (1989). The role of exercise in preventing osteoporosis. *Public Health Report*, **104**, Suppl. 54–8.

Blum, S.M., Sherman, A.R. and Boileau, R.A. (1986). The effects of fitness-type exercise on iron status in adult women. *American Journal of Clinical Nutrition*, **43**, 456–63.

Bray, T.M. and Bettger, W.J. (1990). The physiological role of zinc as an antioxidant. *Free Radical Biology and Medicine*, **8**, 281–91.

Brotherhood, J.R. (1984). Nutrition and sports performance. *Sports Medicine*, **1**, 350–89.

Bucci, L.R. (1989). Nutritional ergogenic aids. In *Nutrition in Exercise and Sport* (eds. J.E. Hickson and I. Wolinsky), pp. 107–84. CRC Press, Boca Raton, Florida.

Burke, L.M. and Read, R.S.D. (1987). Diet patterns of elite Australian male triathletes. *Physician and Sportsmedicine*, **15**, 140–55.

Cade, R., Conte, M., Zauner, C., Mars, D., Peterson, J., Lunne, D., Hommen, N. and Packer, D. (1984). Effects of phosphate loading on 2,3-diphosphoglycerate and maximal osygen uptake. *Medicine and Science in Sports and Exercise*, **16**, 263–8.

Calabrese, L.H., Kirkendall, D.T., Floyd, M., Rapoport, S., Williams, G.W., Weiker, G.G. and Bergfeld, J.A. (1983). Menstrual abnormalities, nutritional patterns, and body composition in female classical ballet dancers. *Physician and Sportsmedicine*, 11, 86–98.

Campbell, W.W. and Anderson, R.A. (1987). Effect of aerobic exercise and training on the trace minerals chromium, zinc, and copper. *Sports Medicine*, 4, 9–18.

Casoni, I., Borsetto, C., Cavicchi, A., Martinelli, S. and Conconi, F. (1985). Reduced hemoglobin concentration and red cell hemoglobinization in Italian marathon and ultramarathon runners. *International Journal of Sports Medicine*, 6, 176–9.

Casoni, I., Guglielmini, C., Graziano, L., Reali, M.G., Mazzotta, D. and Abbasciano, V. (1990). Changes in magnesium concentrations in endurance athletes. *International Journal of Sports Medicine*, 11, 234–7.

Celsing, F., Blomstrand, E., Werner, B., Pihlstedt, P. and Ekblom, B. (1986). Effects of iron deficiency on endurance on muscle enzyme activity in man. *Medicine and Science in Sports and Exercise*, 18, 156–61.

Clarkson, P.M. (1991) Vitamins and trace minerals. In *Prospectives in Exercise Science and Sports Medicine*, Vol. 4 (eds. D.R. Lamb and M.H. Williams), in press. Benchmark Press, Indianapolis.

Clement, D.B. and Asmundson, R.C. (1982). Nutritional intake and hematological parameters in endurance runners. *Physician and Sportsmedicine*, 10, 37–43.

Clement, D.B. and Sawchuk, L.L. (1984). Iron status and sports performance. *Sports Medicine*, 1, 65–74.

Cohen, J.L., Potosnak, L., Frank, O. and Baker, H. (1985). A nutritional and hematological assessment of elite ballet dancers. *Physician and Sportsmedicine*, 13, 43–54.

Conn, C.A., Ryder, E., Schemmel, R.A., Ku, P., Seefeldt, V. and Heusner, W.W. (1986). Relationship of maximal oxygen consumption to plasma and erythrocyte magnesium and to plasma copper levels in elite young runners and controls. *Federation Proceedings*, 45, 972 (abstract).

Costill, D.L. and Miller, J.M. (1980). Nutrition for endurance sport: Carbohydrate and fluid balance. *International Journal of Sports Medicine*, 1, 1–14.

Couzy, F., Lafargue, P. and Guezennec, C.Y. (1990). Zinc metabolism in the athlete: Influence of training nutrition and other factors. *International Journal of Sports Medicine*, 11, 263–6.

Dale, G., Fleetwood, J.A., Inkster, J.S. and Sainsbury, J.R.C. (1986). Profound hypophosphataemia in patients collapsing after a 'fun run'. *British Medical Journal*, 292, 447–8.

Dalsky, G.P., Stocke, K.S., Ehsani, A.A., Slatopolsky, E., Lee, W.C. and Birge, S.J. (1988). Weight bearing exercise training and lumber bone mineral content in postmenopausal women. *Annals Internal Medicine*, 198, 824–8.

Davee, A.M., Rosen, C.J. and Adler, R.A. (1990). Exercise patterns and trabecular bone density in college women. *Journal of Bone Mineral Research*, 5, 245–50.

Deuster, P.A., Kyle, S.B., Moser, P.B., Vigersky, R.A., Singh, A. and Schoomaker, E.B. (1986). Nutritional survey of highly trained women runners. *American Journal of Clinical Nutrition*, 44, 954–62.

Deuster, P.A., Dolev, E., Kyle, S.B., Anderson, R.A. and Schoomaker, E.B. (1987). Magnesium homeostasis during high-intensity anaerobic exercise in men. *Journal of Applied Physiology*, **62**, 545–50.

Dowdy, R.P. and Burt, J. (1980). Effect of intensive, long-term training on copper and iron nutriture in man. *Federation Proceedings*, **39**, 786 (abstract).

Dressendorfer, R.H. and Sockolov, R. (1980). Hypozincemia in runners. *Physician and Sportsmedicine*, **8**, 97–100.

Dressendorfer, R.H., Wade, C.E., Keen, C.L. and Scaff, J.H. (1982). Plasma mineral levels in marathon runners during a 20-day road race. *Physician and Sportsmedicine*, **10**, 113–18.

Drinkwater, B.L., Nilson, K., Chestnut III, C.H., Bremmer, W.J., Shainholtz, S. and Southworth, M.B. (1984). Bone mineral content of amenorrheic and eumenorrheic athletes. *New England Journal of Medicine*, **311**, 277–81.

Drinkwater, B.L., Nilson, K., Ott, S. and Chestnut III, C.H. (1986). Bone mineral density after resumption of menses in amenorrheic athletes. *Journal of the American Medical Association*, **256**, 380–2.

Dufaux, B., Hoederath, A., Streitberger, I., Hollmann, W. and Assmann, G. (1981). Serum ferritin, transferrin, haptoglobin, and iron in middle- and long-distance runners, elite rowers, and professional racing cyclists. *International Journal of Sports Medicine*, **2**, 43–6.

Duffy, D.J. and Conlee, R.K. (1986). Effects of phosphate loading on leg power and high intensity treadmill exercise. *Medicine and Science in Sports and Exercise*, **18**, 674–7.

Ehn, L., Carlmark, B. and Hoglund, S. (1980). Iron status in athletes involved in intense physical activity. *Medicine and Science in Sports and Exercise*, **12**, 61–4.

Eichner, E.R. (1986). The anemias of athletes. *Physician and Sportsmedicine*, **14**, 122–30.

Ellsworth, N.M., Hewitt, B.F. and Haskell, W.L. (1985). Nutrient intake of elite male and female nordic skiers. *Physician and Sportsmedicine*, **13**, 78–92.

Evans, G.W. (1989). The effect of chromium picolinate on insulin controlled parameters in humans. *International Journal of Bioscience Research*, **1**, 163–80.

Fischer, P.W.F., L'Abbe, M.R. and Giroux, A. (1990). Effects of age, smoking, drinking, exercise and estrogen use on indices of copper status in healthy adults. *Nutrition Research*, **10**, 1081–90.

Franz, K.B., Ruddel, H., Todd, G.L., Dorheim, T.A., Buell, J.C. and Eliot, R.S. (1985). Physiological changes during a marathon, with special reference to magnesium. *Journal of the American College of Nutrition*, **4**, 187–94.

Goldfarb, A.H., Todd, M.K., Boyer, B.T., Alessio, H.M. and Cutler, R.G. (1989). Effect of vitamin E on lipid peroxidation at 80% VO_2 max. *Medicine and Science in Sports and Exercise*, **21**, S16 (abstract).

Golf, S.W., Happel, O. and Graef, V. (1984). Plasma aldosterone, cortisol and electrolyte concentrations in physical exercise after magnesium supplementation. *Journal of Clinical Chemistry and Clinical Biochemistry*, **22**, 717–21.

Greenleaf, J.E. and Brock, P.J. (1980). Na^+ and Ca^+ ingestion: plasma volume-electrolyte distribution at rest and exercise. *Journal of Applied Physiology*, **48**, 838–42.

Gutteridge, J.M.C., Rowley, D.A., Halliwell, B., Cooper, D.F. and Heeley, D.M. (1985). Copper and iron complexes catalytic for oxygen radical reactions in sweat from human athletes. *Clinica Chimica Acta*, **145**, 267–73.

Hackman, R.M. and Keen, C.L. (1983). Trace element assessment of runners. *Federation Proceedings*, **42**, 830 (abstract).

Hackman, R.M. and Keen, C.L. (1986). Changes in serum zinc and copper levels after zinc supplementation in running and non-running men. In *Sport Health and Nutrition: 1984 Olympic Scientific Congress Proceedings*, Vol. 2 (ed. F.I. Katch), pp. 89–99. Human Kinetics Publications, Champaign, IL.

Haralambie, G. (1981). Serum zinc in athletes in training. *International Journal of Sports Medicine*, **2**, 135–8.

Haymes, E.M. (1987). Nutritional concerns: need for iron. *Medicine and Science in Sports and Exercise*, **19**, S197–S200.

Hetland, O., Brubak, E.A., Refsum, H.E. and Stromme, S.B. (1975). Serum and erythrocyte zinc concentrations after prolonged heavy exercise. In *Metabolic Adaptation to Prolonged Physical Exercise* (eds. H. Howard and J. Poortmans), pp. 367–70. Birkhausen Verlag, Basel.

Hunt, S.M. and Groff, J.L. (1990). *Advanced Nutrition and Human Metabolism*, pp. 264–348. West Publishing Company, St. Paul.

Kanter, M.M., Lesmes, G.R., Kaminsky, L.A., La Ham-Saeger, J. and Nequin, N.D. (1988). Serum creatine kinase and lactate dehydrogenase changes following an eighty kilometer race. *European Journal of Applied Physiology*, **57**, 60–3.

Keen, C.L. and Gershwin, M.E. (1990). Zinc deficiency and immune function. *Annual Review of Nutrition*, **10**, 415–31.

Kreider, R.B., Miller, G.W., Williams, M.H., Somma, C.T. and Nasser, T.A. (1990). Effects of phosphate loading on oxygen uptake, ventilatory anaerobic threshold, and run performance. *Medicine and Science in Sports and Exercise*, **22**, 250–6.

Krotkiewski, M., Gudmundsson, M., Backstrom, P. and Mandroukas, K. (1982). Zinc and muscle strength and endurance. *Acta Physiologica Scandanavica*, **116**, 309–11.

Lamanca, J.J., Haymes, E.M., Daly, J.A., Moffatt, R.J. and Waller, M.F. (1988). Sweat iron loss of male and female runners during exercise. *International Journal of Sports Medicine*, **9**, 52–5.

Lampe, J.W., Slavin, J.L. and Apple, F.S. (1986). Poor iron status of women runners training for a marathon. *International Journal of Sports Medicine*, **7**, 111–14.

Lane, H.W. (1989). Some trace elements related to physical activity: zinc, copper, selenium, chromium, and iodine. In *Nutrition in Exercise and Sport* (eds. J.E. Hickson and I. Wolinsky), pp. 301–7. CRC Press, Boca Raton, Florida.

Lane, N.E., Bloch, D.A., Jones, H.H., Marshall, W.H., Wood, P.D. and Fries, J.F. (1986). Long-distance running, bone density, and osteoarthritis. *Journal of American Medical Association*, **255**, 1147–51.

Lemon, P.W.R. (1989). Nutrition for muscular development of young athletes. In *Prospectives in Exercise Science and Sports Medicine. Vol. 2: Youth, Exercise, and Sport* (eds. C.V. Gisolfi and D.R. Lamb), pp. 369–400. Benchmark Press, Indianapolis.

Lindsay, R. (1987). Estrogens and osteoporosis. *Physician and Sportsmedicine*, **15**, 91–108.

Lijnen, P., Hespel, P., Fagard, R., Lysens, R., Vanden Eynde, E. and Amery, A. (1988). Erythrocyte, plasma and urinary magnesium in men before and after a marathon. *European Journal of Applied Physiology*, **58**, 252–6.

Loosli, A.R., Benson, J., Gillien, D.M. and Bourdet, K. (1986). Nutrition habits and knowledge in competitive adolescent female gymnasts. *Physician and Sportsmedicine*, **14**, 118–30.

Lukaski, H.C. (1989a). Influence of physical training on human copper nutritional status. *Abstracts of the American Chemical Society*, **197**, 91.

Lukaski, H.C. (1989b). Effects of exercise training on human copper and zinc nutrition. *Advances in Experimental Medicine and Biology*, **258**, 163–70.

Lukaski, H.C., Bolonchuk, W.W., Klevay, L.M., Milne, D.B. and Sandstead, H.H. (1983). Maximum oxygen consumption as related to magnesium, copper, and zinc nutriture. *American Journal of Clinical Nutrition*, **37**, 407–15.

Lukaski, H.C., Bolonchuk, W.W., Klevay, L.M., Milne, D.B. and Sandstead, H.H. (1984). Changes in plasma zinc content after exercise in men fed a low-zinc diet. *American Journal of Physiology*, **247**, E88–E93.

Mader, A., Hartmann, U., Fischer, H.G., Reinhards-Mader, G., Bohnert, K.J. and Hollmann, W. (1990). Magnesiumsubstitution im hohentraining der rud-ernationalmannschaft in vorbereitung auf die olympischen spiele – ergebnisse einer kontrollierten studie. *Magnesium-Bullitin*, **12**, 69–78 (abstract in English).

Marrella, M., Guerrini, F., Tregnaghi, P.L., Nocini, S., Velo, G.P. and Milanino, R. (1990). Effect of copper, zinc and ceruloplasmin levels in blood of athletes. *Metal Ions in Biology and Medicine*. Proceedings of the 1st International Symposium, 16–19 May 1990, pp. 111–13.

Magazanik, A., Weinstein, Y., Dlin, R.A., Derin, M. and Schwartzman, S. (1988). Iron deficiency caused by 7 weeks of intensive physical exercise. *European Journal of Applied Physiology*, **57**, 198–202.

Marieb, E.N. (1989). *Human Anatomy and Physiology*, pp. 814–18. Benjamin/Cummings, Redwood City, CA.

Matter, M., Stittfall, T., Graves, J., Myburgh, K., Adams, B., Jacobs, P. and Noakes, T.D. (1987). The effect of iron and folate therapy on maximal exercise performance in female marathon runners with iron and folate deficiency. *Clinical Science*, **72**, 415–22.

Maughan, R.J., Donnelly, A.E., Gleeson, M., Whiting, P.H. and Walker, K.A. (1989). Delayed-onset muscle damage and lipid peroxidation in man after a downhill run. *Muscle and Nerve*, **12**, 332–6.

McDonald, R. and Keen, C.L. (1988). Iron, zinc and magnesium nutrition and athletic performance. *Sports Medicine*, **5**, 171–84.

Mouton, G., Sluse, F.E., Bertrand, A., Welter, A. and Cabay, J.L. (1990). Iron status in runners of various running specialities. *Archives Internationale de Physiologie et Biochimie*, **98**, 103–9.

Myburgh, K.H., Hutchins, J., Fataar, A.B., Hough, S.F. and Noakes, T.D. (1990). Low bone density is an etiologic factor for stress fractures in athletes. *Ann. International Medicine*, **113**, 754–9.

National Research Council. (1989). *Recommended Dietary Allowances*, 10th Edition. National Academy Press, Washington.

Nelson, M., Black, A.E., Morris, J.A. and Cole, T.J. (1989). Between- and within-subject variation in nutrient intake from infancy to old age: estimating the number of days required to rank dietary intakes with desired precision. *American Journal of Clinical Nutrition*, **50**, 155–67.

Newhouse, I.J., Clement, D.B., Taunton, J.E. and McKenzie, D.C. (1989). The effects of prelatent/latent iron deficiency on physical work capacity. *Medicine and Science in Sports and Exercise*, **21**, 263–8.

Nieman, D.C., Butler, J.V., Pollett, L.M., Dietrich, S.J. and Lutz, R.D. (1989). Nutrient intake of marathon runners. *Journal of the American Dietician Association*, **89**, 1273–8.

Ohno, H., Yahata, T., Hirata, F., Yamamura, K., Doi, R., Harada, M. and Taniguchi, N. (1984). Changes in dopamine-Beta-hydroxylase, and copper, and catecholamine concentrations in human plasma with physical exercise. *Journal of Sports Medicine*, **24**, 315–20.

Ohno, H., Yamashita, K., Doi, R., Yamamura, K., Kondo, T. and Taniguchi, N. (1985). Exercise-induced changes in blood zinc and related proteins in humans. *Journal of Applied Physiology*, **58**, 1453–8.

Ohno, H., Sato, Y., Ishikawa, M., Yahata, T., Gasa, S., Doi, R., Yamamura, K. and Taniguchi, N. (1990). Training effects on blood zinc levels in humans. *Journal of Sports Medicine and Physical Fitness*, **30**, 247–53.

Olha, A.E., Klissouras, V., Sullivan, J.D. and Skoryna, S.C. (1982). Effect of exercise on concentration of elements in the serum. *Journal of Sports Medicine*, **22**, 414–25.

O'Toole, M.L., Iwane, H., Douglas, P.S., Applegate, E.A. and Hiller, W.D.B. (1989). Iron status in ultraendurance triathletes. *Physician and Sportsmedicine*, **17**, 90–102.

Parr, R.B., Porter, M.A. and Hodgson, S.C. (1984). Nutrition knowledge and practices of coaches, trainers, and athletes. *Physician and Sportsmedicine*, **12**, 126–38.

Pate, R.R. (1983). Sports anemia: a review of the current research literature. *Physician and Sportsmedicine*, **11**, 115–31.

Pattini, A., Schena, F. and Guidi, G.C. (1990). Serum ferritin and serum iron changes after cross-country and roller ski endurance races. *European Journal of Applied Physiology*, **61**, 55–60.

Peters, A.J., Dressendorfer, R.H., Rimar, J. and Keen, C.L. (1986). Diet of endurance runners competing in a 20-day road race. *Physician and Sportsmedicine*, **14**, 63–70.

Plowman, S.A. and McSwegin, P.C. (1981). The effects of iron supplementation on female cross country runners. *Journal of Sports Medicine*, **21**, 407–16.

Ricci, G., Masotti, M., DePaoli Vitali, E., Vedovato, M. and Zanotti, G. (1988). Effects of exercise on haematologic parameters, serum iron, serum ferritin, red cell 2,3-diphosphoglycerate and creatine content, and serum erythropoietin in long-distance runners during basal training. *Acta Haematologica*, **80**, 95–8.

Risser, W.L. and Risser, J.M.H. (1990). Iron deficiency in adolescents and young athletes. *Physician and Sportsmedicine*, **18**, 87–101.

Risser, W.L., Lee, E.J., Poindexter, H.B.W., West, M.S., Pivarnik, J.M., Risser, J.M.H. and Hickson, J.F. (1988). Iron deficiency in female athletes: its prevalence and impact on performance. *Medicine and Science in Sports and Exercise*, **20**, 116–21.

Rose, L.I., Carroll, D.R., Lowe, S.L., Peterson, E.W. and Cooper, K.H. (1970). Serum electrolyte changes after marathon running. *Journal of Applied Physiology*, **29**, 449–51.

Rowland, T.W. (1990). Iron deficiency in the young athlete. *Sports Medicine*, **37**, 1153–63.

Rowland, T.W., Deisroth, M.B., Green, G.M. and Kelleher, J.F. (1988). The effect of iron therapy on the exercise capacity of nonanemic iron-deficient adolescent runners. *American Journal of Diseases of Children*, **142**, 165–9.

Sanborn, C.F. (1990). Exercise, calcium, and bone density. *Sports Science Exchange*, Gatorade Sport Science Institute, **2** (24).

Schoene, R.B., Escourrou, P., Robertson, H.T., Nilson, K.L., Parsons, J.R. and Smith, N.J. (1983). Iron repletion decreases maximal exercise lactate concentrations in female athletes with minimal iron-deficiency anemia. *Journal of Laboratory Clinical Medicine*, **102**, 306–12.

Selby, G.B. and Eichner, E.R. (1989). Age-related increases of iron stores in athletes. *Medicine and Science in Sports and Exercise*, **21**, S78 (abstract).

Sherman, A.R. and Kramer, B. (1989). Iron nutrition and exercise. In *Nutrition in Exercise and Sport* (eds. J.E. Hickson and I. Wolinsky), pp. 291–300. CRC Press, Boca Raton, Florida.

Short, S.H. (1989). Dietary surveys and nutrition knowledge. In *Nutriton in Exercise and Sport* (eds. J.E. Hickson and I. Wolinsky), pp. 309–43. CRC Press, Boca Raton, Florida.

Singh, A., Deuster, P.A. and Moser, P.B. (1990). Zinc and copper status in women by physical activity and menstrual status. *Journal of Sports Medicine and Physical Fitness*, **30**, 29–36.

Snyder, A.C., Dvorak, L.L. and Roepke, J.B. (1989). Influence of dietary iron source on measures of iron status among female runners. *Medicine and Science in Sports and Exercise*, **21**, 7–10.

Steel, J.E. (1970). A nutritional study of Australian Olympic athletes. *Medical Journal, Australia*, **2**, 119–23.

Steen, S.N. and McKinney, S. (1986). Nutritional assessment of college wrestlers. *Physician and Sportsmedicine*, **14**, 101–16.

Stendig-Lindberg, G., Shapiro, Y., Epstein, Y., Galun, E., Schonberger, E., Graff, E. and Wacker, W.E. (1988). Changes in serum magnesium concentration after strenuous exercise. *Journal of the American College of Nutrition*, **6**, 35–40.

Van Erp-Baart, A.M.J., Saris, W.M.H., Binkhorst, R.A., Vos, J.A. and Elvers, J.W.H. (1989). Nationwide survey on nutritional habits in elite athletes. Part II. Mineral and vitamin intake. *International Journal of Sports Medicine*, **10**, S11–S16.

Weatherwax, R.S., Ahlberg, A., Deady, M., Otto, R.M., Perez, H.R., Cooperstein, D. and Wygand, J. (1986). Effects of phosphate loading on bicycle time trial performance. *Medicine and Science in Sports and Exercise*, **18**, S11–S12 (abstract).

Weight, L.M., Noakes, T.D., Labadarios, D., Graves, J., Jacobs, P. and Berman, P.A. (1988). Vitamin and mineral status of trained athletes including the effects of supplementation. *American Journal of Clinical Nutrition*, **47**, 186–91.

Welch, P.K., Zager, K.A., Endres, J. and Poon, S.W. (1987). Nutrition education, body composition, and dietary intake of female college athletes. *Physician and Sportsmedicine*, **15**, 63–74.

Wilmore, J.H. and Freund, B.J. (1984). Nutritional enhancement of athletic performance. *Nutrition Abstracts and Reviews, Reviews in Clinical Nutrition*, **54**, 1–16.

Wishnitzer, R., Vorst, E. and Berrebi, A. (1983). Bone marrow iron depression in competitive distance runners. *International Journal of Sports Medicine*, **4**, 27–30.

8

Fluid and electrolyte loss and replacement in exercise*

R.J. Maughan

8.1 INTRODUCTION

Fatigue is an inevitable accompaniment of prolonged strenuous exercise, but the nature of the fatigue process will be influenced by many factors. The most important of these is undoubtedly the intensity of the exercise in relation to the capacity of the individual, and the most effective way to delay the onset of fatigue and improve performance is by training. The primary cause of fatigue in exercise lasting more than 1 h but not more than 4–5 h is usually the depletion of the body's carbohydrate reserves. This time scale covers most ball games such as football, hockey and tennis, and also individual events such as marathon running. Systematic training results in many adaptations to the cardiovascular system and to the muscles, allowing them to increase the extent to which they can use the relatively unlimited fat stores as a fuel and thus spare the rather small amounts of carbohydrate which are stored in the liver and in the muscles. Where the availability of carbohydrate fuel limits exercise, this will result in an improved performance.

Many other factors will, however, influence performance, and among these are the environmental conditions under which the exercise is

*This chapter is based on a review presented to the Gatorade Sports Science Conference in June 1990 and published in *Perspectives in Exercise Science and Sports Medicine, Volume 4: Ergogenics: The Enhancement of Sport Performance*, edited by D.R. Lamb and M.H. Williams. Benchmark Press: Carmel, pp. 35–85, 1991.

Food, Nutrition and Sports Performance
Edited by Clyde Williams and John T. Devlin
Published in 1992 by E & F N Spon, London. ISBN 0 419 17890 2

performed. When the ambient temperature and humidity are high, the capacity to perform prolonged exercise is reduced: in this situation, dehydration and thermoregulatory problems may be a cause of fatigue. At high ambient temperatures, endurance time in laboratory tests may be reduced to less than half of that when the temperature is low; since the rate of carbohydrate utilization is essentially the same under both conditions, it appears that the earlier onset of fatigue is related directly to the increased heat stress rather than to glycogen depletion. At rest, the rate of heat production by the body is low, but at high work rates, metabolic heat production can exceed 80 kJ min^{-1} (20 kcal min^{-1}), and highly trained athletes can sustain these work rates for more than 2 h. The rate of sweating necessary to prevent an excessive rise in body temperature will result in a rapid loss of body water with an associated loss of electrolytes. Fluid ingestion during exercise has the twin aims of providing a source of carbohydrate fuel to supplement the body's limited stores and of supplying water to replace the losses incurred by sweating. In some situations there may also be a need to replace the electrolytes which are lost in sweat. Increasing the carbohydrate content of drinks will increase the amount of fuel which can be supplied, but will tend to decrease the rate at which water can be made available.

Where provision of water is the first priority, as in very prolonged events at a high ambient temperature, the carbohydrate content of drinks will be low, thus restricting the rate at which substrate is provided. The composition of drinks taken should thus be determined by the relative needs to supply fuel and water. This in turn depends on the intensity and duration of the exercise task, on the ambient temperature and humidity, and on the physiological and biochemical characteristics of the individual athlete. Carbohydrate depletion will result in fatigue and a reduction in the exercise intensity that can be sustained, but is not normally a life-threatening situation. Disturbances in fluid and electrolyte balance and in temperature regulation have potentially more serious consequences, and it may be, therefore, that the emphasis for the majority of participants in endurance events should be on proper maintenance of fluid and electrolyte balance.

8.2 AVAILABILITY OF INGESTED FLUIDS

The availability of ingested fluids depends on the rates of gastric emptying and intestinal absorption. The techniques used to measure these processes, and some of the limitations to these techniques, are described by Leiper and Maughan (1988). The first barrier to the availability of ingested fluids is the rate of gastric emptying, which controls the rate at which fluids are delivered to the small intestine and the extent to which they are influenced by the gastric secretions. The rate of emptying is determined by the volume and composition of fluid consumed. The volume of the stomach contents is a major factor in regulating the rate of emptying; emptying follows an exponential time course, and falls rapidly as the volume remaining in the stomach decreases (Leiper and Maughan, 1988; Rehrer *et al.*, 1989a). Where a high rate of emptying is desirable, this can be promoted by keeping the volume high by repeated drinking. Dilute carbohydrate solutions will leave the stomach almost, but not quite, as fast as plain water; the rate of emptying is slowed in proportion to the carbohydrate content, and concentrated solutions will remain in the stomach for long periods. The effect of carbohydrate concentration on the time course of emptying is shown in Fig. 8.1. It has been proposed that the rate of emptying of nutrient solutions is regulated so as to provide a constant rate of energy delivery to the intestine (Brener *et al.*, 1983), but it is clear from Fig. 8.1 that the rate of energy delivery is proportional to the carbohydrate concentration of the drinks; even though the volume emptied is decreased, the amount of glucose emptied is increased with more concentrated solutions.

An increasing osmolality of the gastric contents will tend to delay emptying, and there is some evidence that substitution of glucose polymers for free glucose, which will result in a decreased osmolality for the same carbohydrate content, may be effective in increasing the volume of fluid and the amount of substrate delivered to the intestine. The differences, however, are generally small, with the exception of a report by Foster *et al.* (1980), who found that emptying of a 5% glucose polymer solution was about one-third faster than that of a 5% solution of free glucose: the results of this study may, however, be misleading as no account was taken of the volume of fluid secreted into the stomach, and this is now known to be greater for solutions of free glucose than for polymers (Sole and Noakes, 1989; Rehrer 1990). Sole and Noakes (1989) found no significant difference in emptying rates between 5% polymer and free glucose solutions, and Naveri *et al.* (1989) made the same observation on 3% solutions. With more concentrated solutions, Foster *et al.* (1980) found no differences between polymer and free glucose solutions in the concentration range 10–40%, but Sole and Noakes (1989) found that 15% polymer solutions emptied faster than the corresponding free glucose solution. It thus appears that the results are rather variable, but it is worth noting that there are no reports of polymer solutions being emptied more slowly than free glucose solutions with the same energy density: even when the difference is not significant, there is a tendency for faster emptying of polymer solutions.

The temperature of ingested drinks may also have an influence on the rate of emptying. Costill and Saltin (1974) gave subjects 400 ml of a

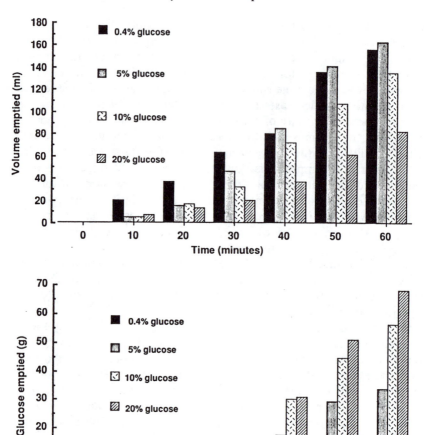

Fig. 8.1 Effects of glucose concentration on the rate of gastric emptying in six healthy male subjects at rest. This study used gamma scintigraphy to measure the time course of gastric emptying of drinks, and illustrates some of the problems which arise when only a single time point measurement is made.

Upper panel: Volume of solution emptied after ingestion of 200 ml of flavoured water (0.4% glucose) or solutions containing 5%, 10% or 20% glucose. The initial rate of emptying is higher for water than for the glucose solutions when such low volumes of drink are given: at 30 min, differences are apparent between all solutions.

Lower panel: Amount of glucose emptied from the stomach when these solutions are consumed. Although the volume emptied is generally greatest for the lowest glucose concentrations, the amount of glucose emptied tends to increase as the glucose concentration increases.

dilute glucose solution at temperatures ranging from 5–35° C: the volume emptied in the first 15 min after ingestion was approximately twice as great for the solution at 5° C as for the solution at 35° C. More recent reports, however, have cast some doubt on the importance of temperature in affecting emptying of liquids. Sun *et al.* (1988) gave isosmotic orange juice at different temperatures, and found that the initial emptying rate for cold (4° C) drinks was slower than for drinks given at body temperature (37° C): the emptying rate for warm (50° C) drinks was not significantly different from that for the other two drinks. McArthur and Feldman (1989) have also recently shown that the emptying rate for coffee drinks given at 4, 37 or 58° C was not different. Other factors, such as pH, may have a minor role to play. Interestingly, in view of the introduction of carbonated sports drinks, there is some evidence that emptying is hastened if drinks are carbonated (Lolli *et al.*, 1952). Highly carbonated drinks, however, are likely to cause gastrointestinal distress and should be avoided.

Absorption of glucose occurs in the small intestine, and is an active, energy-consuming process linked to the transport of sodium. There is no active transport mechanism for water, which will cross the intestinal mucosa in either direction depending on the local osmotic gradients. The rate of glucose uptake is dependent on the luminal concentrations of glucose and sodium, and dilute glucose electrolyte solutions with an osmolality which is slightly hypotonic with respect to plasma will maximize the rate of water uptake (Wapnir and Lifshitz, 1985). Solutions with a very high glucose concentration will not necessarily promote an increased glucose uptake relative to more dilute solutions, but, because of their high osmolality, will cause a net movement of fluid into the intestinal lumen. This results in an effective loss of body water and will exacerbate any pre-existing dehydration. Other sugars, such as sucrose (Spiller *et al.*, 1982) or glucose polymers (Jones *et al.*, 1983, 1987) can be substituted for glucose without impairing glucose or water uptake. In contrast, the absorption of fructose is not an active process in man: it is absorbed less rapidly than glucose and promotes less water uptake (Fordtran, 1975).

Several studies have shown that exercise at intensities of less than about 70% of VO_2 max has little or no effect on intestinal function, although both gastric emptying and intestinal absorption may be reduced when the exercise intensity exceeds this level (Fordtran and Saltin, 1967; Costill and Saltin, 1974). These studies have been reviewed and summarized by Brouns *et al.* (1987).

Some recent results, using an isotopic tracer technique to follow ingested fluids, have suggested that there may be a decreased availability of ingested fluids even during low-intensity exercise (Fig. 8.2).

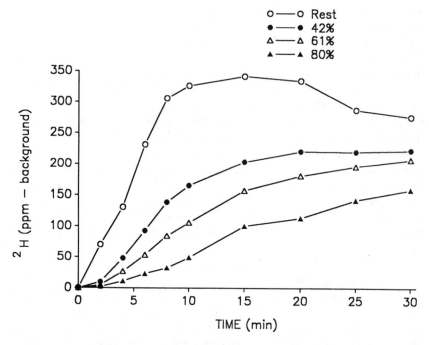

Fig. 8.2 Effect of exercise intensity on the accumulation in blood of a deuterium tracer. Reproduced from Maughan *et al.* (1990) where further details of the experimental method are given.

8.3   METABOLIC EFFECTS OF CARBOHYDRATE INGESTION DURING EXERCISE

Once emptied from the stomach and absorbed in the small intestine, carbohydrates ingested during exercise will enter the blood glucose pool, either directly or after metabolism in the liver. In the later stages of prolonged exercise, a fall in the circulating glucose concentration is commonly observed, and ingestion of glucose during exercise will maintain or raise the blood glucose concentration compared with the situation where no glucose is given (Costill *et al.*, 1973; Pirnay *et al.*, 1982; Erickson *et al.*, 1987). Although there are several studies indicating that maintenance of blood glucose concentration by ingestion of carbohydrate will maintain a higher rate of carbohydrate utilization by muscle and delay the onset of fatigue (see Chapter 3), preventing hypoglycaemia by the administration of CHO will not necessarily delay the point of exhaustion (Felig *et al.*, 1982). Sugars other than glucose are commonly used in the formulation of sports drinks, and there is some justification for their inclusion, as

similar effects are seen with short-chain length (3–10 glucosyl units) glucose polymers (Ivy *et al.*, 1979; Coyle *et al.*, 1983, 1986; Maughan *et al.*,
1987; Coggan and Coyle, 1988; Hargreaves and Briggs, 1988), sucrose
(Sasaki *et al.*, 1987) or mixtures of sugars (Murray *et al.*, 1987; Mitchell
et al., 1988; Carter and Gisolfi, 1989).

One of the aims of ingesting carbohydrate during exercise is to spare
the limited muscle glycogen stores, as there is a good relationship between
the availability of muscle glycogen and endurance capacity (Ahlborg *et
al.*, 1967). It is not clear how effectively this aim can be achieved. It has
been reported that glucose solutions providing 1 g glucose per kg body
weight can reduce the rate of muscle glycogen utilization by about 30%
during 90 min of bicycle exercise at 65–70% of VO_2 max (Erickson *et al.*,
1987). In more prolonged (4 h) exercise consisting of low-intensity cycle
exercise interspersed with high-intensity sprints, Hargreaves *et al.* (1984)
fed subjects either a flavoured placebo or water with a solid feeding of
43 g of sucrose together with small amounts of fat and protein per hour:
the rate of muscle glycogen utilization was not different between the two
trials in the first hour, but over the following 3 h was about 37% lower
on the fed trial. Some other studies, which have employed a variety of
exercise models and have fed different types and amounts of carbohydrate
during exercise, have shown no effect of carbohydrate feeding during
exercise on the rate of muscle glycogen utilization (Fielding *et al.*, 1985;
Coyle *et al.*, 1986; Hargreaves and Briggs, 1988; Noakes *et al.*, 1988). The
reason for these different results is not clear, and may be partly explained
by differences in the type and amount of carbohydrate given, by the
different exercise models used, and by differences in the training status
of the subjects. Nutritional status may also be important, and Flynn *et al.*
(1987) found that CHO feeding during exercise had no effect on the rate
of muscle glycogen breakdown when this was elevated prior to exercise
by a CHO-loading procedure.

The ready availability of ingested carbohydrate as a fuel for the working
muscles is demonstrated by studies which have followed the appearance
in expired air of isotopes of carbon added as tracers (Rehrer, 1990).

8.4 FLUID LOSS AND TEMPERATURE REGULATION

Fluid loss during exercise is linked to the need to maintain body temperature within narrow limits. At rest the rate of energy turnover is low; the
resting oxygen consumption is about 250 ml min^{-1}, corresponding to a
rate of heat production of about 70 W. During exercise, the rate of heat
production can be increased to many times this level. Running a marathon
in 2 h 30 min requires an oxygen consumption of about 4 l min^{-1} to be

sustained throughout the race for a runner with a body weight of 70 kg. When the ambient temperature is higher than skin temperature, heat will also be gained from the environment by physical transfer. In spite of this, marathon runners normally maintain body temperature within 2–3° C of the resting level, indicating that heat is being lost from the body almost as fast as it is being produced.

At high ambient temperatures, the only mechanism by which heat can be lost from the body is evaporation. Evaporation of 1 l of water from the skin will remove 2.4 MJ (580 kcal) of heat from the body. For the 2 h 30 min marathon runner with a body weight of 70 kg to balance his rate of heat production by evaporative loss alone would therefore require sweat to be evaporated from the skin at a rate of about $1.6 \, l \, h^{-1}$. At such high sweat rates, an appreciable fraction drips from the skin without evaporating, and a sweat secretion rate of about $2 \, l \, h^{-1}$ is likely to be necessary to achieve this rate of evaporative heat loss. This is possible, but would result in the loss of 5 l of body water, corresponding to a loss of more than 7% of body weight for a 70 kg runner. The rise of 2–3° C in body temperature which normally occurs during marathon running means that some of the heat produced is stored, but the effect on heat balance is minimal: a rise in mean body temperature of 3° C for a 70 kg runner would reduce the total requirement for evaporation of sweat by less than 300 ml.

It is often reported that exercise performance is impaired when an individual is dehydrated by as little as 2% of body weight, and that losses in excess of 5% of body weight can decrease the capacity for work by about 30% (Saltin and Costill, 1988). These figures, however, are based on rather unreliable data as the original studies did not employ suitable methods of measuring work capacity; these original data are still widely quoted as there are no more recent studies to replace them. Fluid losses are distributed in varying proportions among the plasma, extracellular water and intracellular water. The decrease in plasma volume which accompanies dehydration may be of particular importance in influencing work capacity; blood flow to the muscles must be maintained at a high level to supply oxygen and substrates, but a high blood flow to the skin is also necessary to convect heat to the body surface where it can be dissipated (Nadel, 1980). When the ambient temperature is high and blood volume has been decreased by sweat loss during prolonged exercise, there may be difficulty in meeting the requirement for a high blood flow to both these tissues. In this situation, skin blood flow is likely to be compromised, allowing central venous pressure and muscle blood flow to be maintained but reducing heat loss and causing body temperature to rise (Rowell, 1986).

8.5 ELECTROLYTE LOSS IN SWEAT AND THE EFFECTS ON BODY FLUIDS

The sweat which is secreted on to the skin contains a wide variety of organic and inorganic solutes, and significant losses of some of these components will occur where large volumes of sweat are produced. The electrolyte composition of sweat is variable, and the concentration of individual electrolytes as well as the total sweat volume will influence the extent of losses. The normal concentration ranges for the main ionic components of sweat are shown in Table 8.1, along with their plasma and intracellular concentrations for comparison.

A number of factors contribute to the variability in the composition of sweat: methodological problems in the collection procedure, including evaporative loss, incomplete collection and contamination with skin cells account for at least part of the variability, but there is also a large biological variability.

Table 8.1 Concentration (in mmol l^{-1}) of the major electrolytes in sweat, plasma and intracellular water. These values are taken from a variety of sources, but are based primarily on those reported by Pitts (1959), Lentner (1981) and Schmidt and Thews (1989)

Electrolyte	Sweat	Plasma	Intracellular
Sodium	20–80	130–155	10
Potassium	4–8	3.2–5.5	150
Calcium	0–1	2.1–2.9	0
Magnesium	<2.0	0.7–1.5	15
Chloride	20–60	96–110	8
Bicarbonate	0–35	23–28	10
Phosphate	0.1–0.2	0.7–1.6	65
Sulphate	0.1–2.0	0.3–0.9	10

The sweat composition undoubtedly varies between individuals, but can also vary within the same individual depending on the rate of secretion, the state of training and the state of heat acclimation (Leithead and Lind, 1964). In response to a standard heat stress, the sweat rate increases with training and acclimation and the electrolyte content decreases. These adaptations allow improved thermoregulation while conserving electrolytes.

The major electrolytes in sweat, as in the extracellular fluid, are sodium and chloride (Table 8.1), although the sweat concentrations are invariably lower than those in plasma. Contrary to what might be expected, Costill

(1977) reported an increased sodium and chloride sweat content with increased flow, but Verde *et al.* (1982) found that the sweat concentration of these ions was unrelated to the sweat flow rate. Acclimation studies have shown that elevated sweating rates are accompanied by a decrease in the concentration of sodium and chloride in sweat (Allan and Wilson, 1971; Kobayashi *et al.*, 1980). These apparently conflicting results demonstrate some of the difficulties in interpreting the literature in this area. Differences between studies may be due to differences in training status and degree of acclimation of the subjects used as well as difference in methodology: some studies have used whole-body washdown techniques to collect sweat, whereas others have examined local sweating responses using ventilated capsules or collection bags. The potassium content of sweat appears to be relatively unaffected by the sweat rate, and the magnesium content is also unchanged or perhaps decreases slightly.

Because sweat is hypotonic with respect to body fluids, the effect of prolonged sweating is to increase the plasma osmolality, which may have a significant effect on the ability to maintain body temperature. A direct relationship between plasma osmolality and body temperature has been demonstrated during exercise (Greenleaf *et al.*, 1974; Harrison *et al.*, 1978). Hyperosmolality of plasma, induced prior to exercise, has been shown to result in a decreased thermoregulatory effector response; the threshold for sweating is elevated and the cutaneous vasodilator response is reduced (Fortney *et al.*, 1984). In short term (30 min) exercise, however, the cardiovascular and thermoregulatory response appears to be independent of changes in osmolality induced during the exercise period (Fortney *et al.*, 1988). The changes in the concentration of individual electrolytes are more variable, but an increase in the plasma sodium and chloride concentrations is generally observed in response to both running and cycling exercise. Exceptions to this are rare and occur only when excessively large volumes of drinks low in electrolytes are consumed over long time periods; these situations are discussed further below.

The plasma potassium concentration has been reported to remain constant after marathon running (Meytes *et al.*, 1969; Whiting *et al.*, 1984) although others have reported small increases, irrespective of whether drinks containing large amounts of potassium (Kavanagh and Shephard, 1975) or no electrolytes (Costill *et al.*, 1976; Cohen and Zimmerman, 1978) were given. Much of the inconsistency in the literature relating to changes in the circulating potassium concentration can be explained by the variable time taken to obtain blood samples after exercise under field conditions; the plasma potassium concentration rapidly returns to normal in the post-exercise period (Stansbie *et al.*, 1982). Laboratory studies where an indwelling catheter can be used to obtain blood samples during exercise commonly show an increase in the circulating potassium concentration in the later stages of prolonged exercise. The potassium concentration of extracellular fluid (4–5 mmol l^{-1}) is small relative to the intracellular concentration (150–160 mmol l^{-1}), and release of potassium from liver, muscle and red blood cells will tend to elevate plasma potassium levels during exercise in spite of the losses in sweat.

The plasma magnesium concentration is unchanged after 60 min of moderate-intensity cycling exercise (Joborn *et al.*, 1985), but Rose *et al.* (1970) observed a 20% fall in the serum magnesium concentration after a marathon race and attributed this to a loss in sweat; a fall of similar magnitude was reported by Cohen and Zimmerman (1978). A larger fall in the serum magnesium concentration has been observed during exercise in the heat than at neutral temperatures (Beller *et al.*, 1972), supporting the idea that losses in sweat are responsible. There are, however, reports that the fall in plasma magnesium concentration that occurs during prolonged exercise is a consequence of redistribution, with uptake of magnesium by red blood cells (Refsum *et al.*, 1973), active muscle (Costill, 1977) or adipose tissue (Lijnen *et al.*, 1988). Although the concentration of potassium and magnesium in sweat is high relative to that in the plasma, the plasma content of these ions represents only a small fraction of the whole body stores; Costill and Miller (1980) estimated that only about 1% of the whole body stores of these electrolytes was lost when individuals were dehydrated by 5.8% of body weight, although this obviously represents a greater fraction of the exchangeable body pool.

8.6 FLUID REPLACEMENT DURING EXERCISE

The ability to sustain a high rate of work output requires that an adequate supply of carbohydrate substrate be available to the working muscles, and fluid ingestion during exercise has the twin aims of providing a source of carbohydrate fuel to supplement the body's limited stores and of supplying water to replace the losses incurred by sweating. Increasing the carbohydrate content of drinks will increase the amount of fuel which can be supplied, but will tend to decrease the rate at which water can be made available; where provision of water is the first priority, the carbohydrate content of drinks will be low, thus restricting the rate at which substrate is provided.

Since the rate of rehydration can be increased by the addition of carbohydrate to drinks, it is difficult to separate the effects of water replacement and substrate provision. In one study, water replacement at a rate of 100 ml every 10 min did not improve endurance during cycle exercise at 70% VO_2 max, whereas ingestion of 4% glucose-electrolyte solution did significantly extend exercise time (Maughan *et al.*, 1989).

8.7   EFFECTS OF FLUID INGESTION ON PERFORMANCE

The effects of feeding different types and amounts of beverages during exercise have been extensively investigated using a wide variety of experimental models. Not all of these studies have shown a positive effect of fluid ingestion on performance, but, with the exception of a few investigations where the consumption of the drinks administered was such as to result in gastro-intestinal disturbances, there are no studies showing that fluid ingestion will have an adverse effect on performance. Since the rate of rehydration can be increased by the ingestion of glucose and sodium in low concentrations, it is difficult to separate the effects of water replacement and substrate provision. Several extensive reviews published in recent years have concentrated on the effects of administration of CHO, electrolytes and water on exercise performance (Coyle and Coggan, 1984; Coyle and Hamilton, 1990; Lamb and Brodowicz, 1986; Maughan, 1991; Murray, 1987).

8.7.1   Laboratory studies

Laboratory investigations into the ergogenic effects of the administration of CHO-electrolyte drinks during exercise have usually relied upon changes in physiological function during submaximal exercise or on the exercise time to exhaustion at a fixed work rate as a measure of performance. While this is a perfectly valid approach in itself, it must be appreciated that there are difficulties in extrapolating results obtained in this way to a race situation. It is possible to demonstrate large differences in the time for which a fixed work load can be sustained in laboratory tests when carbohydrate solutions are given during exercise: in one study, for example, a 30% increase (from 3 to 4 h) was seen (Coyle *et al.*, 1986). In a simulated race situation, where a fixed distance had to be covered as fast as possible, the advantage would translate to no more than a few per cent, and in a real competition it would probably be even less. Even a few per cent, however, is often the difference between a world class performance and a mediocre one. To take account of some of these factors, some recent investigations have used exercise tests involving intermittent exercise, simulated races or prolonged exercise followed by a sprint finish. Because different exercise tests and different solutions and rates of administration have been used in these various studies, comparisons between studies are difficult.

Some studies have included a trial where no fluids were given, whereas others have compared the effects of test solutions with trials where plain water or flavoured placebo drinks were given.

Even where the exercise model used is similar, different results have been obtained. These studies have been described and reviewed elsewhere (Maughan, 1991). Of nine seemingly well-controlled trials where continuous cycling exercise for 2 h or more was performed, six showed improvements in exercise performance (measured as an increased time to exhaustion), and three showed no significant effect of administration of CHO-containing drinks. Several studies have employed an experimental model consisting of prolonged intermittent exercise followed by a brief high-intensity sprint, and again the results are not altogether consistent except in that there appear to be no negative effects of fluid ingestion. Williams (1989) and Williams *et al.* (1990) have used an experimental model in which the subject is able to adjust the treadmill speed while running; the subject can then be encouraged either to cover the maximum distance possible in a fixed time or to complete a fixed distance in the fastest time possible. These studies showed an increased running speed in the closing stages of the trials when carbohydrate-containing drinks were given.

8.7.2 Field studies

There are many practical difficulties associated with the conduct of field trials to assess the efficacy of ergogenic aids, which accounts for the fact that few well-controlled studies of the effects of administration of glucose-electrolyte solutions have been carried out in this way. The main problem is with the design of an adequately controlled trial; where a cross-over design is used, this is likely to be confounded by changes in the environmental conditions between trials, and the use of parallel control and test groups raises the difficulty of matching the groups. Many of the early studies purporting to show beneficial effects of ingesting CHO-containing solutions on performance in events such as cycling, canoeing and soccer were so poorly designed that the results are of no value.

Cade *et al.* (1972) gave subjects no fluids or approximately 1 l of hypotonic saline or a glucose-electrolyte solution during a 7-mile course consisting of walking and running at an ambient temperature of 32–34° C. None of the subjects completed the course when no fluid was given, and the mean distance covered was 4.7 miles; when saline was given, they covered 5.5 miles and all subjects completed the 7-mile course when given the glucose-electrolyte solution.

Studies where matched groups of competitors consumed 1.4 l of either water or a glucose-electrolyte solution during a marathon race (Maughan and Whiting, 1985) or 1.4 l of different CHO-containing drinks during marathon and ultramarathon races (Noakes *et al.*, 1988) have shown no differences between the groups in finishing time. In the study of Maughan and Whiting (1985), subjects were matched on the basis of their anticipated finishing times. Many of these individuals had not previously completed a marathon, so these times must be considered unreliable. Nonetheless, mean finishing time for the runners ($n = 43$) drinking the CHO-electrolyte solution was $200 + 40$ min compared with a predicted finishing time of $220 + 35$ min; for the group drinking water ($n = 47$) actual finishing time was $217 + 32$ min and predicted time was $212 + 32$ min. Twenty-four runners (60%) in the CHO-electrolyte group ran faster than expected, compared with 19 (40%) in the water group.

Leatt (1986) gave 1 l of a 7% glucose polymer solution or a flavoured placebo to soccer players during a practice game. During the match, the group who had been given CHO utilized 31% less glycogen than the placebo group. No measure of performance of the two groups was made, but it was proposed that beneficial effects would be experienced in the later stages of the game by the players taking the glucose polymer. In an earlier study, Saltin and Karlsson (1977) showed that other soccer players beginning the game with low muscle glycogen concentration covered less distance during the game, particularly during the second half, and spent more time walking and running at low speed.

8.8 POST-EXERCISE REHYDRATION

Replacement of water and electrolyte losses in the post-exercise period may be of crucial importance when repeated bouts of exercise have to be performed. The need for replacement will obviously depend on the extent of the losses incurred during exercise, but will also be influenced by the time and nature of subsequent exercise bouts. Rapid rehydration may also be important in events such as wrestling, boxing and weight-lifting where competition is by weight category. Competitors in these events frequently undergo acute thermal and exercise-induced dehydration to make weight: the time interval between the weigh-in and competition is normally about 3 h, although it may be longer. The practice of acute dehydration to make weight should be discouraged, but it will persist and so there is a need to maximize rehydration in the time available.

Ingestion of plain water in the post-exercise period results in a rapid fall in the plasma sodium concentration and in plasma osmolality (Nose *et al.*, 1988a). These changes have the effect of reducing the stimulus to drink (thirst) and of stimulating urine output, both of which will delay the rehydration process. In the study of Nose *et al.* (1988a), subjects exercised at low intensity in the heat for 90–110 min, inducing a mean dehydration of 2.3% of body weight, and then rested for 1 h before beginning to drink. Plasma volume was not restored until after 60 min when plain water was ingested together with placebo (sucrose) capsules. In contrast, when sodium chloride capsules were ingested with water to give a saline solution with an effective concentration of 0.45% (77 mmol l^{-1}), plasma volume was restored within 20 min. In the NaCl trial, voluntary fluid intake was higher and urine output was less; 71% of the water loss was retained within 3 h compared with 51% in the plain water trial. The delayed rehydration in the water trial appeared to be a result of a loss of sodium, accompanied by water, in the urine caused by enhanced plasma renin activity and aldosterone levels (Nose *et al.*, 1988b).

In an earlier study where a more severe (4% of body weight) dehydration was induced in resting subjects by heat exposure, consumption over a 3 h period of a volume of fluid equal to that lost did not restore plasma volume of serum osmolality within 4 h (Costill and Sparks, 1973). Ingestion of a glucose-electrolyte solution, however, did result in greater restoration of plasma volume than did plain water: this was accompanied by a greater urine production in the water trial.

It is clear from the results of these studies that rehydration after exercise can only be achieved if the sodium lost in sweat is replaced as well as the water, and it might be suggested that rehydration drinks should have a sodium concentration similar to that of sweat. Since the sodium content of sweat varies widely, no single formulation will meet this requirement for all individuals in all situations. The upper end of the normal range for sodium concentration (80 mmol l^{-1}), however, is similar to the sodium concentration of many commercially produced oral rehydration solutions (ORS) intended for use in the treatment of diarrhoea-induced dehydration, and some of these are not unpalatable. The ORS recommended by the World Health Organization for rehydration in cases of severe diarrhoea has a sodium content of 90 mmol l^{-1}. By contrast, the sodium content of most sports drinks is in the range of 10–25 mmol l^{-1} and is even lower in some cases; most commonly consumed soft drinks contain virtually no sodium (Table 8.2). Many mineral waters also have a low sodium content, but the composition is highly variable.

The requirement for sodium replacement stems from its role as the major ion in the extracellular fluid. It may be speculated that inclusion of potassium, the major cation in the intracellular space, would enhance the replacement of intracellular water after exercise and thus promote rehydration (Nadel *et al.*, 1990), but there is little experimental evidence to support this. Nielsen *et al.* (1986), however, did find some evidence that restoration of plasma volume in the 2 h after dehydration was more rapid when solutions with high sodium content were given but that intracellular rehydration was favoured by drinks with high concentrations of potassium or glucose.

Although there seems no doubt as to the necessity for the presence of sodium in oral rehydration solutions, there has been some debate as to the value of adding other electrolytes to drinks to be consumed during or after exercise. Most commonly available sport drinks contain significant amounts of potassium, magnesium and other electrolytes, often in

Table 8.2 Carbohydrate and electrolyte content of some commonly used sports drinks, a soft drink, the World Health Organization recommended oral rehydration solution (WHO-ORS) and a commercially available hypotonic oral rehydration solution (Dioralyte). Carbohydrate content is expressed in g l^{-1}, as the molecular weight of some of the sugars used is unknown; electrolyte concentrations are expressed in mmol l^{-1}; osmolality is expressed as mosmol kg^{-1}. Most of the solutions contain some additional electrolytes, including magnesium, bicarbonate, citrate and phosphate. Some of the sports drinks are available as powders or as carbonated solutions; the degree of carbonation is generally much less than that of most soft drinks. Carbonation will affect the osmolality, but will not have a major effect on gastric emptying. The composition of Coca-Cola appears to vary widely between different countries.

Sports drink	CHO	Na^+	K^+	Cl^-	Osmolality
Isostar	73	24	4	12	296
Gatorade	62	23	3	14	349
Lucozade Sport	69	23	4	1	280
Pripps Energy	75	13	2	7	260
Coca-Cola	105	3	0	1	650
WHO-ORS	20	90	20	80	331
Dioralyte	16	60	20	60	240

concentrations similar to those estimated to be present in sweat. During prolonged exercise, however, the circulating concentrations of the major electrolytes are generally observed to increase slightly or to remain unchanged when no fluid is taken or when water is ingested. After exercise, electrolyte losses in sweat and any excess loss in urine will be replaced through normal food intake.

This then raises the question as to whether there are possible adverse effects associated with the ingestion of solutions containing these electrolytes. There appear to have been no studies carried out with the aim of establishing whether this is the case, but equally there are no reported cases of problems arising from the consumption of large volumes of sports drinks during exercise. Given the popularity of these drinks, it would be expected that any problems would have become apparent.

There are also some data to suggest that, at least in the case of potassium, large amounts of electrolytes can be ingested during exercise without seriously impairing the body's ability to regulate circulating ion concentrations as long as fluid balance is well maintained. In one trial in which subjects competed in a marathon race, half the subjects ($n = 47$) drank 1.4 l of water and the other half ($n = 43$) drank an equal volume of a glucose-electrolyte solution containing 20 mmol l^{-1} potassium (Whiting *et al.*, 1984). Serum potassium concentration, measured on samples taken immediately after the race, was not different between the two groups. In one unpublished study, we exercised a group of subjects to exhaustion on a cycle ergometer at a work load of 70% of VO_2 max: on one trial they were given no drink, and on the other trials they were given drinks at a rate of 100 ml every 10 min, starting immediately before exercise. One of the drinks was plain water, and the others were glucose-electrolyte solutions containing either 20 or 25 mmol l^{-1} potassium. This concentration is commonly used in solutions used for oral rehydration in cases of diarrhoeal disease, but is considerably higher than the 4–5 mmol l^{-1} present in sweat and in most commercially available sports drinks (Tables 8.1 and 8.2). There was no differences between trials in the serum potassium concentration during exercise at any time up to 1 h. Subjects exercised longer when given the glucose-electrolyte drinks, and serum potassium concentration was slightly higher on these trials at the point of exhaustion, perhaps as a consequence of the greater exercise time (Table 8.3). These results suggest that supplementation with large amounts of potassium during exercise does not represent a significant risk in healthy subjects when renal function is well maintained. When renal function is impaired, however, it may be unwise to ingest large amounts of potassium during exercise.

Table 8.3 Median time to exhaustion (min) and serum potassium concentration (mmol l^{-1}) at the point of exhaustion for 12 subjects exercising a cycle ergometer at 70% of VO_2 max when given no fluid (C), water (W), an isotonic glucose-electrolyte solution containing 20 mmol l^{-1} potassium (I), or a hypotonic glucose-electrolyte solution containing 25 mmol l^{-1} potassium (H) at a rate of 100 ml every 10 min during exercise. Values sharing the same superscript are not different from each other at the 5% level

	Exercise time	Serum potassium
C	80.7[a]	5.5[a]
W	91.1[a,b]	5.3[c]
I	107.3[b]	5.6[d]
H	110.3[b]	5.8[d]

8.9 PRACTICAL ISSUES IN FLUID REPLACEMENT DURING EXERCISE

Many factors affect the need for fluid replacement during exercise. The composition of the fluid, as well as the volume and frequency of drinks, which will confer the greatest benefit during exercise will depend very much on individual circumstances. As with most physiological variables, there is a large inter-individual variability in the rates of fluid loss during exercise under standardized conditions and also in the rates of gastric emptying and intestinal absorption of any ingested beverage. Marathon runners competing under the same conditions and finishing in the same time may lose as little as 1% or as much as 5% of body weight, even though their fluid intake during the race is the same (Maughan, 1985). Under more controlled conditions, Greenhaff and Clough (1989) found that sweat rate during 1 h of exercise at a work load of 70% VO_2 max and an ambient temperature of 23° C ranged from 426–1665 g h^{-1}. It would seem logical that the need for fluid (water) replacement is greater in the individual who sweats profusely, and any guidelines as to the rate of fluid ingestion and the composition of fluids to be taken, must be viewed with caution when applied to the individual athlete.

Sweat rate in activities such as running can be predicted from estimates of the energy cost of running, as used by Barr and Costill (1989), but these do not explain the variation which is observed between individuals. A more reliable method might be for the individual to measure body weight before and after training or simulated competition and to estimate sweat loss from the change in body weight.

Many individuals and organizations have issued recommendations as to the most appropriate fluid replacement regimens (e.g. Olsson and Saltin, 1971; American College of Sports Medicine, 1975, 1984). Olsson and Saltin (1971) recommended 100–300 ml of a 5–10% sugar solution every 10–15 min during exercise; they also suggested that the temperature of ingested fluids should be 25° C. At the extreme ends of this range, this would give an intake each hour of 400–1800 ml of liquid and 20–180 g of sugar. In 1975 the American College of Sports Medicine published a Position Statement on the prevention of heat injuries during distance running, in which an intake of 400–500 ml of fluid 10–15 min before exercise was recommended: although no figures were given, it was also suggested that runners ingest fluids frequently during competition and that the sugar and electrolyte content of drinks should be low (2.5% and 10 mmol l^{-1} sodium, respectively) so as not to delay gastric emptying. A revised version of these guidelines (American College of Sports Medicine, 1984) continued to recommend hyperhydration prior to exercise by the ingestion of 400–600 ml of cold water 15–20 min before the event. The recommendations as to intake during a race were more specific than previously: cool water was stated to be the optimum fluid, although more recent evidence casts doubt on this, and an intake of 100–200 ml every 2–3 km was suggested, giving a total intake of 1400–4200 ml at the extremes. Again, taking these extreme values, it is unlikely that the élite runners could tolerate a rate of intake of about $2\,l\,h^{-1}$, and equally unlikely that an intake of 300 ml h^{-1} would be adequate for the slowest competitors except when the ambient temperature was low.

8.10 EXERCISE INTENSITY AND DURATION

The rate of metabolic heat production during exercise is dependent on the exercise intensity and the body mass; in activities such as running or cycling this is a direct function of speed. The rate of rise of body temperature in the early stages of exercise and the steady state level which is eventually reached are both proportional to the metabolic rate. The rate of sweat production is therefore also closely related to the absolute work load. In many sports, including most ball games, short bursts of high-intensity activity are separated by variable periods of rest or low-intensity exercise.

The time for which high-intensity exercise can be sustained is necessarily rather short: the factors limiting exercise performance where the duration is in the range of about 10–60 min are not clear, but it does seem that fluid and substrate availability are not normally limiting and that performance of continuous exercise on this time scale will not be improved by the ingestion of CHO-containing beverages during exercise. Also, even though the sweat rate may be high, the total amount of water lost by sweating is likely to be rather small. Accordingly there is generally no need for fluid replacement during very high-intensity exercise, although it is difficult to define a precise cut-off point. In a recent study, however, the effects of an intravenous-infusion of saline during cycle ergometer exercise to exhaustion at an exercise intensity equivalent to 84% of VO_2 max were investigated (Deschamps *et al.*, 1989). In the control trial a negligible amount of saline was infused, whereas an infusion rate of about 70 ml min^{-1} was used in the other trial. The saline infusion was effective in reducing the decrease in plasma volume which occurred in the initial stages of exercise, although it did not completely abolish this response, and the core temperature and heart rate at the point of exhaustion were both lower in the infusion trial. There was no effect on endurance time which was the same in both trials. The endurance times were, however, short (20.8 and 22.0 min for the infusion and control trials, respectively), although the range was large (from about 9 to 43 min), and these results support the idea that fluid provision will not benefit exercise performance when the exercise duration is short.

There are likely to be real problems associated with any attempt to replace fluids orally during very intense exercise. The rate of gastric empty-ing, which is probably the most important factor is determining the fate of ingested fluid, is impaired when the exercise intensity is high, as described above. Even at rest, the maximum rates of gastric emptying which have been reported are only about half the saline infusion rate (70 ml min^{-1}) used in the study of Deschamps *et al.* (1989) and are com-monly much less than this. To achieve a high rate of fluid delivery from the stomach, it is necessary to ingest large volumes, and any attempt to do so when the exercise intensity exceeds about 80% of VO$_2$ max would almost certainly result in nausea and vomiting.

At lower intensities of exercise, the duration of exercise is inversely related to the intensity. In an activity such as running, this holds true for populations as much as for individuals. As the distance of a race increases, so the pace that an individual can sustain decreases (Davies and Thomp-son, 1979); equally, in an event such as a marathon race where all runners complete the same distance, the slower runners are generally exercising at a lower relative (as a percentage of VO$_2$ max) and absolute work intensity (Maughan and Leiper, 1983). Because the faster runners are exercising at a higher work load, in absolute as well as in relative terms, their sweat rate is higher, although this effect is offset to some extent by the fact that they generally have a lower body weight: because the faster runners are active for a shorter period of time, however, the total sweat loss during a marathon race is unrelated to finishing time (Maughan, 1985).

The need for fluid replacement is therefore much the same, irrespective of running speed, in terms of the total volume required, but there is a need for a higher rate of replacement in the faster runners. Among the fastest marathon runners, sweat rates of about 30–35 ml min^{-1} can be sustained for a period of about 2 h 15 min by some runners. The highest sustained rates of gastric emptying reported in the literature are greater than this, at about 40 ml min^{-1} (Costill and Saltin, 1974; Duchman *et al.*, 1990). These gastric emptying measurements were made on resting sub-jects, and it is possible that there may be some inhibition of gastric emptying at the exercise intensity (about 75% of VO$_2$ max) at which these élite athletes are running (Costill and Saltin, 1974). In the slower runners, the exercise intensity does not exceed 60% of VO$_2$ max, and gastrointesti-nal function is unlikely to be impaired relative to rest (Mitchell *et al.*, 1989; Rehrer *et al.*, 1989a). In these runners, sweat rates will also be relatively low (Maughan, 1985).

Although in theory, therefore, it should be possible to meet the fluid loss by oral intake, gastric emptying rates of fluids are commonly much lower than the figures quoted above: Noakes *et al.* (1988) have suggested that the maximum fluid intake of élite marathon runners never exceeds about 600 ml h^{-1}, and it is inevitable that most individuals exercising hard, particularly in the heat, will incur a fluid deficit.

8.11 COMPOSITION OF DRINKS

In spite of the definitive statement by the American College of Sports Medicine in its 1984 Position Stand on the prevention of thermal injuries in distance running that cool water is the optimum fluid for ingestion during endurance exercise, some of the evidence presented above indicates that there may be good reasons for taking drinks containing added substrate and sodium chloride. In prolonged exercise, performance is improved by the addition of an energy source in the form of carbohydrate; the type of carbohydrate does not appear to be critical, and glucose, sucrose and oligosaccharides have all been shown to be effective in improving endurance capacity.

Some recent studies have suggested that long-chain glucose polymer solutions are more readily used by the muscles during exercise than are glucose of fructose solutions (Noakes, 1990), but others have found no difference in the oxidation rates of ingested glucose or glucose polymer (Massicote *et al.*, 1989; Rehrer, 1990). Massicote *et al.* (1989) also found that ingested fructose was less readily oxidized than glucose or glucose polymers. Fructose in high concentrations is best avoided on account of the risk of gastrointestinal upset. The argument advanced in favour of the ingestion of fructose during exercise, namely that it provides a readily available energy source but does not stimulate insulin release and consequent inhibition of fatty acid mobilization, is in any case not well founded: insulin secretion is suppressed during exercise.

The optimum concentration of sugar to be added to drinks will depend on individual circumstances. High carbohydrate concentrations will delay gastric emptying, thus reducing the amount of fluid that is available for absorption: very high concentrations will result in secretion of water into the intestine and thus actually increase the danger of dehydration. High carbohydrate concentrations (perhaps > 10% for simple sugars and > 15% for glucose polymers) may also result in gastrointestinal disturbances. Where there is a need to supply an energy source during exercise, however, increasing the sugar content of drinks will increase the delivery of carbohydrate to the site of absorption in the small intestine: although the volume emptied from the stomach is reduced as the sugar concentration increases, the amount of sugar emptied is increased, and so is the rate of carbohydrate oxidation by the muscles.

The available evidence indicates that the only electrolyte that should be added to drinks consumed during exercise is sodium, which is usually added in the form of sodium chloride. Sodium will stimulate sugar and water uptake in the small intestine and will help to maintain extracellular fluid volume. Most soft drinks of the cola or lemonade variety contain virtually no sodium (1–2 mmol l⁻¹); sports drinks commonly contain 10–25 mmol l⁻¹; oral rehydration solutions intended for use in the treatment of diarrhoea-induced dehydration, which may be fatal, have higher sodium concentrations, in the range 30–90 mmol l⁻¹. A high sodium content, although it may stimulate jejunal absorption of glucose and water, tends to make drinks unpalatable, and it is important that drinks intended for ingestion during or after exercise should have a pleasant taste in order to stimulate consumption. Specialist sports drinks are generally formulated to strike a balance between the twin aims of efficacy and palatability, although it must be admitted that not all achieve either of these aims. Many commercially available products also contain added vitamins although there is no evidence to support any benefit from their inclusion.

When the exercise duration is likely to exceed 3–4 h, there may be advantages in adding sodium to drinks to avoid the danger of hyponatraemia, which has been reported to occur when excessively large volumes of low-sodium drinks are taken. It has often been reported that the fluid intakes of participants in endurance events are low, and it is recognized that this may lead to dehydration and heat illness in prolonged exercise when the ambient temperature is high. Accordingly, the advice given to participants in endurance events is that they should ensure a high fluid intake to minimize the effects of dehydration and that drinks should contain low levels of glucose and electrolytes so as not to delay gastric emptying (American College of Sports Medicine, 1984). In accordance with these recommendations, most CHO-electrolyte drinks intended for consumption during prolonged exercise also have a low electrolyte content, with sodium and chloride concentrations typically in the range of 10–20 mmol l⁻¹. While this might represent a reasonable strategy for providing substrates and water (although it can be argued that a higher sodium concentration would enhance water uptake and that a higher carbohydrate content would increase substrate provision), these recommendations may not be appropriate in all circumstances.

Physicians dealing with individuals in distress at the end of long-distance races have become accustomed to dealing with hyperthermia associated with dehydration and hypernatraemia, but it has become clear that a small number of individuals at the end of very prolonged events may be suffering from hyponatraemia in conjunction with either hyperhydration (Noakes *et al.*, 1985, 1990; Frizell *et al.*, 1986; Saltin and Costill, 1988) or dehydration (Hiller, 1989).

All the reported cases have been associated with ultramarathon or prolonged triathlon events; most of the cases have occurred in events lasting in excess of 8 h, and there are few reports of cases where the exercise duration is less than 4 h. Noakes *et al.* (1985) reported four cases of exercise-induced hyponatraemia; race times were between 7 and 10 h, and post-race serum sodium concentrations were between 115 and 125 mmol l^{-1}. Estimated fluid intakes were between 6 and 12 l, and consisted of water or drinks containing low levels of electrolytes; estimated total sodium chloride intake during the race was 20–40 mmol. Frizell *et al.* (1986) reported even more astonishing fluid intakes of 20–24 l of fluids (an intake of almost 2.5 l h^{-1} sustained for a period of many hours, which is in excess of the maximum gastric emptying rate that has been reported) with a mean sodium content of only 5–10 mmol l^{-1} in two runners who collapsed after an ultramarathon run and who were found to be hyponatraemic (serum sodium concentration 118–123 mmol l^{-1}). Hyponatraemia as a consequence of ingestion of large volumes of fluids with a low sodium content has also been recognized in resting individuals. Flear *et al.* (1981) reported the case of a man who drank 9 l of beer, with a sodium content of 1.5 mmol l^{-1}, in the space of 20 min; plasma sodium fell from 143 mmol l^{-1} before to 127 mmol l^{-1} after drinking, but the man appeared unaffected.

In these cases, there is clearly a replacement of water in excess of losses with inadequate electrolyte replacement. In competitors in the Hawaii Ironman Triathlon who have been found to be hyponatraemic, however, dehydration has also been reported to be present (Hiller, 1989). Fellmann *et al.* (1988) reported a small but statistically significant fall in serum sodium concentration, from 141 to 137 mmol l^{-1}, in runners who completed a 24 h run, but food and fluid intakes were neither controlled nor measured.

These reports are interesting and indicate that some supplementation with sodium chloride may be required in extremely prolonged events where large sweat losses can be expected and where it is possible to consume large volumes of fluid. This should not, however, divert attention away from the fact that electrolyte replacement during exercise is not a priority for most participants in most sporting events. Sodium is also necessary for post-event rehydration, which may be particularly important when the exercise has to be repeated within a few hours: if drinks containing little or no sodium are taken, plasma osmolity will fall, urine production will be stimulated and most of the fluid will not be retained. When a longer time interval between exercise sessions is possible, replacement of sodium and other electrolytes will normally be achieved as a result of intake from the diet without additional supplementation.

It is often stated that there is an advantage to taking chilled (4° C) drinks as this accelerates gastric emptying and thus improves the availability of ingested fluids. The most recent evidence, however, suggests that the gastric emptying rate of hot and cold beverages is not different. In spite of this, there may be advantages in taking cold drinks, as the palatability of most carbohydrate-electrolyte drinks is improved at low temperatures.

8.12 ENVIRONMENTAL CONDITIONS

The ambient temperature and wind speed will have a major influence on the physical exchange of heat between the body and the environment. When ambient temperature exceeds skin temperature, heat is gained from the environment by physical transfer, leaving evaporative loss as the only mechanism available to prevent or limit a rise in body temperature. The increased sweating rate in the heat will result in an increased requirement for fluid replacement. Other precautions such as limiting the extent of the warm-up prior to competition and reducing the amount of clothing worn will help to reduce the sweat loss and hence reduce the need for replacement. For endurance events at high ambient temperatures, there may also be a need to reduce the exercise intensity if the event is to be successfully completed.

When the humidity is high, and especially in the absence of wind, evaporative heat loss will also be severely limited. In this situation, exercise tolerance is likely to be limited by dehydration and hyperthermia rather than by the limited availability of metabolic fuel. Suzuki (1980) reported that exercise time at a work load of 66% VO_2 max was reduced from 91 min, when the ambient temperature was 0° C, to 19 min when the same exercise was performed in the heat (40° C). In an unpublished study in which six subjects exercised to exhaustion at 70% VO_2 max on a cycle ergometer, we found that exercise time was reduced from 73 min at an ambient temperature of 2° C to 35 min at a temperature of 33° C: exercise time in the cold was increased by ingestion of a dilute glucose-electrolyte solution, but in the heat, the exercise duration was too short for fluid intake to have any effect on performance. Although fatigue at these work intensities is generally considered to result from depletion of the muscle glycogen stores, this is clearly not the case when the ambient temperature is high, as this would require the rate of muscle glycogen utilization to be increased two-fold in the heat and this did not occur.

From these studies, we can conclude that the supply of water should take precedence over the provision of substrate during exercise in the heat. There may therefore be some advantage in reducing the carbohydrate content of drinks, to perhaps 2–8%, and in increasing the sodium content, to something in the range 30–50 mmol l^{-1}. Conversely, when exercise is undertaken in the cold, fluid loss is less of a problem, and the energy content of drinks might usefully be increased. Loss of fluid and electrolytes via sweat and urine may be enhanced at altitude, and there may be a need for an emphasis on an increased intake of liquids, especially during the early stages of acclimation.

8.13 STATE OF TRAINING AND ACCLIMATION

It is well recognized that both training and acclimation will confer some protection against the development of heat illness during exercise in the heat. Although this adaptation is most marked in response to training carried out in the heat (Senay, 1979), endurance training at moderate environmental conditions will also confer some benefit. Among the benefits of training is an expansion of plasma volume (Hallberg and Magnusson, 1984). Although this condition is recognized as a chronic state in the endurance-trained individual, an acute expansion of plasma volume occurs in response to a single bout of strenuous exercise: this effect is apparent within a few hours of completion of exercise and may persist for several days (Davidson *et al.*, 1987; Robertson *et al.*, 1988). This post-exercise hypervolaemia should be regarded as an acute response rather than an adaptation, although it may appear to be one of the first responses to occur when an individual embarks on a training regimen.

Circulating electrolyte and total protein concentrations are normal in the endurance-trained individual in spite of the enlarged vascular and extracellular spaces, indicating an increased total circulating content (Convertino *et al.*, 1980).

The increased resting plasma volume in the trained state allows the endurance-trained individual to maintain a higher total blood volume during exercise (Convertino *et al.*, 1983), allowing for better maintenance of cardiac output, albeit at the cost of a lower circulating haemoglobin concentration. In addition, the increased plasma volume is associated with an increased sweating rate which limits the rise in body temperature (Mitchell *et al.*, 1976). These adaptive responses appear to occur within a few days of exposure to exercise in the heat, although, as pointed out above, this may not necessarily be a true adaptation. In a series of papers reporting the same study, Mitchell *et al.* (1976), Wyndham *et al.* (1976) and Senay *et al.* (1976) followed the time course of changes in men exposed to exercise (40–50% VO_2 max for 4 h) in the heat (45° C) for 10 days. Although there were marked differences between individuals in their responses, resting plasma volume increased progressively over the first 6 days, reaching a value about 23% greater than the control, with little change thereafter. The main adaptation in terms of an increased sensitivity of the sweating response, an increased sweating rate and an improved thermoregulatory response (with body temperature lower by 1° C and heart rate lower by 30 beats min^{-1} in the later stages of exercise) occurred slightly later than the cardiovascular adaptations, with little change in the first 4 days.

Although there is clear evidence that acclimation by exercise in the heat over a period of several days will improve the thermoregulatory response during exercise, this does not affect the need to replace fluids during the exercise period. Better maintenance of body temperature is achieved at the expense of an increased water (sweat) loss. Although this allows for a greater evaporative heat loss, the proportion of the sweat which is unevaporated and which therefore drips wastefully from the skin is also increased (Mitchell *et al.*, 1976). The athlete who trains in a moderate climate for a competition to be held in the heat will, however, be at a disadvantage on account of his inability to sustain a high sweat rate.

REFERENCES

Ahlborg, B., Bergstrom, J., Brohult, J., Ekelund, L.-G., Hultman, E. and Mashio, E. (1967). Human muscle glycogen content and capacity for prolonged exercise after different diets. *Forsvarsmedicin*, **3**, 85–99.

Allan, J.R. and Wilson, C.G. (1971). Influence of acclimatization on sweat sodium secretion. *Journal of Applied Physiology*, **30**, 708–12.

American College of Sports Medicine. (1975). Position statement on prevention of heat injuries during distance running. *Medicine and Science in Sports and Exercise*, **7**, vii–ix.

American College of Sports Medicine. (1984). Position stand on prevention of thermal injuries during distance running. *Medicine and Science in Sports and Exercise*, **16**, ix–xiv.

Barr, S.I. and Costil, D.L. (1989). Can the endurance athlete get too much of a good thing? *Journal of the American Dietetic Association*, **89**, 1629–32.

Beller, G.A., Maher, J.T., Hartley, L.H., Bass, D.E. and Wacker, W.E.C. (1972). Serum Mg and K concentrations during exercise in thermoneutral and hot conditions. *Physiologist*, **15**, 94.

Brener, W., Hendrix, T.R. and McHugh, P.R. (1983). Regulation on the gastric emptying of glucose. *Gastroenterology*, **85**, 76–82.

Brouns, F., Saris, W.H.M. and Rehrer, N.J. (1987). Abdominal complaints and gastrointestinal function during long-lasting exercise. *International Journal of Sports Medicine*, **8**, 175–89.

Cade, R., Spooner, G., Schlein, E., Pickering, M. and Dean, R. (1972). Effect of fluid, electrolyte, and glucose replacement on performance, body temperature, rate of sweat loss and compositional changes of extracellular fluid. *Journal of Sports Medicine and Physical Fitness*, **12**, 150–6.

Carter, J.E. and Gisolfi, C.V. (1989). Fluid replacement during and after exercise in the heat. *Medicine and Science in Sports and Exercise*, **21**, 532–9.

Coggan, A.R. and Coyle, E.F. (1988). Effect of carbohydrate feedings during high-intensity exercise. *Journal of Applied Physiology*, **65**, 1703–9.

Cohen, I. and Zimmerman, A.L. (1978). Changes in serum electrolyte levels during marathon running. *South African Medical Journal*, **53**, 449–53.

Convertino, V.A., Brock, P.J., Keil, L.C., Bernauer, E.M. and Greenleaf, J.E. (1980). Exercise training-induced hypervolemia: role of plasma albumin, renin and vasopressin. *Journal of Applied Physiology*, **48**, 665–9.

Convertino, V.A., Keil, L.C. and Greenleaf, J.E. (1983). Plasma volume, renin, and vasopressin responses to graded exercise after training. *Journal of Applied Physiology*, **54**, 508–14.

Costill, D.L. (1977). Sweating: its composition and effects on body fluids. *Annals of the New York Academy of Sciences*, **301**, 160–74.

Costill, D.L. and Miller, J.M. (1980). Nutrition for endurance sport. *International Journal of Sports Medicine*, **1**, 2–14.

Costill, D.L. and Saltin, B. (1974). Factors limiting gastric emptying during rest and exercise. *Journal of Applied Physiology*, **37**, 679–83.

Costill, D.L. and Sparks, K.E. (1973). Rapid fluid replacement following thermal dehydration. *Journal of Applied Physiology*, **34**, 299–303.

Costill, D.L., Bennett, A., Branam, G. and Eddy, D. (1973). Glucose ingestion at rest and during prolonged exercise. *Journal of Applied Physiology*, **34**, 764–9.

Costill, D.L., Branam, G., Fink, W. and Nelson, R. (1976). Exercise induced sodium conservation: changes in plasma renin and aldosterone. *Medicine and Science in Sports and Exercise*, **8**, 209–13.

Coyle, E.F. and Coggan, A.R. (1984). Effectiveness of carbohydrate feeding in delaying fatigue during prolonged exercise. *Sports Medicine*, **1**, 446–58.

Coyle, E.F. and Hamilton, M. (1990). Fluid replacement during exercise: Effects on physiological homeostasis and performance. In *Perspectives in Exercise Science and Sports Medicine*. Vol. 3, *Fluid homeostasis during exercise* (eds. C.V. Gisolfi and D.R. Lamb), pp. 281–308. Benchmark Press, Carmel.

Coyle, E.F., Hagberg, J.M., Hurley, B.F., Martin, W.H., Ehsani, A.H. and Holloszy, J.O. (1983). Carbohydrate feeding during prolonged strenuous exercise can delay fatigue. *Journal of Applied Physiology*, **55**, 230–5.

Coyle, E.F., Coggan, A.R., Hemmert, M.K. and Ivy, J.L. (1986). Muscle glycogen utilization during prolonged strenuous exercise when fed carbohydrate. *Journal of Applied Physiology*, **61**, 165–72.

Davidson, R.J.L., Robertson, J.D., Galea, G. and Maughan, R.J. (1987). Haematological changes associated with marathon running. *International Journal of Sports Medicine*, **8**, 19–25.

Davies, C.T.M. and Thompson, M.W. (1979). Aerobic performance of female marathon and male ultramarathon athletes. *European Journal of Applied Physiology*, **41**, 233–45.

Deschamps, A., Levy, R.D., Cosio, M.G., Marliss, E.B. and Magder, S. (1989). Effect of saline infusion on body temperature and endurance during heavy exercise. *Journal of Applied Physiology*, **66**, 2799–804.

Duchman, S.M., Blieler, T.L., Schedl, H.P., Summers, R.W. and Gisolfi, C.V. (1990). Effects of gastric function on intestinal composition of oral rehydration solutions. *Medicine and Science in Sports and Exercise*, **22** (Suppl.), S89.

Erickson, M.A., Schwartzkopf, R.J. and McKenzie, R.D. (1987). Effects of caffeine, fructose, and glucose ingestion on muscle glycogen utilization during exercise. *Medicine and Science in Sports and Exercise*, **19**, 579–83.

Felig, P., Cherif, A., Minigawa, A. and Wahren, J. (1982). Hypoglycaemia during prolonged exercise in normal men. *New England Journal of Medicine*, **306**, 895–900.

Fellmann, N., Sagnol, M., Bedu, M., Falgairette, G., van Praagh, E., Gaillard, G., Jouanel, P. and Coudert, J. (1988). Enzymatic and hormonal responses following a 24 h endurance run and a 10 h triathlon race. *European Journal of Applied Physiology*, **57**, 545–53.

Fielding, R.A., Costill, D.L., Fink, W.J., King, D.S., Hargreaves, M. and Kovaleski, M.E. (1985). Effect of carbohydrate feeding frequencies on muscle glycogen use during exercise. *Medicine and Science in Sports and Exercise*, **17**, 472–6.

Flear, C.T.G., Gill, C.V. and Burn, J. (1981). Beer drinking and hyponatraemia. *Lancet*, **2**, 477.

Flynn, M.G., Costill, D.L., Hawley, J.A., Fink, W.J., Neufer, P.D., Fielding, R.A. and Sleeper, M.D. (1987). Influence of selected carbohydrate drinks on cycling performance and glycogen use. *Medicine and Science in Sports and Exercise*, **19**, 37–40.

Fordtran, J.S. (1975). Stimulation of active and passive sodium absorption by sugars in the human jejunum. *Journal of Clinical Investigation*, **55**, 728–37.

Fordtran, J.S. and Saltin, B. (1967). Gastric emptying and intestinal absorption during prolonged severe exercise. *Journal of Applied Physiology*, **23**, 331–5.

Fortney, S.M., Wenger, C.B., Bove, J.R. and Nadel, E.R. (1984). Effect of hyperosmolality on control of blood flow and sweating. *Journal of Applied Physiology*, **57**, 1688–95.

Fortney, S.M., Vroman, N.B., Beckett, W.S., Permutt, S. and LaFrance, N.D. (1988). Effect of exercise hemoconcentration and hyperosmolality on exercise responses. *Journal of Applied Physiology*, **65**, 519–24.

Foster, C., Costill, D.L. and Fink, W.J. (1980). Gastric emptying characteristics of glucose and glucose polymers. *Research Quarterly*, **51**, 299–305.

Frizell, R.T., Lang, G.H., Lowance, D.C. and Lathan, S.R. (1986). Hyponatraemia and ultramarathon running. *Journal of the American Medical Association*, **255**, 772–4.

Greenhaff, P.L. and Clough, P.J. (1989). Predictors of sweat loss in man during prolonged exercise. *European Journal of Applied Physiology*, **58**, 348–52.

Greenleaf, J.E., Castle, B.L. and Card, D.H. (1974). Blood electrolytes and temperature regulation during exercise in man. *Acta Physiologica Polonica*, **25**, 397–410.

Hallberg, L. and Magnusson, B. (1984). The aetiology of sports anaemia. *Acta Medica Scandinavica*, **216**, 145–8.

Hargreaves, M. and Briggs, C.A. (1988). Effect of carbohydrate ingestion on exercise metabolism. *Journal of Applied Physiology*, **65**, 1553–5.

Hargreaves, M., Costill, D.L., Coggan, A., Fink, W.J. and Nishibata, I. (1984). Effect on carbohydrate feedings on muscle glycogen utilization and exercise performance. *Medicine and Science in Sports and Exercise*, **16**, 219–22.

Harrison, M.H., Edwards, R.J. and Fennessy, P.A. (1978). Intravascular volume and tonicity as factors in the regulation of body temperature. *Journal of Applied Physiology*, **44**, 69–75.

Hiller, W.D.B. (1989). Dehydration and hyponatraemia during triathlons. *Medicine and Science in Sports and Exercise*, **21**, 219–21.

Ivy, J., Costill, D.L., Fink, W.J. and Lower, R.W. (1979). Influence of caffeine and carbohydrate feedings on endurance performance. *Medicine and Science in Sports*, **11**, 6–11.

Joborn, H., Akerstrom, G. and Ljunghall, S. (1985). Effects of exogenous catecholamines and exercise on plasma magnesium concentrations. *Clinical Endocrinology*, **23**, 219–26.

Jones, B.J.M., Brown, B.E., Loran, J.S., Edgerton, D. and Kennedy, J.F. (1983). Glucose absorption from starch hydrolysates in the human jejunum. *Gut*, **24**, 1152–60.

Jones, B.J.M., Higgins, B.E. and Silk, D.B.A. (1987). Glucose absorption from maltotriose and glucose oligomers in the human jejunum. *Clinical Science*, **72**, 409–14.

Kavanagh, T. and Shephard, R.J. (1975). Maintenance of hydration in 'post-coronary' marathon runners. *British Journal of Sports Medicine*, **9**, 130–5.

Kobayashi, Y., Ando, Y., Takeuchi, S., Takemura, K. and Okuda, N. (1980). Effects of heat acclimation of distance runners in a moderately hot environment. *European Journal of Applied Physiology*, **45**, 189–98.

Lamb, D.R. and Brodowicz, G.R. (1986). Optimal use of fluids of varying formulations to minimize exercise-induced disturbances in homeostasis. *Sports Medicine*, **3**, 247–74.

Leatt, P. (1986). *The effect of glucose polymer ingestion on skeletal muscle glycogen depletion during soccer match-play and its resynthesis following a match.* MSc Thesis, University of Toronto.

Leiper, J.B. and Maughan, R.J. (1988). Experimental models for the investigation of water and soluble transport in man: implications for oral rehydration solutions. *Drugs*, **36**, Suppl. 4, 65–79.

Leithead, C.S. and Lind, A.R. (1964). *Heat Stress and Heat Disorders*. Cassell, London.

Lentner, C. (ed.) (1981). *Geigy Scientific Tables*. 8th edn. Ciba-Geigy Limited, Basel.

Lijnen, P., Hespel, P., Fagard, R., Lysens, R., Vanden Eynde, E. and Amery, A. (1988). Erythrocyte, plasma and urinary magnesium in men before and after a marathon. *European Journal of Applied Physiology*, **58**, 252–6.

Lolli, G., Greenberg, L.A. and Lester, D. (1952). The influence of carbonated water on gastric emptying. *New England Journal of Medicine*, **246**, 490–2.

Massicote, D., Peronnet, F., Brisson, G., Bakkouch, K. and Hillaire-Marcel, C. (1989). Oxidation of a glucose polymer during exercise comparison with glucose and fructose. *Journal of Applied Physiology*, **66**, 179–83.

Maughan, R.J. (1985). Thermoregulation and fluid balance in marathon competition at low ambient temperature. *International Journal of Sports Medicine*, **6**, 15–19.

Maughan, R.J. (1991). Effects of CHO-electrolyte solution on prolonged exercise. In *Ergogenics: The Enhancement of Sport and Exercise Performance* (eds. D.R. Lamb and H.H. Williams). Benchmark Press, Carmel.

Maughan, R.J. and Leiper, J.B. (1983). Aerobic capacity and fractional utilization of aerobic capacity in elite and non-elite male and female marathon runners. *European Journal of Applied Physiology*, **52**, 80–7.

Maughan, R.J. and Whiting, P.H. (1985). Factors influencing plasma glucose concentration during marathon running. In *Exercise Physiology*. Vol. 1 (eds. C.D. Dotson and J.H. Humphrey), pp. 87–98. AMS Press, New York.

Maughan, R.J., Fenn, C.E., Gleeson, M. and Leiper, J.B. (1987). Metabolic and circulatory responses to the ingestion of glucose polymer and glucose/electrolyte solutions during exercise in man. *European Journal of Applied Physiology*, **56**, 356–62.

Maughan, R.J., Fenn, C.E. and Leiper, J.B. (1989). Effects of fluid, electrolyte and substrate ingestion on endurance capacity. *European Journal of Applied Physiology*, **58**, 481–6.

Maughan, R.J., Leiper, J.B., McGaw, B.A. (1990). Effects of exercise intensity on absorption of ingested fluids in man. *Experimental Physiology*, **75**, 419–21.

McArthur, K.E. and Feldman, M. (1989). Gastric acid secretion, gastrin release, and gastric temperature in humans as affected by liquid meal temperature. *American Journal of Clinical Nutrition*, **49**, 51–4.

Meytes, I., Shapira, Y., Magazanik, A., Meytes, D. and Seligsohn, U. (1969). Physiological and biochemical changes during a marathon race. *International Journal of Biometeorology*, **13**, 317.

Mitchell, D., Senay, L.C., Wyndham, C.H., van Rensburg, A.J., Rogers, G.G. and Strydom, N.B. (1976). Acclimatization in a hot, humid environment: energy exchange, body temperature, and sweating. *Journal of Applied Physiology*, **40**, 768–78.

Mitchell, J.B., Costill, D.L., Houmard, J.A., Flynn, M.G., Fink, W.J. and Beltz, J.D. (1988). Effects of carbohydrate ingestion on gastric emptying and exercise performance. *Medicine and Science in Sports and Exercise*, **20**, 110–15.

Mitchell, J.B., Costill, D.K., Houmard, J.A., Fink, W.J., Robergs, R.A. and Davis, J.A. (1989). Gastric emptying: influence of prolonged exercise and carbohydrate concentration. *Medicine and Science in Sports and Exercise*, **21**, 269–74.

Murray, R. (1987). The effects of consuming carbohydrate-electrolyte beverages on gastric emptying and fluid absorption during and following exercise. *Sports Medicine*, **4**, 322–51.

Murray, R., Eddy, D.E., Murray, T.W., Seifert, J.G., Paul, G.L. and Halaby, G.A. (1987). The effect of fluid and carbohydrate feedings during intermittent cycling exercise. *Medicine and Science in Sports and Exercise*, **19**, 597–604.

Nadel, E.R. (1980). Circulatory and thermal regulations during exercise. *Federation Proceedings*, **39**, 1491–7.

Nadel, E.R., Mack, G.W. and Nose, H. (1990). Influence of fluid replacement beverages on body fluid homeostasis during exercise and recovery. In *Perspectives in Exercise Science and Sports Medicine*. Vol. 3, *Fluid homeostasis during exercise* (eds. C.V. Gisolfi and D.R. Lamb), pp. 181–205. Benchmark Press, Carmel.

Naveri, H., Tikkanen, H., Kairento, A.-L. and Harkonen, M. (1989). Gastric emptying and serum insulin levels after intake of glucose-polymer solutions. *European Journal of Applied Physiology*, **58**, 661–5.

Nielsen, B., Sjogaard, G., Vgelvig, J., Knudsen, B. and Dohlmann, B. (1986). Fluid balance in exercise dehydration and rehydration with different glucose-electrolyte drinks. *European Journal of Applied Physiology*, **55**, 318–25.

Noakes, T.D. (1990). The dehydration myth and carbohydrate replacement during prolonged exercise. *Cycling Science*, **1**, 23–9.

Noakes, T.D., Goodwin, N., Rayner, B.L., Branken, T. and Taylor, R.K.N. (1985). Water intoxication: a possible complication during endurance exercise. *Medicine and Science in Sports and Exercise*, **17**, 370–5.

Noakes, T.D., Adams, B.A., Myburgh, K.H., Greeff, C., Lotz, T. and Nathan, M. (1988). The danger of an inadequate water intake during prolonged exercise. A novel concept re-visited. *European Journal of Applied Physiology*, **57**, 210–19.

Noakes, T.D., Norman, R.J., Buck, R.H., Godlonton, J., Stevenson, K. and Pittaway, D. (1990). The incidence of hyponatremia during prolonged ultra-endurance exercise. *Medicine and Science in Sports and Exercise*, **22**, 165–70.

Nose, H., Mack, G.W., Shi, X. and Nadel, E.R. (1988a). Role of osmolality and plasma volume during rehydration in humans. *Journal of Applied Physiology*, **65**, 325–31.

Nose, H., Mack, G.W., Shi, X. and Nadel, E.R. (1988b). Involvement of sodium retention hormones during rehydration in humans. *Journal of Applied Physiology*, **65**, 332–6.

Olsson, K.E. and Saltin, B. (1971). Diet and fluids in training and competition. *Scandinavian Journal of Rehabilitation Medicine*, **3**, 31–8.

Pirnay, F., Crielaard, J.M., Pallikarakis, N., Lacroix, M., Mosora, F., Krzentowski, G., Luyckx, A.S. and Lefebvre, P.J. (1982). Fate of exogenous glucose during exercise of different intensities in humans. *Journal of Applied Physiology*, **53**, 1620–4.

Pitts, R.F. (1959). *The Physiological Basis of Diuretic Therapy*. C.C. Thomas, Springfield, Illinois.

Poortmans, J. (1984). Exercise and renal function. *Sports Medicine*, **1**, 125–53.

Refsum, H.E., Meen, H.D. and Stromme, S.B. (1973). Whole blood, serum and erythrocyte magnesium concentrations after repeated heavy exercise of long duration. *Scandinavian Journal of Clinical and Laboratory Investigation*, **32**, 123–7.

Rehrer, N.J. (1990). *Limits to Fluid Availability During Exercise*. Vrieseborsch, Haarlem.

Rehrer, N.J., Beckers, E., Brouns, F., ten Hoor, F. and Saris, W.H.M. (1989a). Exercise and training effects on gastric emptying of carbohydrate beverages. *Medicine and Science in Sports and Exercise*, **21**, 540–9.

Robertson, J.D., Maughan, R.J. and Davidson, R.J.L. (1988). Changes in red cell density and related parameters in response to long distance running. *European Journal of Applied Physiology*, **57**, 264–9.

Rose, L.I., Carroll, D.R., Lowe, S.L., Peterson, E.W. and Cooper, K.H. (1970). Serum electrolyte changes after marathon running. *Journal of Applied Physiology*, **29**, 449–51.

Rowell, L.B. (1986). *Human Circulation*. Oxford University Press, New York.

Saltin, B. and Costill, D.L. (1988). Fluid and electrolyte balance during prolonged exercise. In *Exercise, Nutrition, and Metabolism* (eds. E.S. Horton and R.L. Tenjung), pp. 150–8. Macmillan, New York.

Saltin, B. and Karlsson, J. (1977). Die Ernahrung des sportlers. In *Zentrale Themen der Sportmedizin* (ed. W. Hollmen). Springer-Verlag, Berlin.

Sasaki, H., Maeda, J., Usui, S. and Ishiko, T. (1987). Effect of sucrose and caffeine ingestion on performance of prolonged strenuous running. *International Journal of Sports Medicine*, **8**, 261–5.

Schmidt, R.F. and Thews, G. (eds.) (1989). *Human Physiology*. 2nd edn. Springer-Verlag, Berlin.

Senay, L.C. (1979). Effects of exercise in the heat on body fluid distribution. *Medicine and Science in Sports*, **11**, 42–8.

Senay, L.C., Mitchell, D. and Wyndham, C.H. (1976). Acclimatization in a hot humid environment: body fluid adjustments. *Journal of Applied Physiology*, **40**, 786–96.

Sole, C.C. and Noakes, T.D. (1989). Faster gastric emptying for glucose-polymer and fructose solutions than for glucose in humans. *European Journal of Applied Physiology*, **58**, 605–12.

Spiller, R.C., Jones, B.J.M., Brown, B.E. and Silk, D.B.A. (1982). Enhancement of carbohydrate absorption by the addition of sucrose to enteric diets. *Journal of Parenteral and Enteral Nutrition*, **6**, 321.

Stansbie, D., Tomlinson, K., Potman, J.M. and Walters, E.G. (1982). Hypothermia, hypokalaemia and marathon running. *Lancet*, **2**, 1336.

Sun, W.M., Houghton, L.A., Read, N.W., Grundy, D.G. and Johnson, A.G. (1988). Effect of meal temperature on gastric emptying of liquids in man. *Gut*, **29**, 302–5.

Suzuki, Y. (1980). Human physical performance and cardiocirculatory responses to hot environments during sub-maximal upright cycling. *Ergonomics*, **23**, 527–42.

Verde, T., Shephard, R.J., Corey, P. and Moore, R. (1982). Sweat composition in exercise and in heat. *Journal of Applied Physiology*, **53**, 1540–5.

Wapnir, R.A. and Lifshitz, F. (1985). Osmolality and solute concentration – their relationship with oral rehydration solution effectiveness: an experimental assessment. *Pediatric Research*, **19**, 894–8.

Whiting, P.H., Maughan, R.J. and Miller, J.D.B. (1984). Dehydration and serum biochemical changes in runners. *European Journal of Applied Physiology*, **52**, 183–7.

Williams, C. (1989). Diet and endurance fitness. *American Journal of Clinical Nutrition*, **49**, 1077–83.

Williams, C., Nute, M.G., Broadbank, L. and Vinall, S. (1990). Influence of fluid intake on endurance running performance: a comparison between water, glucose and fructose solutions. *European Journal of Applied Physiology*, **60**, 112–19.

Wyndham, C.H., Rogers, G.G., Senay, L.C. and Mitchell, D. (1976). Acclimatization in a hot, humid environment: cardiovascular adjustments. *Journal of Applied Physiology*, **40**, 779–85.

9

Heat – sweat – dehydration – rehydration: a praxis oriented approach

F. Brouns

The presentation of this chapter is quite different to that of normal scientific review. The reason is that the gap between science and practice must be bridged. Scientific knowledge has been made applicable for people with less scientific background. Therefore it was decided to present the current status of knowledge in easy to understand figures and graphs. The text has been reduced to the most relevant key findings of research for sports practice. Reference to these findings is to a large extent made in the preceding chapter by Maughan.

With increasing exercise intensity, oxygen consumption increases to cover the increased requirement for metabolic processes. Every litre of oxygen used during exercise will result in approximately 16 kJ heat

BODY HEAT		
Exercise intensity	$\longrightarrow$	Heat production
1 litre oxygen uptake	$\longrightarrow$	$\pm$ 16–20 kJ heat
Rest	$\longrightarrow$	5–7 kJ min^{-1}
Exercise	$\longrightarrow$	75–90 kJ min^{-1}

Fig. 9.1 Exercise intensity determines heat production.

Food, Nutrition and Sports Performance
Edited by Clyde Williams and John T. Devlin
Published in 1992 by E & F N Spon, London. ISBN 0 419 17890 2

production and 4 kJ energy for mechanical work. As a result, the amount of heat liberated under resting conditions may be increased >10 fold under maximal exercise circumstances (see Fig. 9.1).

BODY HEAT

Exercise ——→ Heat production 75–90 kJ min^{-1}

↓

Body core temp ↑ 1° C every 5–7 min

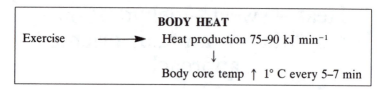

Fig. 9.2 Produced heat affects body core temperature.

Under maximal exercise circumstances, the amount of heat produced may lead to an increase in body core temperature of 1° C every 5–7 min. It is obvious that the heat produced must be eliminated in order to avoid severe hypothermia and health risks (Fig. 9.2).

BODY HEAT

Heat flux depends on:

- Temperature gradient tissue/blood
- Rate of blood flow (exercise 20–25 fold ↑)
- Temperature gradient blood/skin

Fig. 9.3 Factors affecting heat flux.

The heat produced in the muscles will increase muscle tissue temperature drastically. It is the circulating blood which is relatively cool compared to the exercising muscle tissue, which takes up most of the heat. Therefore, the maximal possible transport of heat depends on the difference in temperature between muscle tissue and blood and the rate of blood flow through the muscle. The latter may be increased 20–25 fold during exercise as a result of increased cardiac stroke volume and decreased peripheral resistance. The blood will transport the heat to the periphery where the relatively cool skin forms a second temperature gradient which will lead to a heat flux from blood to skin (Fig. 9.3).

BODY COOLING

Sweat evaporation 1 ml	——→	2.5 kJ heat loss
Max sweat rate 30 ml min^{-1}	——→	75 kJ min^{-1}
Max heat production	——→	90 kJ min^{-1}

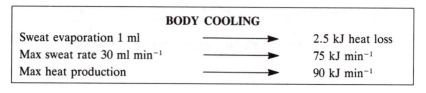

Fig. 9.4 Continued heat production will increase body core temperature.

Continued heat production will increase body core temperature. As a result, sweat production will be increased in order to wet the skin for cooling purposes. Each ml of sweat evaporating from the skin will lead to a heat loss of 2.5 kJ (Fig. 9.4).

At theoretical maximal evaporation rates of approximately 180 ml h^{-1} in a 70 kg male, this will lead to a heat elimination which equals about 80% of maximal heat production. Therefore, at maximal exercise intensities the remaining heat must be eliminated by direct cooling of the skin, i.e. by surrounding air or water (radiation and convection).

	BODY HEAT
Total thermal load	• Exercise intensity
	• Environmental temperature
	• Environmental evaporative power

Fig. 9.5 Factors which determine total thermal load.

The total thermal load depends on exercise intensity, environmental temperature and evaporative power. The higher the exercise intensity, the higher will be the heat production. The warmer the environment, the less will be the heat loss by radiation and convection. Humidity of the immediate surroundings further influences the possibilities for sweat to be evaporated and to cool the skin (Fig. 9.5).

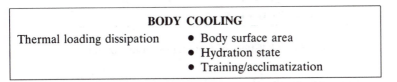

	BODY COOLING
Thermal loading dissipation	• Body surface area
	• Hydration state
	• Training/acclimatization

Fig. 9.6 Factors influencing thermal heat dissipation.

In addition, body surface, hydration status and status of training and acclimatization will influence the possible thermal heat dissipation. Also the type of clothing will determine how well sweat can be evaporated. Additionally a large body surface will have a larger 'evaporative and thus cooling capacity'. A status of severe dehydration may limit sweat production and skin blood flow and therefore evaporative capacity. In addition, improved training status and adequate acclimatization will lead to improved heat elimination when exercising in the heat (Fig. 9.6).

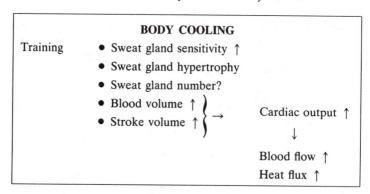

Fig. 9.7 Effect of training on thermoregulation.

There are indications that training improves quantitative sweat secretion and also induces a more 'economical sweating' by improving the sensitivity of sweat glands to thermal load. As a result, the 'trained and acclimatized' sweat glands will respond with an earlier onset of sweat secretion.

Training additionally increases total blood volume which, via an increased stroke volume, will improve cardiac output at a certain heart frequency. As a result, blood flow in muscle and skin, and with it heat flux, will be improved (Fig. 9.7).

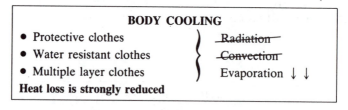

Fig. 9.8 Effect of clothing on body cooling.

Heat flux through the skin and heat elimination by sweat evaporation may become severely reduced by inappropriate clothing. Multiple layer clothing, nylon training suits or protective clothing (American football, ice-hockey, fencing) may almost totally block sweat evaporation. Also convection and radiation will be severely impaired so that total heat dissipation will be reduced to critical levels. As such, inadequate clothing should be seen as a potential health risk. Adequate but protective clothing may lead to health risks in warm environments (see Fig. 9.8).

Because sweat evaporation is a major route of heat elimination, it is clear that a status of severe dehydration, which will impair blood flow as well as sweat production, will lead to hyperthermia by a reduction of heat flux. Because dehydration depends on quantitative sweat loss and the

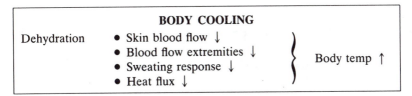

Fig. 9.9 Dehydration can affect body core temperature.

latter is determined by exercise intensity, duration, environmental temperature and clothing, both coach and athlete should be aware of the effects and interaction of these factors (see Fig. 9.9).

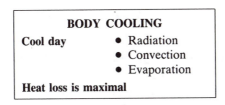

Fig. 9.10 Heat loss is maximal on cool days.

On a windy cool day with normal or low humidity cooling of the body by the various routes is maximal. Under these environmental circumstances high-speed runners producing maximal amounts of heat may experience optimal competition circumstances because much of the heat is eliminated by radiation and convection and only limited amounts by sweating. Low-speed runners, however, who produce little heat, may become overcooled if they are clothed inadequately. Fluid loss will be moderate under these circumstances (see Fig. 9.10).

On a wet day with high humidity evaporation of the sweat will be depressed and sweat will more or less continuously drip from the body, a very ineffective means of cooling the body. In this circumstance, heat elimination may become severely impaired if the temperature is also high, limiting radiation and convection. Therefore, races in these climatological

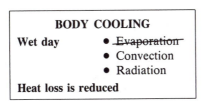

Fig. 9.11 Heat loss can be reduced on a wet day.

circumstances may be a potential threat to health of the endurance athlete. Fluid loss will be maximal under these circumstances and adequate rehydration is of utmost importance for maintaining health. When it is raining, in a cool environment, this will not be the case due to direct cooling from the rain (see Fig. 9.11).

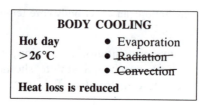

Fig. 9.12 Heat loss is low on hot days.

On a hot day with normal or low humidity, heat loss by radiation and convection may be minimal. In this circumstance sweat evaporation becomes the prime route of heat elimination. Under such circumstances, sweat production may reach maximal levels and athletes may lose up to 1.5–2.0 l of sweat per h. It seems evident that adequate fluid intake in order to avoid dehydration and related depressed heat flux is of paramount importance for the health of the athlete involved in endurance exercise in the heat (Fig. 9.12).

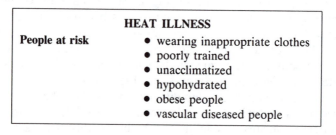

Fig. 9.13 People at risk of heat-induced illness.

Because training status, acclimatization, body surface, hydration status, evaporative power and clothing may influence heat flux, it becomes evident that these factors also characterize athletes of potential risk for experiencing heat stress, heat exhaustion or heat stroke (Fig. 9.13).

Based on an extensive number of studies, it can be stated that there are no differences in gastric emptying between: rest and exercise up to 70% VO_2 max and between trained and untrained people. However, gastric emptying will be influenced by the energy/carbohydrate content of

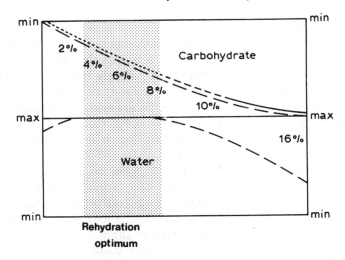

Fig. 9.14 Fluid and carbohydrate supply in relation to climatological circumstances: effects on bioavailability. The curve symbols given indicate the carbohydrate concentration to be used: hot >26 °C; and warm and humid >22 °C (. . . .); warm 20–28 °C (– – – –); moderate to cold <22 °C (———).

the drink. The more concentrated the drink is, the more will gastric emptying be slowed down. In other words, low-concentrated drinks leave the stomach at high speed, but supply only little amounts of carbohydrate. More concentrated drinks leave the stomach at low speed, but supply more carbohydrate due to the high concentration. Based on our knowledge about sweating and dehydration, it is therefore proposed to consume low-concentrated drinks when exercising in the heat, when fluid losses are substantial, whereas more concentrated drinks may be consumed when sweat loss is depressed and carbohydrate supply may be the most important factor for maintaining optimal performance. When exercise lasts <30 min there is no need for fluid or carbohydrate ingestion (Fig. 9.14).

Electrolytes (minerals) are excreted with sweat. The amount of electrolytes lost depends on a number of factors. At higher sweat rates (e.g.

Table 9.1 Whole body sweat electrolyte content and compensation range

Electrolyte	Cl	Na	K	Ca	Mg
Average (mmol/l)	28.6	32.7	4.4	1	0.79
Average (mg/l)	1014	752	173	40	19
Range (mg/l)	533–1495	413–1091	121–225	(13–67)	(4–34)
				×3.33	×2.86
Compensation range	500–1500	400–1100	120–225	45–225	10–100

when exercising in the heat) some electrolytes are excreted in higher quantities. Well-trained people have developed the ability to minimize the excretion of electrolytes by the sweat glands. The electrolyte composition of passively induced sweat (sauna) differs slightly from the composition of actively induced sweat (sport). The amount of electrolytes excreted by different regions of the body differs. For these reasons it seems impossible to determine the one and only electrolyte composition of human sweat.

However, a reasonable overall picture can be obtained by determination of whole body sweat electrolyte losses under different conditions. This excludes the effect of overestimation of excretion based on regional sweat sampling. From the available literature the studies in which sweat was accurately determined by a whole body washdown procedure under different circumstances such as exercise- and sauna-induced sweat loss were selected. A mean electrolyte loss as well as the standard deviation from this mean was calculated. Correction for bioavailability taking for absorption of Na, Cl, K 100%, Ca 30% and Mg 35%, finally resulted in an optimal range for replacement of electrolyte losses under daily circumstances. Since rehydration drinks for sport are designed to replace losses induced by sweating it is advised that the electrolyte content of these drinks should not exceed the electrolyte levels as presented above. This will ensure that, independent of the quantity of fluid intake, an overload of minerals to the blood resulting in too high blood electrolyte levels and hyperosmolality will not take place (Table 9.1).

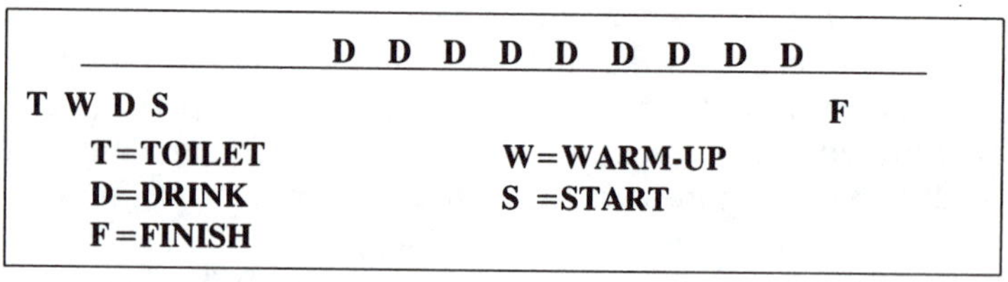

```
                    D  D  D  D  D  D  D  D  D
   T  W  D  S                                      F
         T = TOILET              W = WARM-UP
         D = DRINK               S  = START
         F = FINISH
```

Fig. 9.15 Avoidance of dehydration during sports activity.

During sports activity the hydration status will be influenced by a number of factors, such as pre-competition fluid intake and fluid intake during competition in relation to fluid losses. The best procedure to follow is to visit a toilet 30–45 min prior to the start in order to urinate and to defaecate. This is important because both factors may influence drink behaviour during competition. Perform a warm-up and stretching activity according to your personal wishes after this.

Ingest 300–600 ml of fluid 3–5 min prior to the start and continue drinking at every post whenever sweat loss may be substantial. The amount of fluid to be ingested depends on fluid loss by sweating and will be affected

Fig. 9.16 Fluid balance is important during endurance events in the heat.

by palatability and tolerance to 'volume ingestion'. Fluid choice depends on climatological circumstances. Athletes should practise drinking during exercise in training sessions (Fig. 9.15).

Any athlete can get an idea about his fluid loss during endurance activities by regularly taking body weight (nude) prior to and immediately after exercise. This is important for anyone who wants to compete at his personal best level. Some people are heavy sweaters, others are less. This means that it is impossible to give a general guideline as to how much an athlete should drink.

In general it is observed that mean maximal fluid intakes amount to 400–600 ml h^{-1}, but small runners who sweat little or large runners who sweat heavily may ingest or tolerate much less or more than these amounts. In general, it may be assumed that net weight loss after activity minus 1 kg reflects the amount of fluid which is missing for optimal fluid balance. Athletes should know that the feeling of thirst becomes suppressed during exercise. Not having thirst is no indication of not being dehydrated. (*Note*: Weight loss (kg) − 1 kg = litres of fluid not ingested.)

REFERENCES TO TABLE 1

Armstrong, L.E., Hubbard, R.W., Szlyk, P.C., Mathew, W.T. and Sils, I.V. (1985). Voluntary dehydration and electrolyte losses during prolonged exercise in the heat. *Aviation Space Environmental Medicine*, **56**, 765–70.

Claremont, A.D., Costill, D.L., Fink, W. and Van Handel, P. (1976). Heat tolerance following diuretic induced dehydration. *Medical Science Sports*, **8**, 239–43.

Cohn, J.R. and Emmet, E.A. (1978). The excretion of trace metal in human sweat. *Annual Clinical Laboratory Science*, **8**, 270–5.

Consolazio, C.F., Matoush, L.R.O., Nelson, R.A., Isaac, G.J. and Canham, J.E. (1966). Comparison of nitrogen, calcium and iodine excretion in arm and total body sweat. *American Journal of Clinical Nutrition*, **18**, 443–8.

Costa, F., Galloway, D.H. and Margen, S. (1969). Regional and total body sweat composition of men fed controlled diets. *American Journal of Clinical Nutrition*, **22**, 52–8.

Costill, D.L., Coté, R. and Fink, W. (1976). Muscle water and electrolytes following varied levels of dehydration in man. *Journal of Applied Physiology*, **40**, 6–11.

Dill, D.B., Jones, B.F., Edwards, H.T. and Oberg, S.A. (1933). Salt economy in extreme dry heat. *Journal of Biology and Chemistry*, **100**, 755–67.

Dill, D.B., Hall, F.G. and Edwards, H.T. (1938). Changes in composition of sweat during acclimatization to heat. *American Journal of Physiology*, **123**, 412–19.

Johnston, F.A., McMillan, T.J. and Evans, E.R. (1950). Perspiration as a factor influencing the requirement for calcium and iron. *Journal of Nutrition*, **42**, 285–96.

Kleeman, C.R., Bass, D.E. and Quinn, M. (1953). The effect of an impermeable vapor barrier on electrolyte and nitrogen concentrations in sweat. *Journal of Clinical Investigations*, **32**, 736–45.

Malhotra, M.S., Sridharan, K., Venkataswamy, Y., Rai, R.M., Pichan, G., Radhakrishan, U. and Grover, S.K. (1981). Effect of restricted potassium intake on its excretion and on physiological responses during heat stress. *European Journal of Applied Physiology*, **47**, 169–79.

Thapar, G.S., Shenolikar, I.S. and Tulpule, P.G. (1976). Sweat loss of nitrogen and other nutrients during heavy physical activity. *Indian Journal of Medical Research*, **64**, 590–6.

Vellar, O. (1969). Nutrient losses through sweating. Thesis, Oslo.

Index